Prescription for Wealth

Financial Planning for the Health Care Professional

Dr. Terry Curran

CROWNE ROCK

PRESCRIPTION FOR WEALTH

Financial Planning for the Health Care Professional

This is a book for health care professionals —

Acupuncturists
Audiologists
Chiropractors
Dentists
Dental Hygienists
Dietitians
Medical Doctors
Naturopaths
Nurses
Physiotherapists
Pharmacists
Psychologists
Occupational Therapists
Speech Language Pathologists
Veterinarians
Any Other Altruistic Health Care Professional

Printed in Canada

CROWNE ROCK

PUBLISHING

R.R. #6, Site 11A, C18

Vernon, B.C. V1T 6Y5

Canadian Cataloguing in Publication Data

Curran Terry G., 1960-

Prescription for Wealth: financial planning for the health care professional

Includes index.

ISBN 0-9681405-0-5

1. Finance, Personal — Canada. I. Title.

HG179.C87 1997 332.024'01'0971 C96-900820-1

Crowne Rock Publishing

R.R. #6, Site 11A, C18

Vernon, B.C. V1T 6Y5

CONTENTS

LIST OF TABLES

PREFACE

Why would a neurologist want to write a book on personal financial planning?

Like a lot of health care professionals who complete their training at 30-something, I found myself with a hefty debt load after completing my fellowship at the age of 31. I then accepted the position of Associative Professor at Memorial University of Newfoundland, which meant that I instantly acquired a handsome salary and for the first time in my life felt very rich. My income went from $36,000 per year, while renting in downtown Toronto, with a comfortable 38% tax rate to over $100,000 per year with a 54% tax burden. My introduction to the "marginal tax rate" was truly baptism by fire.

In my usual curious way, I tried to decide the best way to budget my new fortune: Should I pay off my loan? Buy a badly needed new or nearly new car? Buy a house? Maximize my RRSP contributions? I also wondered if there were legitimate ways to reduce my tax bill such as those "great tax shelters" that some of my professors had been talking about throughout my residency years.

Seeking advice from my older and "wiser" mentors left me with more questions than answers. There were generally two groups with different attitudes: those who knew little or nothing and were leaving it up to a bank manager or representative and those who were "experts" in specific areas. But upon close questioning, I realized that most of these "experts" were insufficiently informed and likely to make poor financial decisions, supporting the adage that a little knowledge can be dangerous. There was a myriad of suggestions put forth, but I became leery when these same "medical expert investors" had little or no comprehension of how, for example, inflation would affect their different investments or what the final tax implication would be.

There was no consistent advice on what I thought was important, such as the pros and cons of a self-directed RRSP; how to evaluate term, whole, or universal life insurance; whether to maximize the RRSP or pay off the mortgage first; whether to buy an expensive home versus a modest one and invest the difference; and where the best place for investing inside and outside the RRSP was.

The variability of answers was flabbergasting and lead me to the conclusion that the majority of health care professionals are, indeed, their own worst enemies when it comes to personal financial planning. Ironically, a common theme among most of them was the hope to retire in their fifties, but on questioning them they had no idea of how much they would need to save or what type of return they would require to achieve this goal!

Having being raised in a frugal family and environment in Newfoundland, I decided to do some investigating to see if I could find some answers. This interest has lead to *much* reading (my wife would say compulsive), and I am now proud to state that I have a very broad and indepth knowledge of different types of investing and all aspects of personal financial planning.

Great! But why the book you ask? There are several reasons. First, I have spent a significant amount of time learning about *all* aspects of personal financial planning. I started my own research with the now-classic book, *The Wealthy Barber,* by David Chilton, but found that the more I read the more questions I had. Thanks to my Tourette's obsessive-compulsive gene, I could not be content with just the tip of the iceberg — I needed to see the whole thing.

I soon realized the vastness of the topic of personal financial planning, which lead to my reading many books on specific topics, mainly because I could not find any one book that covered all areas of interest. I also subscribed to numerous investment newsletters. My "obsession" has also lead me to enroll in the Canadian Securities Course and the Chartered Financial Planner Program.

I realize that the average health care professional has neither the time, patience, or desire to emulate my obsessive behavior, and so I saw a niche that needed filling. I thought it would be very useful and practical if there were a *single* book available that covered all these basic financial and investment issues that health care professionals will have to address at some point in their careers.

In this book I have tried to cover in reasonable detail all aspects of personal financial planning with emphasis on the health care professional. I have also kept in mind that no other book has been aimed specifically at the above-average income earner with below-average financial knowledge. (For the purposes of this book, high-income earning is considered anything above $60,000 per year because that is the level when the 50%-plus tax assault begins.) Most health care professionals earn more than that: the average Canadian family income for university graduates is close to $80,000, and 25% of this group make more than $100,000.

Second, it is a running joke in the financial community that health care professionals are notoriously bad investors (especially surgeons and dentists rumor has it). I would like to change this perception, both to assuage my own ego and to sincerely share information that is going to be increasingly important for all of us. The ideal situation would be for personal financial planning to be introduced during the student years of every health care professional, even being part of the curriculum. I know that scenario is unlikely to be realized, but it is my hope that more health care professionals will start to learn the basics before graduating, and for this reason sections of this book are written specifically for the student.

Finally, I was outraged by the number of people in their fifties and sixties who are "opting out" of Canada and taking their money with them because they fear that the inevitable future tax hit required to service the "elderly boom" and baby boom debt will create retirement poverty (e.g., *Maclean's* October 9/1995 issue had the headline: "Offshore Billions — How Canadians are stashing their money in foreign tax havens").

It can be stifling to consider the amount of money that will pass through the hands of a health care professional over 20 to 30 years. And that is the problem; the money passes *through* our hands. All of us could be millionaires many times over with proper financial planning and without having to leave the country.

In the following chapters, I will show you how to earn more, keep more, and lose less through proper financial planning. I have written this book to accommodate the health care professional student in university, early and mid-career health care professionals, and those nearing retirement. I advise you to read all of it, but depending on your age, certain chapters will be of greater interest than others.

I hope you find that this book not only has sound practical advice, but some ethical merit as well, as it encourages you to invest in your country and to retire as a healthy and wealthy Canadian.

Good luck.

ACKNOWLEDGMENTS

I am grateful to the many financial specialists and friends who have provided guidance and constructive criticism for this book. Some of these are Jennifer Hardy of Hardy & Associates, Michael Peck, Mario Romei of Romei & Plummer, Fred K. Soderberg, C.F.P. of First Capital Financial Planners, and Fred Whitbread. I would also like to express my appreciation to my editor, Ruth Wilson, for her guidance and patience.

I would like to dedicate this book to my wife and family who tolerated my obsessiveness and mental absence while writing, and, lastly, to those health care professionals who have become proactive in learning more about personal financial planning.

1

INTRODUCTION

WHY THE HEALTH CARE PROFESSIONAL?

For most of us, our attraction to the health care profession started with altruism, which according to *Webster's Dictionary* is "unselfish devotion to the welfare of others." Most of us held the moral view that helping others and enjoying work was the most important thing in life. Most of us, after a few years in our field, likely still feel this way, but are quickly realizing that present and future personal financial matters are rapidly becoming the third most important thing in life after family and job satisfaction.

The old adage that "in this world, nothing is certain but death and taxes" has been more than just a pithy proverb for the health care professional. Since graduation day we may have been winning the battle against death, thanks to excellence and dedication, but we have been losing the tax battle a at record pace. The financial malaise that exists among health care professionals is unsurpassed by any other professional group. Typically, health care professionals spend 5 to 15 busy years in post-secondary education, and the pace escalates when they start working and raising a family. Most are too busy or too tired to educate themselves about that third most important thing in their life.

It is at that early stage of their careers that personal financial planning is most important, but most health care professionals just never get around to it. I would bet that 50% of those reading this book have yet to take the basic steps of writing a will and purchasing adequate disability and life insurance. This is in stark contrast to other professionals. If you ask your accountant or lawyer when they arranged these essential matters, you will realize that health care professionals are taking up the rear when it comes to proper financial planning. This inaction can cost you tens of thousands of dollars over your lifetime.

It is estimated that 40% to 50% of Canadians spend less than two hours per year on personal financial planning. Women, in particular, make up a large portion of this alarming statistic. About 40% of all health care professionals are women, and the number of women earning more than $50,000 grew by 75% between 1985 and 1990. Even so, a recent Angus Reid poll showed that almost 80% of women surveyed had little or no comprehension of what a mutual fund was. These numbers point to an epidemic of ignorance and I think it is time for change!

There are many other good reasons for wanting to treat the financial malaise of health care professionals. It is said that 90% of all divorces are caused by arguments over money. It is also said that 40% of North Americans are sleeping less in order to work and earn more; the same number want to spend more time with their families.

Health care professionals already make enough money (although some would disagree), but they lack the basic knowledge on how to keep and invest it properly. With proper and effective personal financial planning, you can set and achieve important personal goals such as working less and spending more time with your family. For me, the goal of retirement by age 45 to 48 is very important, and I am now confident that I will achieve that goal because I have proactively created a financial plan and I am applying good investment principles.

It is possible for most health care professionals to achieve similar goals regardless of their age because of the high income they earn. My plan requires an investment portfolio that will provide at least $60,000 per year before taxes during retirement. This means that over the next 10 to 13 years I will have to bank about $1.8 million assuming a 10% return on my investment with an inflation rate of 4%.

How about you? Do you have any idea of what you will require to retire? I bet you have an idea about *when* you would like to retire, but will you be able to?

In the following chapters I will show you how to create a financial plan that will allow you to achieve your financial goals. This book is meant to educate, not to dictate. By using it, you will be able to make personal decisions with a sound understanding of what the financial implications are or will be.

GETTING READY FOR CHANGE IN THE 21st CENTURY

There will be many changes occurring in the 21st Century, some good and others not so good. All of the changes will have an impact on health care professionals, but none as hard as the economic changes that are fast approaching.

Those who are aware of these changes and plan accordingly will fare much better than those who "roll with the punches." The baby boom "good old days" of wealth and prosperity are now behind us. Because of Canada's increasing debt as well as the aging population, there will be a major restructuring of the health care system, Old Age Security (OAS), and the Canada Pension Plan (CPP).

Let's have a look at some of these coming changes and why they will — and must — occur.

We Canadians now have a national debt crisis. In fact, Canada has the second highest net debt interest payment as a percentage of the gross domestic product (GDP) of all the G7 members second only to Italy. Additionally, the annual deficit (i.e., the shortfall difference between what the government takes in and what it spends) for 1994/95 was approximately $38 billion. The national debt, which is the accumulation of these annual deficits plus the accruing yearly interest, was approximately $580 billion in early 1996 and the *combined* federal and provincial debt was almost a whopping $800 billion. This astounding level of debt gives us the dubious distinction of owing the most per capita of all the industrialized countries in the world and means that every Canadian man, woman, and child now owes $25,000 if we were to divide the debt on an individual basis.

The present focus has just been on reducing the deficit; we cannot even think about the debt at this point which continues to spiral upward at a rate of $5 million per hour. Just to service this debt (not reduce it) Canadian taxpayers are paying $47 billion per year in interest charges!

Attempts are being made by current federal and provincial governments to put the financial house back in order. Paul Martin, federal minister of finance, remains on course with his 1996 budget projections. His target deficit for 1996/97 is $24 billion or 3% of the GDP. The plan for 1997/98 is 2% or $17 billion. But these figures are all based on today's projections of continued economic growth, low inflation, and low interest rates. If any part of the equation changes, it is likely there will be further tax increases and a decrease in spending.

If the governments do not take this deficit/debt issue seriously and stay on track, there are potential grave consequences. Rating agencies such as Moody's and Standard & Poors may send out the message that Canada is in financial trouble by down rating the government bonds. By rating Canada poorly, foreign investors may see lending money to Canada as a greater risk and will demand a higher return from the government. This, in turn, would be passed onto Canadians as higher interest and mortgage rates.

As Canada is already over-extended in foreign debt, which accounts for 40% of Canada's current debt, it is unlikely that we will be borrowing more in the future, which means the government will have three options to deal with the deficit/debt: spend less, increase taxes, or do both.

The Impact On The Health Care Professional

Canadians spend the equivalent of 10% of their GDP on health care already, which is at least 1% to 2% more than most European countries and second only to the United States, which is up to 12% of their GDP. The government will have no choice but to reduce this figure in the near future in an attempt to manage the growing debt. As a result, you will see less hiring of health care professionals by governments in both hospitals and schools, which will force new graduates to become self-employed and will create more stress for those already in the system. There will be hospital and school closures in every province resulting in layoffs in all disciplines of the health field. Already since early 1990, there have been hundreds of thousands of layoffs as companies and governments restructure to face tough economic times.

Hospitals, which account for 40% of the total health care expenditures, will be hit the hardest in the medicare cuts. I also suspect that we will see a cut in salaries as well through a variety of schemes. Capitation or population-based reimbursement is the likely way of the future for physicians and chiropractors. And before this happens, fee-for service billings will continue to be rolled back by lowering the maximum billing ceilings.

Despite the recent example in Ontario of the government's efforts to reduce taxes, it is inevitable that all levels of government will have to increase taxes again as the "elderly boom" swells and there are less taxpayers to pay the bills of the 100-year-old healthy retirees (see next section). I think that we will see increases in taxes of all types, especially personal and property taxes. It is also possible we will be taxed on the sale of our homes as currently happens in the United States. You may also see an inheritance tax imposed in addition to the present probate fees in an attempt to reap some benefit from the already wealthier older baby boomers (now age 45 to 50) who stand to inherit billions from their parents.

For these reasons alone, it is likely that health care professionals will not see any increase in before-tax (and definitely after-tax) income for another 7 to 10 years. If there is a national trend toward salaried health care professionals or systems such as capitation (at least for medical doctors and chiropractors), then our average salary will most likely decrease. Continuing inflation will create a further setback to our future buying power. The bottom line and recurrent theme from the government will be "pay more taxes but get less in return."

Meeting The Challenge

The big challenge for health care professionals will be the demand for more of us to be self-employed, emphasizing the need to better understand all aspects of financial matters especially personal financial planning. But that is not the only challenge. There is another debt crisis that we Canadians are personally responsible for. The government debt can be blamed on others, but only we can be blamed for our own personal debt. Canadians have created personal debt of unprecedented levels making us among the world leaders of debt on a per capita basis. Even during the boom years of the 1970s and 1980s, few of us managed to save, and now the percentage of savings from the net income of a Canadian family is at an all time 23-year low. The Canadian total household debt as of 1995 was 88% of yearly disposable after-tax income. This compares to 55% in 1985.

It is estimated that only 1 in 10 Canadians is taking their financial future seriously, and this is reflected by the statistics showing that only 40% to 50% of Canadians contribute to their RRSP and frequently it is just a token contribution. It is my observation that most health care professionals are much more proficient at buying large, rapidly depreciating "toys" such as boats and luxury automobiles than investing in *appreciating* investments.

THE LINING IN THE CLOUDS

So there you have it: we will pay more in taxes, make less income, and we are already overextended on personal debt!

But it is not all bad news. There will also be significant Canadian prosperity in the 21st Century, and health care professionals are properly positioned to take advantage of it. The new economy that Nuala Beck talks about in her bestselling book, *Shifting Gears,* will be technology driven, and some of the major drivers will be in the health care and pharmaceutical sectors. This is in part due to the exponential growth of medical knowledge occurring, but also because of the "elderly boom" that will occur and by its sheer numbers create a tremendous supply and demand for quick and good health care.

Our present health care system cannot cope with the current demands and will certainly not be able to deal with these future demands after Ottawa decreases the health care expenditure by $10 billion over the next few years. The cuts will create great opportunities for the health care private sector. It is important to make sure that we are the owners and operators of this future private health care industry and *not* just the employees.

Health care professionals will likely still work for hospitals and schools but on a contractual self-employed basis rather than as employees, similar to dentists and veterinarians. Many health care professionals who are currently employed are already "moonlighting" privately which is a good way to test the waters and reap some great tax breaks. For those who are already self-employed, or thinking about becoming so, learning more about personal financial planning will serve the dual purpose of helping your present business and future personal financial affairs.

The bulk of business in the future will come from the aging wealthy population that wants good service *today* and not the "bandaid" government service that is currently offered after a two to three month waiting period. Physicians and chiropractors (and other health care professionals) will definitely become exposed to a two-tier system, and more and more will be operating their own private billing practices. Many ophthalmologists and radiologists are already ahead of the game with their own private clinics in some provinces which cater directly to the aging wealthy population (e.g., cataracts, imaging aging bones and spines). There are other private clinics in place in Ontario and Alberta that are targeting U.S. patients, which could be an area of great future growth for Canadian health care professionals.

The government is currently denying that a two-tier system will evolve, but this claim is nothing more then vote soliciting lip service. The two-tier system already exists! When the 10 million baby boomers start retiring and demanding good health care, the simple fact will be that the much smaller succeeding workforce will not be able to afford the large volume or level of health care demand, and a two-tier system will emerge by necessity. Canadian entrepreneurs will not stand for patients going to the United States for service when it can be offered at home. In fact, I would be willing to bet that many Canadian hospitals will be looking at providing health care to U.S. patients as a means of balancing their budgets.

These factors will continue to provide high demand and good job opportunities for health care professionals. But those who start *now* to learn more about operating their own businesses and understanding economic and financial matters will have a head start on the new economy. The best place to start is with your own personal financial planning. Dealing with the different financial aspects of being self-employed will then fall into place much easier.

BABY BOOMERS GROW OLD — AND LIVE LONGER!

The baby boomers have started entering their "golden years," which will soon create an "elderly boom." Most of the older boomers have seen tremendous wealth pass through their hands but, unfortunately, only 10% have managed to adequately plan for the future. Many health care professionals who planned on early retirement will have to continue to work until age 65 to 70 because of excessive expenditures, poor saving habits, and poor investments.

The other problem is that the numbers behind them are shrinking and there are significantly fewer younger Canadians to pay the bills. Projections up to the year 2020 show an increase of 65% in the number of people age 65 to 79 and over a 100% increase for those over 80 years.

The average 65-year-old Canadian now lives to be 76 and the average 50-year-old will likely see 85. This means that the average health care professional in his or her fifties must plan for at least 21 years of retirement financing. But there is more. Three specific features of health care professionals make them very vulnerable in retirement.

First, almost 70% of Canadians are already retiring before the age of 65 creating a longer period for which their investments must support them. The mean age of retirement for physicians is currently 58 and similar for most of the other health care professionals. But remember, the health care professionals who are retiring today are benefiting from some of the government retirement programs and most were "pre-boomers" brought up to "save for a rainy day." Many health care professionals younger than 55 also want to retire this early, or even earlier, but that means creating an even longer retirement plan *without* government help *and* with a lot of debt!

Second, with the rapidly expanding medical knowledge, especially in the area of anti-aging genes, it is likely that by the year 2010 the average life expectancy will be 96. And remember that this is the average, meaning that for 15% it will be even longer. For those who lead healthy lives, life expectancy could easily be 105 years, and retiring at the age of 45 to 50 would mean banking enough for 55 years of retirement living! And the longer the plan, the more imperative it is to *have a plan in place* and to understand the factors that can affect the plan such as inflation (see chapter 2).

Third, health care professionals do not have a great track record when it comes to taking care of their financial affairs and being proactive in their investing and retirement planning. The good news is that you have already taken a positive step toward alleviating this third area of vulnerability by reading this book!

Taking Control

I realize that I have started this book with a lot of gloom and doom, but I think it is appropriate because of the financial malaise that exists in Canada, both at the individual and government level. Fortunately, you have already taken the first step toward taking control of your personal finances by reading this book.

The corporate sector has already changed gears to prepare for the 21st Century. Most major corporations are trimming and tightening the infrastructure to face the future. Most provincial governments are starting to get on line as well with aggressive budgets like those of Ralph Klein and Mike Harris; currently seven provinces now have balanced budgets.

The benefits from the changing focus of spending to saving will help the economy as the baby boomers pour money into the stock market and mutual funds. This is one place where great opportunities will arise for those health care professionals savvy enough to be able to understand these types of investments, and the following chapters will show them the way.

Additionally, as previously discussed, health care professionals have two advantages working in their favour:

1. *above-average income to allow good investing, and*
2. *a good future industry to be working in.*

With appropriate personal financial planning, all health care professionals can prosper in the future despite negative changes to the economy. Many health care professionals will be able to take advantage of the changes by providing good private health care to Canadians and Americans.

When you combine these factors with the country's strong infrastructure, the highly skilled workforce, and the abundance of natural resources, Canada will continue to remain the best country in the world to live. As you will see in future chapters, there are many other areas that health care professionals can improve upon along the road to financial independence. The remaining chapters will show you how to spend less, save more, and optimize your investment portfolio allowing effortless creation of healthy wealth.

The 21st Century will bring changes to the health care system that will potentially cause hardship for some health care professionals, but with appropriate education and awareness there will also be opportunities for tremendous growth. Now is the time for health care professionals to learn more about personal financial planning!

NOTES:

2

SEVEN BASIC BUT ESSENTIAL PRINCIPLES

What is your financial goal? To make a million dollars? Without thinking about it too deeply, most people would probably agree that if they had a million dollars to invest, they would be set for life.

Making a million dollars is relatively easy for most health care professionals. The hard part is trying to keep that million. Health care professionals spend anywhere from 6 to 15 university years focusing on a particular area of interest that quickly leads into a busy professional career leaving little if any time to think about financial planning — which is what you need to do if you want to keep that million dollars.

There are seven basic but essential principles that you must understand to achieve optimal personal financial planning and "healthy wealth." In this chapter, I review each of these principles; later, throughout the book, a discussion of each principle is integrated into other topics where pertinent.

COMPOUND INTEREST AND TIME

Simply put, compound interest is the amount earned on the principal investment plus the interest already accrued, creating exponential growth over time. The more frequently the interest compounds, the better; monthly compound interest is better than semiannual compound interest.

Learning the Rule of 72 will help you remember the effect that time and compounding has on your investment. It states that the time it takes for money to double is 72 divided by the annual interest rate. For example, with a return rate of 5%, your investment will double in 14.4 years; with a rate of 10% it will take 7.2 years; with 12%, 6 years; and with 15%, 4.8 years. A 30-year-old health care professional could become a millionaire by age 63 by saving only $500 a month at a conservative rate of 8%. But if the rate were 13%, he or she would reach the same goal by the age of 55.

Table 1 shows this relation between time and return rate. You can see that compounding interest is even more impressive if you can get a higher rate of return, which I will show you how to achieve in a later chapter. The effect of compounding is even more spectacular if used within an RRSP because you do not pay any taxes (until you withdraw the money) allowing even more money to compound. The earlier you avail yourself of these contributions, the more spectacular is the compounding growth.

For students who do not believe they can afford to put anything toward their RRSP, consider the following example showing why you should try very hard to make early contributions. If you contribute $2,000 per year into an RRSP which earns 12% from the age of 22 to 27 and then stop, you will have over $1 million by the age of 65. But if you procrastinate and start at age 28, you would have to contribute *every* year up to age 65 to earn the same amount. The message is that compounding interest works miracles if you *start early* and *seek the highest return* that you can reasonably tolerate. (There are a number of safe mutual funds that you will learn about later that have average 10- to 15-year returns of 15%, so a return of 10% to 12% is a possibility even for the risk-intolerant health care professional.)

Table 1
The Effect of Compounding on a One-Time Investment of $10,000

Return Rate	5 years	10 years	15 years	20 years	25 years
5%	$12,763	$16,289	$20,789	$26,533	$33,864
8%	14,693	21,589	31,722	46,610	68,485
10%	16,105	25,937	41,772	67,275	108,347
13%	18,424	33,946	62,543	115,231	212,305
15%	20,114	40,456	81,371	163,665	329,190

INFLATION

You cannot achieve your personal financial goals if you do not have an appreciation of what inflation is or, more important, what it does. Inflation is the "silent killer" in the financial world that is unmatched in the health field simply because it cannot be eradicated or contained. Inflation is what caused the average price of a three-bedroom Canadian home to skyrocket from $50,000 in 1976 to the present $150,000 or why a movie and popcorn cost $4 then but $12 now.

Inflation is measured by the Consumer Price Index (CPI), which fluctuates from year to year and is influenced by a variety of commodities. We cannot know exactly what inflation will be in 1997 or 1998, but we can make a good guess based on past figures. In the last 20 years, inflation has averaged approximately 6.5% per year and if we look at just the last 10 years it has been lower at approximately 4%.

Let's look at how inflation affects your investment's *real* return. Assume you invest $50,000 in a guaranteed investment certificate (GIC) with an annual return of 8%. This would be worth approximately $235,000 in 20 years before taxes. But, of course, we have to look at the after-tax amount because that is what you get to keep.

At the 50% tax bracket (which is where most health care professionals are), your return is reduced to $110,000. Now the silent killer hits. Even if we assume a modest annual inflation rate of only 3%, this will further reduce your real return or future buying power (in 20 years) to approximately $60,000! That's right — your $50,000 invested today will be worth only $60,000 20 years from now.

Let's look at another example using a higher inflation rate. Suppose you have a projected monthly income from your retirement investments of $1,000 with a 6% annual inflation. In 10 years, that monthly $1,000 would allow you only $540 of purchasing power and in 20 years only $300. Put another way, to keep your same monthly purchasing power, you would need to increase your investment returns up to $1,800 in 10 years and $3,200 in 20 years.

To get an idea of the effect of inflation, you can reverse the Rule of 72. Instead of dividing 72 by the annual interest rate, divide it by the inflation rate to find out how long it takes your money to be reduced in half. For example, with an annual inflation of 6%, $100 today would be reduced in half ($50) in 12 years and another half ($25) in 24 years. For 5%, the time would be 14.4 years and so on.

It is even more important to consider inflation now than in the past because of salary freezes that many health care professionals are experiencing and will likely see again in the near future. In the 1970s and 1980s there were steady and regular salary increases which frequently offset inflation, but these increases are not happening today. Fortunately, this is not a big problem right now because inflation is quite low, but we can only assume that it will increase again in the future which will then decrease our real take home pay — we will have to do more with less.

The bright side to this picture is that the older you are or the closer to retirement you are, the less effect inflation will have. (Although keep in mind that even retiring next year at the age of 65 still requires a big nest egg to provide for 20-plus years of retirement.) The other bright side is that in later chapters you are going to learn about growth investments that are better hedges against inflation then those investments that many health care professionals may have been exposed to.

A final optimistic note on inflation is that it may not affect everybody the same way. Some people believe that we put too much emphasis on inflation and the CPI. In their interesting book, *Your Money or Your Life,* Joe Dominguez and Vicki Robin argue that inflation as measured by the CPI may be falsely high for some individuals depending on lifestyle. In other words, you can have some control over inflation by choosing how you live. If you choose, for example, to relax at your cottage, which is already paid for, rather than vacation in the United States, inflation will affect you less.

Although *Your Money or Your Life* is an interesting read, I believe it is still prudent for health care professionals to assume an annual inflation rate of at least 4% when doing retirement projections. Better to err on the side of caution.

PERSONAL DEBT

Personal debt (e.g., amounts owing on credit cards, line of credit, bank loans, car loans, department store accounts, and mortgages) is significantly more pernicious than people generally appreciate, especially for health care professions in the 50% tax bracket. While carrying some debt is inevitable from time to time, it is essential that you understand how it can eat away at your savings and how best to minimize and control it.

Remember that any interest you pay on personal debt is with after-tax dollars. That means if you allow a monthly $25 to $50 interest charge to occur on your credit card, it is the same as $50 to $100 earned or pre-tax dollars thrown away every month. The monthly mortgage payment of $1,500 translates into $3,000 earned or billed.

If you cannot avoid some personal debt, it should always be in the form of a bank loan or, even better, on your line of credit (LOC) because the interest charged is significantly less. The beauty of the LOC is that it is usually just 1% to 2% above the bank's prime rate. Compare that to the interest rates most credit cards charge of 18% to 20% or department store cards with rates of 25% to 28%. Remember, this is paid with pre-tax dollars.

Sadly, more than 45% of credit card users do not pay off their balance monthly. Did you know that if you do not pay off the *full* amount each month on your credit card, the bank charges you the interest on the whole amount regardless of the percentage you paid? You will be paying the bank with pre-taxed dollars at a whopping 40% interest charge to you! If you cannot pay off your credit card each month, then *stop using it* or at least use your LOC to pay for it and you will pocket a handsome return risk free.

Another mistake frequently made is carrying personal debt while at the same time having money (outside an RRSP) available to pay that debt in "the emergency fund." This makes no financial sense for two reasons. First, you have to earn a 40% return on this "emergency fund" to match the financial benefit of paying off any personal debt (credit cards) which is next to impossible.

Second, the LOC should be the only emergency fund required by health care professionals. A compromise is to take your "emergency fund" and pay off your personal debt and then borrow the same amount and invest it. You save in two ways:

1. *You pay off your outrageous interest-bearing personal debt.*
2. *You get to deduct the interest you are paying on the borrowed money because it is being used for investment purposes.*

DOLLAR-COST AVERAGING AND THE PAC PLAN

Dollar-cost averaging (DCA) is one of the most widely and successfully used investment principles. This simple but crucial principle is most beneficial to investors who do not have the time to be closely following their investments such as busy health care professionals.

Dollar-cost averaging is a system used to purchase fluctuating growth instruments such as mutual funds or stocks which most, if not all, health care professionals should own. The idea is to buy them on a regular basis with a small fixed amount of cash (e.g., once per month with $1,000) rather than infrequent large purchases (e.g., annually with $12,000).

The frequent small purchases will usually do better in the long run because you will be buying more mutual funds or stocks when they are cheaper and less when they are more expensive, which means your average purchase price will be less than with the lump sum approach. As well, dollar-cost averaging provides a more affordable means of buying investments and it can be an excellent way of saving money because the pattern of regular monthly investments easily becomes a habit.

In fact, I often advise against the traditional loading up of RRSPs at the beginning of the RRSP season and instead recommend a regular monthly buying plan. However, if you do have the lump sum available and if the mutual funds or stocks are particularly cheap in early RRSP season (because of high interest rates) then buying your total RRSP at the beginning of the year is also a reasonable plan and slightly more profitable because of the extra compounding and interest earned.

Dollar-cost averaging allows you to sleep at night knowing that you are getting a good bang for the buck even with market fluctuations. And the best way to achieve dollar-cost averaging is through a pre-authorized contribution (PAC) program. By arranging a PAC with the bank, mutual fund company, or financial planner, your account of choice will automatically be debited every month (or whatever period you desire) by a predetermined amount.

I believe that a PAC program is *mandatory* for every health care professional for several reasons. First, it takes advantage of the "pay yourself first" idea. You won't miss the funds that are regularly being saved and invested in (or outside) your RRSP. Second, it is a forced savings plan and, third, it allows you to take advantage of the dollar-cost averaging if you are investing in growth-type investments.

PRUDENT SPENDING AND SAVING

The principle of not spending more than you earn may be a simple one, but it is exceedingly difficult for many health care professionals to follow. I know from speaking to my colleagues and financial advisers that the more health care professionals earn the more they seem to spend, with the net result being larger debt. Even though they may earn millions of dollars through their working careers, they frequently fail to hold on to it. The real winners are those who can control their spending in the early years to increase their early savings which can then allow the magic of compounding interest to do its work.

Unfortunately, Canadians are not very good when it comes to savings. In the early 1980s, we were saving about $18 for every $100 earned but this has now dropped to $6! This decrease is, of course, a direct reflection of our excessive appetites for spending and our high personal debt load. Our savings levels do not compare well to other countries. The Japanese, for example, manage to save 12% to 15% of their earned income.

For most Canadians, the largest expenses centre around shelter, food, and transportation. You can save a great deal of money in housing expense (see chapter 3), but the only way to save in food and transportation is through prudent spending. There is nothing wrong in spending big dollars on these items — or on luxury items or vacations for that matter. But spending at any level should be compatible with an overall personal financial plan.

The question that is repeatedly asked is "How much should I save"? Most financial planning books say the answer is 10% of your gross earnings. (ie. after taxes) For the self-employed health care professional with a 25% to 35% overhead expense, this means 10% *after* these expenses. I can guarantee you that any health care professional who can put away 10% of his or her gross income after expenses and invest it at 10% to 12% will retire a very young and happy individual.

But most of us have great difficulty putting away this type of money. For those who are 30 to 40 years old, finding even 5% can prove difficult because of the financial demands of the mortgage, children, and other routine expenses. There is, however, a virtually fullproof way of putting away 5% that every health care professional should use and that is the pre-authorized contribution plan (PAC) discussed earlier.

If you are still unable to put away 5% of your gross earnings, then you had better re-examine your lifestyle and spending choices. Additionally, I am sure that you will find ways to save money and, therefore, have more to invest by reading the chapters on insurance and mortgages. Just remember that by putting away 5% to 10%, you will be living on 90% to 95% of your income. If you can't do that now, then what percentage of your present income do you plan to retire on? Most of us will be living on 60% to 70% of our present income at retirement, and if you can do it then, you can do it now!

A FINANCIAL PLAN

Most financial planning books have elaborate spread sheets to help the reader develop a financial plan, but I believe that it is because of these tedious and boring calculations that the planning never happens. I think this is particularly true for younger health care professional investors who have difficulty thinking about age 65 when they have not even bought a house.

Nevertheless, it is important to think about your plan, so to keep you interested, I will use the KISS principle (keep it simple, stupid) to pose three basic questions:

1. *What is your short-term financial plan over the next one to five years (e.g., buying a house, investing in an RRSP, etc.)?*
2. *What is your intermediate plan over the next 5 to 10 years (e.g., paying off the mortgage, saving for children's education, maximizing RRSPs)?*
3. *What is your long-term plan over the next 10 years and beyond (e.g., investing in vacation property, retiring, travelling)?*

Before you go on in this book, write down short answers to each of these questions. For now, you need to simply realize that all these goals have a price tag attached to them. To achieve your goals, you need to have some idea of what level of investments will be required and what the return will be.

I cover these questions and answers in later chapters, and the details of developing your plan are discussed in chapters 12 and 13 after you have learned more about personal financial planning.

TAKE RESPONSIBILITY

The final and most important principle is to take action. Having a plan is not enough; you must be proactive and see the plan through. The only way to do this is by having a basic understanding of all aspects of financial planning and never forget that *no one* cares about your investments more than you do! If you want results *you have to do your own homework.*

The less investment knowledge you have, the less real respect you will get from the different people who will be spending and investing your money. All health care professionals get wide smiles and firm handshakes from these people, but that's not enough if you want to write your own prescription for wealth. There is no doubt in my mind that less-than-scrupulous investors take advantage of financially ignorant health care professionals. We all know stories about the terrible tax shelters that many health care professionals have fallen victim to, but there are many other more subtle and routine ways that financial "experts" take advantage of health care professionals. It may be as simple as charging you a higher commission fee on mutual fund purchases (because you did not know that you could ask for lower) or doing that one extra trade or switch in your portfolio every year, which of course generates commissions and less money for you.

Banks are the same: just by mentioning a lower mortgage rate to your banker, he or she will likely take off 1/4% to 1/2% at the time of purchasing or renewing, which translates into major savings over time. The same is true for interest rates you can negotiate on GIC purchases and on the rate of your personal line of credit. Or how about being sold a universal life insurance policy in your early thirties rather than the more appropriate term insurance?

If you take responsibility and learn more about personal financial planning, then these inappropriate and expensive scenarios will not happen to you and you will be substantially better off financially.

NOTES:

3

YOUR HOME

Buying and owning a home is the dream of many Canadians, and more than 65% of families have managed to realize that dream. Health care professionals are no different than other families, except that they often buy large expensive homes.

Because buying a home is probably the most expensive investment you will ever make, it is common sense to understand the basics of the transaction so that you aren't left paying more than you should — up to $100,000 in extra payments on the average home if you leave it all up to the banks! Armed with proper knowledge, you can save literally thousands of dollars.

Real estate has always been an excellent investment. Many of Canada's estimated 500,000 millionaires have earned their wealth simply by owning their own home. Most of these people struck it rich because of the great real estate appreciation that has occurred over the last 10 to 20 years as well as the tax-free investment that the principal residence offers. The majority of these millionaire home owners were just average income earners.

While general real estate appreciation will likely not keep pace with previous years, you can still build wealth by making careful choices when purchasing a home. It is important that you find out how to minimize interest payments, which means that you need to understand mortgages. The 20 minutes of reading time invested now could save you big bucks over the years. Remember, inadequate consumer mortgage knowledge is part of the reason that banks have become so rich!

Note that all references in this chapter (except where otherwise indicated) are to a home as your principal residence, which receives different tax treatment than investment real estate purchases, which are covered in chapter 9.

TO BUY OR NOT TO BUY?

There are many arguments about owning versus renting, but these arguments apply mostly to the low- and middle-income Canadians who often have to stretch their budgets for the down payment and the monthly mortgage payments. Most health care professionals will not have this financial restriction after a few years in practice.

Adherents of renting argue that in the short run, renting is cheaper and allows you to invest the difference in other areas. This is especially true in times of high interest rates and escalating home prices. However, in the long run, you will likely be far ahead financially if you buy rather then rent especially if you adhere to the principles in this chapter.

I believe that most, if not all, health care professionals should consider buying a home and the earlier the better so you can pay it off quicker which will then free up money for other types of investments. Canadian homes are now more affordable in most regions than they have been for the past 10 to 15 years because of recent market set backs and low mortgage rates. This is especially true in Atlantic Canada and Alberta.

Some experts, such as University of Toronto economist David Foot, believe that prices for many types of city housing will remain flat and even decrease over the next few years because of the demographic slow down of house buying in the post baby boom years. But in his book, *Boom Bust and Echo,* Foot also argues that there will be a surge in the demand and value of other types of homes, such as rural properties, condos, "adult community living" homes, and smaller one-level homes because that is where the baby boomers will want to retire. So if you are planning on buying a home now, you should be thinking about whether it will sell in 10 to 15 years. I wouldn't recommend buying a "monster home," as the demand for larger houses is likely to drop.

The other major reason for buying your own home is the substantial tax savings on the capital gains when you sell, which can be a great source of profit. In the long run, I think Canadian housing prices will again start to appreciate when we see a return of inflation as well as the increased housing demand when the children of baby boomers reach house-buying age. The uncertainty is whether the taxation laws will change in the future. The debt-burdened Canadian government may consider imposing a tax on the sale of the principal residence, which means that buying now and getting some capital appreciation under the wire before such changes are entertained is even more important.

Note that there are a few regions in Canada, primarily in Vancouver, where housing prices are outrageously high and the same logic may not apply. It is difficult to know what to do in these places of focused house inflation. I suspect that in 1997 that there will be 10% to 15% price correction in British Columbia if all goes well at the time of Hong Kong's transition to Chinese government; if not, then prices may actually go higher. If you are thinking about buying in the Vancouver area in 1997, you may be better off waiting it out to see how things resolve themselves.

If you are still uncertain as to whether you should buy or rent, then you may be interested in a computer spreadsheet developed by Canada Mortgage and Housing Corp. For $20.00, you can get this software by calling 1-800-668-CMHC. This allows you to compare the long term difference to buying versus renting, taking into account the many different variables discussed in this chapter.

BUY YOUNG

If you are still a health care student, you probably aren't thinking yet about buying a home. But if possible, do consider it as an option; it is an excellent investment. (This strategy is less likely to be possible for students in Vancouver and Toronto simply because the average home price is too high.)

Let's go through a possible scenario for a first-time purchase. You, as a student, purchase a three-bedroom home with a basement suite for $150,000. You have been paying $400 rent per month which you can now calculate as "income" paid to yourself. You advertise for a roommate to live with you upstairs for $400 per month, and you rent out the basement suite for another $400 per month, giving you a total income of $1,200 per month.

As a first-time home owner you have to put down "only" 5% or $7,500 on your purchase, leaving you with a mortgage of $142,500. The present monthly mortgage payments on that amount with a five-year term rate of 8.5% amortized over 25 years would be $1,130 per month (plus an extra 2.5% mortgage insurance). As you are earning $1,200 from renters, including your own rent, these numbers work so far. The real hurdle is finding the $7,500 down payment.

Examine your options. You could borrow the money from your parents or a well-to-do relative. You could approach the bank for a loan using your parents as co-signers on the premise that you are a good risk client.

You could also consider splitting the down-payment, and the ownership, with another health care professional student. You could borrow money from your RRSP (if you have one) under the Home-Buyer's Plan (covered in detail in the next chapter).

Now let's look what happens when you're ready to sell in five years after you have finished your degree and would like to spend a year in Asia. The house has appreciated at a rate of 5% per year (this is variable depending on where you live) and is now worth $191,442. Remember that you put down only 5% ($7,500) so you now have turned this $7,500 into $41,442 by simply putting your own roof over your head. But there is more: your loan from the bank in the form of a mortgage was for $142,750 amortized over 25 years with a fixed term of 8.5% over five years. After five years of monthly repayments you now owe about $132,010. Therefore, with the $191,442 you must pay the bank $132,010 leaving you with a total gain of $59,432! There is also the sales commission but there are ways to reduce this which we discuss later.

Under normal circumstances, all of this gain would be yours to pocket, but in this case your rental income must be reported as earned income, which may lower your gain somewhat depending on other income and deductions you have. The upside to earning this income is that it will free up RRSP contribution space.

You would only consider buying a home as proposed here if you were planning on holding it for five years or more. This type of home should fit nicely into future housing demands allowing you to sell it with some healthy appreciation. (Again, keep in mind this scenario will not work in all parts of Canada. Regions with higher real estate costs make this plan less workable.) The other advantage to buying a home is that it is the best forced savings plan you can find — short of owing money to a loan shark!

The other details and costs (property tax, utilities, etc.) that affect a house purchase are covered later in this chapter. Additionally, you may want to read the section on real estate as an investment in chapter 9. (For more interesting reading on smart student investing, you may want to read *The Debt-Free Graduate* by Murray Baker. Many health care professional students may find it useful and amusing, especially if frugality is part of their vocabulary.)

THE BASICS OF BUYING A HOUSE

How Much Can I Afford?

To determine how much you can afford when you apply for a mortgage, the lending institution will refer to a standard set of guidelines: either the gross debt service (GDS) or the total debt service (TDS). The GDS ratio allows for up to 32% of the family's gross monthly income to pay for mortgage, taxes, and utilities. So, a gross monthly income of $10,000 would allow for a maximum $3,000 monthly mortgage payment. From this figure you can calculate the maximum house price you can afford.

The TDS ratio looks at all your debt such as outstanding Visa bills and car payments which together with mortgage payments should be less than 40% to 45% of your gross monthly income. For the health care professional, these figures are very rough because most of us also have 25% to 40% overhead to pay from our gross income. Therefore, if you want to use these ratios more realistically, first subtract your overhead and start with that number.

How Much Should I Spend?

So now you know what you can afford to spend, but the more important question is what *should* you spend? It is important to remember that the less you spend on your mortgage, the more you can afford to save and invest elsewhere for the future.

Health care professionals are known for their selection of "monster homes," which continually consume their paycheque each month frequently pushing them to carry large amounts of debt on their line of credit and other credit cards. A question you might want to consider is whether you really want or need that kind of home. Will the house and its location be appealing in 20 to 25 years when it is time to sell? The next house-buying population will be the children of baby boomers who will start looking around the year 2005 and chances are they will not be looking at large homes. Other home buyers at that time will be the aging boomers themselves, who will be looking to scale down.

In formulating a sound financial plan, it is important to try and buy the right house from the beginning so that you can stick with the same home for many years. Historically, Canadians go through three to four homes in their adult years, frequently in an attempt to "buy up" to realize the capital gains on the house appreciation. Unfortunately many people then turn around and buy a more expensive home usually with a bigger mortgage.

If the price of upper-end Canadian homes is going to "bust" like author Garth Turner argues will happen in his recent book *2015 — After The Boom,* then the owners of these monster home are going to become "house poor and cash poor."

I think that Canadians in the future will not be buying and selling as much as our parents did and they will look for modest-size homes, which is a smart financial move for several reasons. The associated costs of moving can be very high; real estate commissions, movers' bills, transfer taxes, legal fees, etc. average $20,000 to $25,000, most of which is paid with after-tax dollars. If you stay in the same home, you will have it paid off much quicker, freeing up money sooner and allowing your other investments to grow.

Many health care professionals are overexposed to real estate with up to 65% to 80% of their total assets invested in their homes. Such concentration in one area of financial investment limits your ability to diversify your portfolio, which is a key to successful financial planning. Remember that when the real estate market tumbles, it is the big ones that tumble the hardest. While it may rebound eventually, you might have to postpone retirement for 5 to 10 years if your home is your biggest or only nest egg.

Because I am suggesting that your first or second home should be your final one, you must make sure that what you buy fits the bill. The only way to do this is to create a wish list of options for your ideal home. It is important to try and find a home with as many of the features on your list as possible. Not only will you enjoy your home more if you are satisfied with it from the beginning, you will also be less inclined to do expensive renovations in the future, which will save you money because the return on most renovations is very low. If you want a pool, then make sure you find a house with one already installed and save yourself 80% of the cost of having to do it yourself. Likewise, buying a home with a finished basement will save you 52% of the cost of later renovations. (There are some renovations, such as kitchen renovations, that are quite rewarding to do and which will give you a 70% to 80% return on your money when you sell. See chapter 9.)

When Should I Buy?

As has already been discussed, you should buy as early in your life as financially possible. But there is also an optimal season to buy.

History shows that the cheapest months to purchase a home are November, December, and January and you can save 10% to 15% if you buy during this period. People who sell in this period are usually more flexible because the home has frequently been on the market for some time; others are simply more desperate to sell because they either have to or because the realtor is anxious to make a sale because things are slow.

The Right Price to Pay

There are several ways to evaluate the price of a home, but the simplest is to compare it to others in the area to get an idea of "fair market value." This approach is referred to as *comparative market analysis.*

To start with, your realtor should show you the asking and selling prices for similar homes in the area for the last year. You should also look and compare home prices in other areas of the community for additional input. After 15 to 20 home visits, you will be surprised by how accurately you can predict the asking price.

Keep in mind that the asking price is just that; it is not carved in stone. This price was decided on by the listing realtor and the owner. There is no doubt that certain realtors list high which is attractive to the sellers because they want as much as possible for their home. This scheme, however, can be counter productive for the listing realtor if his or her listings are consistently too high and not selling. In local areas you will get a feel for which realtors list high and which are more on the mark. You want to make sure that you are paying "fair market value" or even preferably below; the only way to do this is to put in the hours and see what is out there.

Another way to estimate what a home is worth is by hiring a professional property appraiser for about $200. Appraisers use several different methods to come to their conclusion. Make sure the appraiser is registered as a Canadian Residential Appraiser or with the Accredited Appraiser Canadian Institute. (The bank will also have an appraiser assess the home, which will cost you about $200, but this is done after the fact and of little value in helping you make an offer. The unofficial rule of thumb I have heard is that banks give you a dollar value 5% less than the true fair market value of the home.)

Another reasonable system is to find out what the *reproduction cost* of the home is. The price of the lot is easy enough to find out. The price to build the home will require calling a few contractors and asking them what the average cost is to build a moderate or upscale home similar to the one that you are interested in. A typical estimate may be $80 to $100 per square foot to which you add the cost of the land. You should also take into account a depreciating factor of 5% per year for the age of the house when using this system.

Once you have decided on what the home is worth, you should then start with a bid that is 5% to 8% less than this price *or* less than what you want to pay as these two values may be different. There is nothing wrong with wanting to pay less than what the home is worth, in fact this is what you should aim for.

There are many "tricks" that can be used to bring down the asking price. By making a firm but non-antagonizing case that the kitchen and bathrooms are 10 years old, for example, and will require immediate remodeling, you should be able to lower the price by $5,000 to $10,000. If the sellers have already bought, then they likely need the sale, in which case I recommend starting your bid 20% below the asking price. Empty homes and "early possession" advertising also usually means a better chance for a lower price as does "owner transferred" and "estate sales." Your bargaining power with new homes is usually less because of the deeper pocket of the builder/developer.

It is always nice to get a good price on the home but the most important factor is that you like it and that you can afford it. If the home is perfect for you and your family but slightly overpriced, then you will have to decide if it is worth paying the extra money. If it is a "keeper" for 10 to 20 years then the answer is yes, but if you will be buying again in 3 to 5 years then the answer is to keep looking.

New or Used?

Whether to buy a new home or a "used" one is a very personal decision that all home buyers have to consider. You should look at both options initially to get an idea of the fair market value of each. As a general rule, you get more bang for your buck if you buy a used home, especially if it is three to seven years old.

The advantage of buying a new home is that you may have input on the design and layout. The disadvantage is the extra cost for items such as the GST, landscaping, drapery, appliances, etc. Some new homes do come with these items, but if not then they should be considered in your budget.

The major disadvantage of buying something older than 10 years is that the wear and tear will start costing you money (i.e., new paint, new kitchen, appliances, etc.).

WORKING WITH A REAL ESTATE AGENT

As with most commissioned jobs, there is a wide range of competency among real estate agents. Some just offer a polite taxi service, where others take their job very seriously and provide great assistance with both buying and selling. As a rule the agent is more important when it comes to selling than buying.

It is wise to pick a realtor who has been in the business for a minimum of five years; this in itself speaks highly for the person as many realtors "retire prematurely" after their first year. Also, choose one who works full time, not part time. There is no cost to you if you are buying a home, and you will find a lot of realtors willing to taxi you around.

When looking at homes to buy, do not discuss your financial affairs with your agent; the less he or she knows the better it is for you. Do not tell the agent what your upper limit is even if you are asked. Remember that while you want the best price, the agent prefers a quick sale, which will certainly happen if you pay enough.

Don't tell the agent which place you "have fallen in love with" because you will get the slanted "good buy" or "good value" line from the realtor which is of no interest to you. Instead just look and ask questions in the presence of the realtor not indicating whether you like the home or not. Remember, your realtor will be talking to the selling realtor and the bottom line for both is a sale that can work for you or against you. By keeping your cards close to your chest, you will come out ahead (although many realtors would disagree with me on this.)

If you are selling your home, then you must pay a commission to the agent which is shared with the agent's company. The commission is usually 6% to 7% on the first $100,000 and 2.5% to 3.5% on the portion of the price above $100,000. The individual agent can pay up to 50% of the commission earned back to the company to cover overhead. The smaller, local independent realtors often get to keep more of the sales commission. Re/Max has started a new trend where the individual agents pay a flat rate or "tenant's" fee for the use of the office and then they get to keep up to 95% of the commission.

It is important for you to know what the agent's arrangement is when it is time to sell as there may be more of an incentive for the Re/Max agent to sell than for others. The commission is negotiable and should be discussed in advance, especially if you have more than one property to sell and decide to use the same agent for both.

As a seller, you also need to decide the type of listing you wish to use. The most popular is the Multiple Listing Service (MLS) because of the greater exposure it gives your property, which increases the chances of finding a buyer. Other types of listings are open and exclusive, which in general I do not recommend because of the lower exposure your property will receive.

The Offer to Purchase Contract

The offer to purchase is the contract drawn up with your initial offer to the seller. Besides the offering price, the crucial part of the contract is the list of "subject clauses." The subject clauses are those things that provide information you need before you can commit to the sale. For example, the most important subject is "approval by lawyer," giving you time to have the offer reviewed for any potential legal pitfalls. The other important subject clauses to consider are "subject to home inspection by a professional inspector," "subject to bank approval," and "subject to engineer's report," which should also be put in if applicable.

Realtors often resist subject clauses because they see them as more hurdles which decreases the chances of a sale; it is up to you to make sure the clauses you need are included. You should also list in the contract what chattels (i.e., movable possessions) you want to assume with the purchase (e.g., curtains, washer, dryer, stove, pool accessories, etc.) to avoid any disagreements later.

The contract also states the amount of deposit, which is usually 5% to 10% of the purchase price. It should be placed in trust with your realtor's company or with your lawyer and the current interest rate should be paid on it after 30 days.

THE HOME INSPECTION

A professional home inspection is a necessity for any used home that you are interested in, be it for personal use or investment purposes. Unfortunately, only 30% to 40% of Canadians use this service which is less than the number of people who get a used car examined by a mechanic before buying! This is hard to understand when you look at the dollar difference.

You should ask each home inspector for references, an example of a finished home report, and a summary of his or her experience in the field before deciding on who to hire. In British Columbia, Alberta, Ontario, and Quebec, the home inspector should be a member of the Canadian Association of Home Inspectors. For $200 to $300, they will spend three to five hours examining the home from top to bottom and provide you with a report summarizing any deficiencies as well as future costs you can expect to incur (e.g., furnace cleaning/repair, fridge replacement, etc.). You can use this information to proceed confidently with the home purchase, to renegotiate a lower price, or, most important, to get out of a catastrophe waiting to happen (e.g., faulty foundation).

You should accompany the home inspector to learn about the house, but also to make sure that he or she does a thorough job. Finally, do not use a home inspector who waives responsibility by using a disclaimer. Health care professionals must carry insurance to protect from human error; so should home inspectors.

Never allow your realtor to limit the home inspection clause in any way. Buying a house is a time of great financial constraints and every dollar will be needed to close the deal.

MORTGAGES

This section discusses the different mortgage options and the reasons why health care professionals should take mortgage matters into their own hands. By being proactive and arranging a proper mortgage and repayment plan, you can save tens of thousands of dollars.

Mortgages are extremely expensive for two reasons. First, they are paid with after-tax dollars, which for health care professionals means every $1,000 paid on the mortgage equals $2,000 earned. Second, the amount of interest paid over the life of a mortgage is astronomical. Most people have no idea how much of their monthly payment goes toward the interest, not the principal. On average, on a monthly basis, the interest part of your payments is greater than the principal repayment for 15 to 19 years on a mortgage amortized over 25 years!

Consider this scenario to understand why paying off your mortgage as quickly as possible should be one of your priority investment plans. Let's assume that you have a mortgage at 8% and you are in the 50% marginal tax bracket. To get a better investment return than making extra payments on your mortgage, you would have to earn more than 16% in interest income *consistently* because that 16% return would be taxed at 50% decreasing your after-tax return to 8%! This kind of return is hard to find especially on a consistent basis; but the extra mortgage payment is *guaranteed* and is available to you every month (with most institutions) for the term of the mortgage.

It is amazing how many health care professionals are so pleased with themselves because they have $10,000 socked away in a non-RRSP vehicle for "that emergency," but they haven't paid off their mortgage. Even if you are getting a reasonable 10% interest income return before taxes, which is reduced to 5% after taxes, you aren't coming close to the type of benefit you could have from pre-paying your mortgage. If this describes your situation, then I think you have now found an "emergency" on which to spend your money.

Mortgage Basics

A mortgage is a contract between you (the mortgagor) and the lender (the mortgagee) where you receive "cash" to purchase your home and in return the lender gets paid a very handsome interest rate. Additionally, the agreement gives the lender security in the form of a mortgage document filed against the home in case you default on your payment.

A mortgage has an *amortization period* and an initial payment schedule agreement or *term* attached to it. The amortization period is the length of time it will take to pay off the mortgage entirely assuming the interest rate taken with your first term. Most amortization periods run 25 years, but I do not recommend such a long period for health care professionals.

The term of the mortgage is the period of time agreed to by the purchaser where periodic payments are made with a specific interest rate. Then the remaining mortgage is either paid off or another term is negotiated — with either the same or a different lending institution. Most terms run 3 to 5 years but can go from six months to 10 years (even 25 years at one institution). The longer the term, the higher the interest rate will be.

The advantage of a longer term is the peace of mind of knowing in advance what your payments will be. If you choose a short term, then you will have the potential stress of renegotiating more often with the risk that interest rates will be higher. The choice between short and long is a very individual decision which must be based on many factors such as current interest rates, your other financial obligations, your present stress level, your ability to closely follow the markets, etc.

A mistake that people often make when it is time to renegotiate the term is opting for an amortization period that is the same length as the previous one. While this will decrease your monthly payments, it will mean you are paying more over the long run to the banks. When renewing a term it is imperative to renegotiate an amortization period that is less the previous term. For example, if you are nearing the end of a 5-year term on a 25-year amortization, you should renegotiate the next 3- to 5-year term with a 20-year amortization period (or less). The financial savings effect of shortening your amortization period is astounding (see Table 2).

Before making your final decision on choosing a term, it is worth knowing that present 3- to 5-year mortgage rates are three percentage points below the average rate for the last 25 years (as of June 1996)! This is cheap money by most standards even with the low inflation.

Table 2
Effect of Shortening the Amortization Period (assuming $100,000 mortgage at 8% interest)

Amortization	Monthly payment	Total Interest paid	Interest saved (vs. 25 year)
25 yrs	$763	$129,098.54	—
20 yrs	$828	$98,927.31	$30,171.23
15 yrs	$948	$70,692.37	$58,406.17
10 yrs	$1,206	$ 44.794.25	$84,304.29

By paying just an extra $65 per month ($828-$763), you save $30,171.23!)

Types of Mortgages

There are many different types of mortgages available from many different institutions, but for the health care professional who is financing a principal residence, there are really only two options: the conventional mortgage and the high-ratio mortgage. You will qualify for a conventional mortgage if you have a 25% down payment on the home. If you do not, then you must pay insurance to obtain a high-ratio mortgage. In that case, you can get a mortgage for up to 90% of the purchase price, but the more you mortgage the more interest you pay. (If you are a first-time home buyer, you can mortgage up to 95% of the cost of the home.)

By law, any mortgage with a down payment of less than 25% must be insured by either the Canada Mortgage and Housing Corporation (CMHC) or Mortgage Insurance Company of Canada (MICC). The insurance for the high-ratio mortgage is anywhere from 0.5% to 2.5% of the principal which is frequently and quietly tacked onto the borrowed amount. You would save thousands of dollars if you pay this insurance up front, but few have the cash to do so.

You may be able to arrange a conventional mortgage even if you do not have the 25% cash down payment in the bank. If you are lucky enough to have a rich parent who can loan you the funds, then you are all set. Other methods include taking out a second mortgage for the 25% which is not a bad idea if you expect to be making a good salary in the near future and can pay the second loan quickly. Getting the second mortgage may require the help of a mortgage broker and because there is less security for the lender you will pay more on the interest. If you have money in an RRSP, then you may be able to use some of it to put toward your 25% down payment under the Home-Buyer's Plan (see chapter 4). Or you might arrange a vendor-take-back mortgage for the 25% which is discussed below.

Insurance on the high-ratio mortgage is quite expensive and should be avoided if possible or at least paid for up front. The CMHC has some good free information available for potential home buyers which can be obtained by calling 1-800-668-CMHC.

Another option is to assume the mortgage that already exists on the house. If the rate is better than what you can get at your institution, then an assumed mortgage may be an attractive option that can save you money on legal fees, appraisal, and registration. When opting for this type of mortgage, you frequently still have to seek another mortgage from your financial institution to make up any shortfall.

Another type of mortgage that is gaining popularity because of the high insurance interest being charged on high-ratio mortgages is the *vendor-take-back*. In this arrangement, the vendor helps the buyer out by providing their own "mortgage" instead of the financial institution. The vendor-take-back mortgage can be for part or all of the mortgage cost. The advantage to the buyer is less hassle, lower rates, less down payment and cheaper administrative costs. The advantage for the seller is that it is easier to unload the property and there is great security in the form of repossessing the property if there is a default on the payment. Often it is just a portion of the purchasing price with the remainder coming from your down payment and a first mortgage from your institution. In essence the vendor is assuming a second mortgage. The rates and terms are negotiable but this type of mortgage is not usually assumable or as flexible as other types. The seller may want to keep the vendor-take-back mortgage for the monthly cash flow or may want to sell it to a mortgage broker.

Overall the vendor-take-back mortgage is better for the buyer than for the seller especially if it is a principal residence for both parties. There is the risk of default for the seller and the interest income is taxed as personal income rather then capital gains which is less favourable.

Other home lending schemes you may hear about include home equity loans and reverse mortgages. Both of these are methods of getting money out of the equity built up in your home, but are generally not appropriate for buying a first or second home as a principal residence.(see chapter 9)

For those health care professionals who can incorporate their practices, there are other options available regarding mortgages which are covered in chapter 11 under taxes and incorporating. Additionally there are potential ways to make your mortgage interest deductible which are also covered in chapter 11.

If you want more information about some of the alternative types of mortgages mentioned, you might want to consider looking into the services of a mortgage broker. A mortgage broker is someone who specializes in creative financing and more recently has been also taking a share of the more traditional mortgage market, which has become increasingly competitive. A broker is an excellent resource for those who do not have the time to research the market; often their services are free because the eventual lending institute pays their bill rather than you.

Options for Your Mortgage

There are many other options to choose from after you have settled on the conventional versus high-ratio mortgage and the long versus short term. These are critical issues that the health care professional should give thought to before sitting down with a banker.

The first decision is whether to opt for an *open* or closed mortgage. A closed mortgage locks you in at a certain rate and you are, therefore, protected from future interest rate hikes. This choice provides peace of mind because you know your expenses in advance.

An open mortgage is said to give you more flexibility with extra payments, paying off the mortgage at any time, moving the mortgage to another institution, or locking in when the rates are quite low. You cannot do this in a closed mortgage except on the maturity date or by paying a penalty (except for the extra payments that are now allowed). For the greater flexibility of an open mortgage, you pay an extra 1/4% to 3/4%.

Conventional thinking says that you would consider an open mortgage if you thought interest rates were going to go down and you did not want to lock in at the present higher rates or if you just like the thrill of following the interest rates and mortgage rates on a daily basis (yes, some do!). However, as stated above, the competition has made closed mortgages so attractive that I do not think it is worth paying the extra percentage for the open. If you do want flexibility (e.g., you suspect the rates to fall or you know an inheritance is coming to you), then a better option might a short closed term of six months.

The second decision you will have to make is whether to go with a *fixed-* or *variable-rate* mortgage. A fixed-rate mortgage means that the interest rate being charged on the mortgage will remain the same for the whole term regardless of what happens to the banks interest rates. A variable-rate mortgage means that the interest rate on your mortgage fluctuates in accordance with the bank's interest rate which is dictated by the money-market rates (T-bills). Your monthly payments remain fixed, but the amount of the payment that goes toward the principal varies. You win if the interest rates go down (more against the principal) but you lose if the rates go up.

Banks will automatically give you a fixed-rate mortgage if you do not bring the topic up, which is a good thing for most health care professionals who do not have the time to be following daily interest rates. (You can, for an extra charge, have some insurance against rate increases by opting for the new *cap-rate variable* mortgage which sets a ceiling on how high an interest rate you may pay if you have guessed wrong.)

A recent popular hybrid of these different options is the *convertible* mortgage. In essence, this is a closed mortgage with a fixed rate for terms of 6 to 12 months (hence the "6-month convertible"), but one in which you can convert your mortgage at any time to a longer term with either an open or closed feature. It gives you the benefit of the lower short-term rates and the freedom to lock in at any time (if rates drop or start to go up) without a penalty, but again it requires a vigilant watch of the interest rates for which many health care professionals do not have the time or inclination. Be careful, however, as some institutions allow you to only convert to a limited term.

Extra payment privileges come in at least two forms and should be a mandatory option for all closed mortgages. Most mortgage institutions will allow you to pay down up to 10% of the original mortgage once per year as a lump sum payment or anniversary payment. Some institutions only allow this lump sum payment based on the current balance which is less attractive. Additionally, most also allow extra monthly payments — either 10% to 15% extra on each monthly payment or even double-up payments each month.

These extra payments will not be pushed on you or even advertised; it is up to you to be proactive and ask about them as they can make a drastic difference in the amount you pay for your home over the life of a mortgage. Table 3 shows you the incredible interest savings from double-up payments as well as the remarkable "shortening" effect it has on the amortization period. When this is combined with the annual lump sum payment, the effect is even more dramatic.

If we look at a $100,000 mortgage amortized over 25 years and make just one 15% lump payment on the first anniversary of the mortgage, it shortens the mortgage to 16 years and saves you about $62,000 in interest! If you then increased the monthly payments by 15%, you would further reduce the mortgage to 12 years and save another $3,500. Remember that your monthly mortgage payment consists of principal (good) and interest (bad). If you make extra payments they go directly against the principal (the amount you borrowed). By lowering the principal you also lower the interest payment. As stated earlier, it is hard (if not impossible) to get an investment better than the idiot-proof simple extra-mortgage payment.

Table 3
Effect of Double-up Payments on Mortgage (assuming $100,000 mortgage at 8% interest)

# of double ups	Total interest paid	Interest saved	Shortening of amortization period
none	$129,098.54	—	—
one	$98,863.53	$30,285.06	approx. 5 yrs.
two	$81,925.83	$47,172.71	approx. 7 yrs.
three	$61,486.75	$67,611.69	approx. 12 yrs.

The *payment schedule* should always be weekly or biweekly rather than the standard monthly mortgage payment in order to take advantage of the one or two extra payments per year. A $100,000 mortgage amortized over 25 years with weekly payments shortens the amortization period to 19 years and saves you about $38,000.

Look into *transferable* or *portable* mortgages, which allow you to transfer your existing mortgage to another home in case you move before the existing term is up. You would take this mortgage only if the rate on that term is better than the present going rate; otherwise you would want to consider paying off the existing mortgage plus the penalty (if it is cheaper) with the money from the sale.

It is also important to make sure that your mortgage is *assumable.* This option is useful when it is time to sell your home and your existing mortgage makes it attractive to a potential buyer. The buyer will, of course, have to meet the requirements of the institution holding the mortgage; and it is important to make sure that you are not held accountable if the new buyer defaults on your old mortgage.

Some institutions offer an *early renewal* or *no-fee renewal* option which allows you to renew your term in the last year of the present term "prematurely." This option is useful if the rates are on the rise in your last year allowing you to secure a lower rate. You should demand that this option be written into the mortgage contract and use it as a bargaining tool when comparing mortgages at the different institutions (it is important to compare at least three different institutions).

A *pre-approved* mortgage is something that every health care professional should seek before actually looking at homes. It will focus you on looking within a certain price range that the institution has approved which will save you time and headaches. More important, it will allow you to lock in to a low rate while you look in case the rates are on the increase. Most institutions will allow you to lock in for 90 days.

Mortgage and Home-purchase Fees

It is important to know in advance what fees you face in a real estate transaction because some are negotiable and they will form part of your checklist when you go shopping for a mortgage. These extra costs do add up, often sending you scrambling at the last minute to find extra cash. Remember that the mortgage business is very competitive, which you should take advantage of, to get the best deal possible, especially if you are planning on real estate investing where every dollar saved is important.

Here is a list of the common fees associated with buying a home:

1. *The mortgage application fee is usually about $75 and can be waived if you ask.*
2. *An appraisal fee may cost you $200 to $250. The appraisal is sought by the lending institution to make sure that the purchase price (and mortgage) is appropriate for the home. Royal LePage charges only $75 and some of the trusts and credit unions may charge less. This is also negotiable especially if you are thinking about moving your mortgage to another institution.*
3. *The home and property must be surveyed which will cost you $150 to $250. It is worth trying to get an old survey report if possible which you might be able to shoulder onto the real estate agent. Some people believe that the realtor should pay for the survey.*
4. *Mortgage insurance is required and added to your monthly payment if your down payment is less than 25%.*
5. *The GST applies to purchases of new homes. The GST amount for a new home that will be used as the principal residence is calculated on a sliding scale with a partial rebate based on the purchase price. The rebate is nothing for homes priced over $450,000. For homes priced between $350,000 and $450,000, you will pay*

about 4.5% GST (rather than the usual 7%). The rebate for homes less than $350,000 is 36% of the tax paid to a maximum rebate of $8,750. If you are buying the new home as an investment property, you will not get any rebate regardless of the price.

6. *Legal fees should be discussed beforehand with the lawyer. The usual range is $650 to $900 on homes less than $200,000 but above this the sky is the limit. Many lawyers charge a percentage of the purchase price.*
7. *The transfer tax or property purchase tax differs in each province. In British Columbia it is a whopping 1% of the purchase price which must be paid at the time of closing. This is the biggest and most unexpected hit for the average home buyer and comes directly out of your pocket.*
8. *The final cost is the property tax, which requires you to pay a percentage equal to that portion of that year the house is yours and then full payment every year after. The amount is variable from region to region but usually is 1% to 2% of the property's value. In most provinces there is a rebate or percentage reduction for a principal residence but not for investment or leisure properties.*

Mortgage Renewal

The most important issue concerning mortgage renewal is to remember *when* the term is up; otherwise the institution will just repeat the same term on your behalf regardless of what the current rates are.

The next most important thing is to start watching rates 12 months prior to your renewal date. If there is a financial catastrophe lurking on the horizon, then you may be better getting out of the mortgage prematurely with a penalty and locking in a rate and term suitable for the upcoming couple of years. If your mortgage is due for renewal in 1997/98, this is an essential point to keep in mind. The financial markets are not likely to respond well to another Quebec referendum, and you could pay financially for the political disruption caused. It may be to your advantage to consider breaking your mortgage in 1997 and locking in at the present very favourable rates if you are pessimistic about the results of a referendum.

Another option is to secure a guaranteed rate from an institution several months before your mortgage is due especially if the rates might be higher at the time of your renewal. Most banks will guarantee you today's rate for up to three months. As well, some institutions will also give you the flexibility to renew for no fee in the last year or so of your mortgage if you have asked for it before signing the contract.

If you have not negotiated a no-fee renewal, you should think about *blending.* This is something that the lending institutions will not openly discuss and some mortgage clerks may actual deny exists. It does exist, but will require you being proactive to make it happen, frequently requiring a visit to the bank's upper management.

Blending is where you average your present term rate with the newer lower rate to give you a lower rate *without* a penalty. The term will have to be longer than your present one so the bank is assured of your business for another couple of years. I am told that the Bank of Montreal will openly allow this blending option for a small fee which would likely be waived if you asked.

You should always check with a few other institutions to get the best rate at term renewal time. Don't hesitate to move your business if your current lender will not match the offer. Remember that 1/2% means a significant saving over 15 to 20 years. There may be charges for moving the mortgage, but these are generally quite small and usually they are absorbed by the new lender.

There are a number of other perks now being offered by different lending institutions to lure your business such as cash rewards of 1% of your mortgage (Canada Trust), paying the first three months of interest for you if a five-year term is chosen (T.D. Bank), cash bonus of $500 or 10,000 Aeroplan points (CIBC), etc. These perks can offset any penalty you are charged if you are breaking your mortgage. Prepare a list and compare what each institution is offering; it is well worth the one to two hours of your time. Even better, do it over the phone or ask a mortgage broker to look into it for you.

When to Break the Mortgage

If you are currently (i.e., late 1996) carrying a mortgage that is 10% (even 9%) or above, then you should look into the cost of breaking the present term prematurely and paying the penalty in order to capture a lower interest rate. This can frequently save you a lot of money over the course of the new mortgage. You should, at the same time, call two other institutions to see what they would give you if you moved the mortgage over to them. They will not defray any of the penalty cost, but most will take 1/2% to 3/4% off the posted rate and pick up the appraisal fee and the legal fees plus any transfer fees to get your business.

There are two different ways that lending institutions penalize for breaking mortgages prematurely. The first is the *three months' interest penalty* which is the sum of three months' interest on your mortgage. A ballpark figure for a $100,000 mortgage at 9.5% over 25 years with 2 years remaining on a 5-year term would be about $3,000 in interest penalties. While this is a lot of up-front cash, keep in mind that you make it back in less than a year if your rate goes down to 7.5%. Over three to four years the savings are far greater.

The second type of penalty is the *interest rate differential* which is the difference that the bank stands to lose by your switching to a lower rate. Most bankers will tell you to apply the penalty money directly against the present mortgage instead of breaking. This may be more beneficial financially, but you should ask the banker to give you a computer printout of each of these options and compare. Remember, as a rule, the average banker's job is to lend money, not to save you money (although there are exceptions).

KISS PRINCIPLE — Mortgages

1. *Get three different quotes before choosing a lending institution.*
2. *Arrange biweekly (or weekly) payments rather than monthly.*
3. *Start with a 20-year amortization (even better 15-year) because the health care professional has the money and this is the best forced savings plan available.*
4. *Try and make extra payments whenever possible.*
5. *Avoid the mortgage life insurance offered by the bank and instead build this into your own life insurance policy.*
6. *In the last 6 to 12 months of your present mortgage term, shop around and gently threaten to move your mortgage if you do not get a lower rate. Use the many bonuses available for transferring your mortgage to another lender as a bargaining tool.*
7. *Choose a closed-fixed mortgage rate because the rates are very low, but concentrate on extra payments. Consider an open mortgage (and/or short term) only if*

you are expecting a rate drop, expecting a lump sum of cash, or thinking of selling soon.

8. *If you are considering a variable rate, be prepared to follow the rates daily.*
9. *Take the mortgage from the institution that compounds the interest the least frequently.*
10. *When writing up the offer to purchase, put in a clause for approval by your lawyer so he or she can look it over. This is especially important for investment properties.*
11. *Consider breaking your present mortgage and demand a blend if your present rate is too high (greater than 9.5% as of August 1996).*

DO I BUY UP OR RENOVATE?

It used to be common belief that purchasing larger homes, or "buying up," was a great way to increase the value of your house and capitalize on the tax-free growth. This was especially true for those fortunate enough to be able to do a lot of the building or renovations themselves; this "sweat equity" resulted in big payoffs. Unfortunately, most busy health care professionals do not have the time, knowledge, even inclination for this type of sweat equity work.

Most people move into larger, more expensive homes or renovate their existing homes at times of life changes — and expanding family, for example. Historically, 65% of Canadians have moved up and 35% have renovated. I think in the future we will see a reversal of this pattern for a variety of reasons, and such a reversal will have financial benefits.

First, a lot of areas of the country will not see the same real estate appreciation that has occurred in the past 10 to 20 years. Second, from a financial viewpoint, renovating wins hands down over buying up especially if it requires an increase in your mortgage.

For example, if you are thinking of getting a larger home that will require another $100,000 mortgage and your house appreciates 4% per year, then in 20 years this would appreciate to approximately $220,000. But remember that you are making monthly mortgage interest payments which would decrease your return depending on how quickly you pay off the extra mortgage (not to mention the cost of moving).

Alternatively, you could put the $100,000 (the monthly extra payment earmarked for mortgage) in an equity mutual fund with a return of 13%.

This translates into approximately 8% return after taxes (40% tax bracket) which would give you close to $450,000 after taxes in 20 years! Recognizing that you would not put all the money earmarked for the extra mortgage into this equity fund because some of it will go into renovations, this example still demonstrates that it is a lot cheaper to renovate or build up than to move. So it is my belief that it is best to try and buy the right house from the beginning and stick with it, or if you need a different home, then at least try and stay away from increasing the mortgage.

Remember, too, that it is also possible that we may see some form of taxation on principal residences in the future. It may not be beneficial then to have a larger home as any tax would likely be based on the value of the home. Finally, as has been already mentioned, and will be covered in more detail in chapter 12, putting all your eggs in one financial basket doesn't provide you with a healthy asset mix allocation.

RECREATION PROPERTIES

As a rule recreational properties are almost never good financial investments. First, if you take the $25,000 to $50,000 that you use to acquire the property and compare this to a good equity mutual fund you will see the substantial differences. The return on recreation properties in most places in Canada over the last 10 to 20 years has shown a gain of 7% to 9% at best versus 13% to 15% on a good equity fund.

Second, there are the extra costs that accompany recreation property. If you buy a cottage, you'll probably buy a boat, water skis, etc. If you buy a ski chalet, you'll buy ski passes. And don't forget property tax, insurance, etc. Of course, if you are buying a recreation property as a lifestyle decision, then you have to think about more than finances. With disability stress claims for health care professionals up astronomically in the last five years, maybe more of us should invest less in huge fancy homes and more in a relaxing vacation property.

Other people, however, believe that the demand and, therefore, the price of cottages and ski chalets may go up over the next 10 years as the retiring baby boomers look for more peace and solitude in rural areas. The American statistics tend to support this notion showing that boomers are buying up vacation properties in droves. The percentage of people buying these properties has tripled in the last few years and most believe that the peak demand by these boomers will occur over the next 5 to 15 years.

The best draws are places that can be accessed in both summer and winter, apparently as a potential retirement location which then may be claimed as the final principal residence. Will this happen in Canada? Although I do not have any national statistics, if you look at resorts like Whistler the findings are similar with sky rocketing sales and appreciation. The average-priced condo in 1985 was $99,000 and in 1994 it was $190,000. The average-priced chalet in 1985 was $125,000 and in 1994 it was $385,000.

There also seems to be a trend for couples who are fed up with urban living to sell their city homes and buy in the country. Some commute daily; others rent a condo in the city where they stay three or four nights a week and spend the rest in the country. Because of the significant difference in home prices between the two locations, this arrangement can be cheaper, even with the additional rent. And what a great way to retire!

I believe that you should consider investing in recreation property only after you have made a reasonable dent in both your principal residence mortgage and your RRSP. Ideally the location should be a place where you might consider retiring (or others can if you sell) which would then allow you the possibility of claiming it as the principal residence some day after you sell your present home. Ideally it should be accessible year round or at least by the time you retire. If it is reasonably accessible, you could consider renting it out one or two months of the year to offset your expenses. Another option is owning a duplex arrangement which would cut your expenses significantly.

Time shares are another type of recreation property that a lot of health care professionals get involved in. As a rule, these are not good investments and, unfortunately, health care professionals in particular have fallen prey to problems associated with them. All too often these purchases are rushed decisions creating many questions and anxiety after the fact.

There are several variations of time shares or "vacation ownerships" to choose from. There is the *right to use,* where you do not own but basically rent for a set week or two per year. When the term expires you are out. The other is *fee-simple ownership,* which does give you a percentage ownership. You may be 1 of 40 who owns that particular property with all sharing it at different times.

The major problem with time shares is the lack of regulations especially for those outside of Canada. If you are interested, take your time and rent the property (or area) a few times before diving in. Some companies now offer an *exchange* program where you can trade locations, but you still run into restrictions of fixed dates with no money back if you leave early or the frustration of not being able to extend at the last minute.

A final word: most financial advisers do not recommend buying vacation property in the United States because of the increasingly complex tax regulations on any rental income as well as estate tax that you will have to pay at the time of your death if you still own the property.

4

REGISTERED RETIREMENT SAVINGS PLAN (RRSP)

Without a doubt, RRSPs are one of the best "guaranteed investments" for high tax-paying health care professionals. Even with the recent changes to the RRSP legislation (i.e., capping the maximum level of investment for the foreseeable future), contributions to a plan should remain a priority in your personal financial plan.

All Canadians benefit when contributing to RRSPs, but health care professionals in the 50%-plus tax bracket benefit the most because of the excellent immediate tax savings, the prolonged tax deferral break, and the tax-free growth that is allowed. The typical example used to bring home this point is that someone in the 50%-plus tax bracket making an RRSP contribution of $5,000 with pre-tax dollars will see that translate into a savings of $2,500 in the form of a tax refund. The tax deferral that is allowed is basically a "free loan" from the government, and when you repay it you can pay less taxes if you plan properly.

Despite the benefits, only 40% to 50% of eligible Canadians contributed in 1994/95 and even then the average contribution was only 25% of the allowable maximum. The figures, however, do show an improving trend with 5.3 million Canadians contributing a record $21 billion in 1994, which was up 9% from 1993. We still have a long way to go, however, as 50% of contributors have less than $10,000 in their RRSPs, and only 13% currently have more than $50,000 in RRSP savings, which is simply not enough!

In this chapter, I do not cover the effects of private pension plans on RRSPs as most health care professionals are or will be self-employed in the future. If you are currently employed with a pension plan and would like to learn more about this aspect of RRSPs, I recommend Steven Kelman's book, *RRSPs 1996*.

Tables 4 and 5 at the end of this chapter demonstrate the growth of RRSPs with different contribution levels as well as the amazing effect of time and compounding on different rates of return.

THE FUNDAMENTALS OF RRSPS

Contribution Period

Most people think of January and February as "RRSP season," but the contribution period for any one year is that year plus the first two months of the following year. So, for example, you can make contributions to your 1996 RRSP any time from January 1, 1996 to February 28, 1997. The "extra" two months is a bonus for procrastinators, and unfortunately the majority of the contributions do occur in the last 30 to 60 days available.

The disadvantage of delaying, however, is that you lose the sheltered compound growth for the previous months. Contributing early in the year rather then in the last two months of the allowable contribution period can make a big difference. For example, if you assume a modest contribution of $2,500 per year with an average return of 8%, the difference between contributing early or late can add up to $200,000 over 35 years. By using the PAC (preauthorized contribution) program discussed in chapter 2, you will still be ahead by $108,000.

Contribution Amount

You can contribute each year 18% of the previous year's earned income to a maximum of $13,500 in 1996. (This maximum translates to an annual income of approximately $75,000.) Because the contribution amount is based on the previous year's income, you will not be able to make a large contribution in your first "employed" year as a health care professional; on the other hand, you will still be able to contribute in your first year of retirement even though you have earned little income.

The rules concerning contribution amounts are subject to change with each federal budget. In the last budget the government said that the $13,500 level would be in place for the next several years, but you should probably prepare for that amount to decrease in the future. The optimal method of investing in RRSPs, therefore, is to contribute the maximum amount early in your career and early in the year. The difference between contributing $5,000 versus $10,000 per year for 25 years is approximately $560,000 (assuming a 10% annual return). But because of tax-free compounding growth, this additional $560,000 only costs you an extra $125,000 in contributions.

The Carry-Forward Rule

The carry-forward rule, which came into effect in 1991, allows you to carry forward any unused portion of your RRSP contribution after and including 1991. This is most helpful for the younger health care professionals starting out who cannot afford to maximize their RRSPs early in their careers.

Many financial experts believe that the carry-forward rule will not last because people may intentionally not contribute for years knowing that they are going to receive a large sum of money (e.g., inheritance or family gift) which they can then put into their RRSPs.

When Can I Start to Contribute?

You can begin contributing to an RRSP whenever you start earning income. This can be any age, but the income must be earned and there are definitions of what is and is not considered "earned." It may be worth considering paying your teenagers a salary for legitimate work around your office, if this is possible for you, so that they are receiving "earned income" and can set up RRSPs at an early age; this is certainly something you should be arranging with your spouse if he or she does not receive other forms of earned income. By starting at a young age, your children will see tremendous growth on even very small contribution amounts because of the long compounding effect.

A minor is allowed to earn up to $6,456 per year without paying taxes because of the personal tax credit. This income should still be reported in order to allow him or her to start an RRSP. Even if the RRSP is not activated, the young person can build up the unused RRSP with the carry-forward rule. You might also then consider topping up the amount by making an "excess contribution" for the children as discussed below.

Spousal RRSPs

A spousal RRSP is created when the higher-income earning spouse puts part or all of his or her yearly RRSP contribution into the spouse's RRSP. The total contribution to both RRSPs cannot exceed your maximum yearly limit. The "receiving" spouse can still make his or her own contribution (but doesn't have to) up to the personal limit. The tax break for the spousal contribution is given to the high-income earning spouse. (Note: as of 1993, a common-law spouse is recognized for the RRSP spousal plan.)

A spousal RRSP is one of the best ways of "income splitting," which is a technique that should be used if there is a disparity in your incomes or if you expect there to be at the time of retirement. For example, if your expected retirement income is $80,000 per year, then you will be paying taxes with a 52% marginal rate (taxes will be $28,500). But if the income is split between the two spouses at $40,000, then your marginal tax rate will be only 40% (and taxes will be $10,320 x 2 = $20,640) meaning a lower total family tax bite. As well, both spouses would be eligible for the federal pension income tax credit after age 65 when you can convert your RRSP to an annuity or RRIF (see chapter 13). The spousal plan can also provide a way to continue contributing (and therefore defer taxes) past the age of 69 if your spouse is younger than you.

If you invest in a spousal RRSP, you do need to think ahead, because if you take funds out of the plan before three years after the last contribution, the withdrawal will be taxed on *your* income, not your spouse's. It does not matter whether it was you or your spouse who made the last contribution. (You can, however, get access to the money within three years by collapsing the RRSP into an annuity or RRIF, but there are some limitations which your accountant can tell you about — see chapter 13.)

You cannot transfer funds from your established RRSP into a spousal plan; rather the spousal plan must be set up in advance to allow for direct deposits. Transferring or "rolling over" the assets is possible upon your death as long as the spouse is named beneficiary.

Some people fear the repercussions of investing in spousal plans because of the high divorce rate. However, current law would most likely split all family assets in the case of a divorce unless there was a prenuptial agreement stating otherwise.

Excess Contributions

A legal tax "loophole" that smart investors took advantage of was to over contribute (up to $8,000 until recently) to their RRSPs to increase their tax-sheltered gains. As of January 1996, this "legal" over contribution amount has been reduced to $2,000. Anything over this triggers a 1% penalty per month on the amount of over contribution.

For those who are in the position of already having the extra $8,000 inside their RRSPs, you must put it toward the subsequent contribution years until the amount is reduced to the allowed $2,000 over contribution.

If you have the extra cash to "over contribute," then you should take advantage of this allowance, but remember that you do not get the immediate tax deduction, just the tax-free growth. Also remember that it will have to be deducted from your total yearly RRSP at some point in the future. Finally, this over contribution is a great opportunity to put excess cash in the children's RRSP at an early age as long as they have earned reported income (e.g., from jobs such as a paper route).

Cashing Your RRSPs

You can cash or unwind your RRSP at any age, but you are required by law to do so by age 69 (recently reduced from age 71). You have several options for unwinding the RRSP for retirement which are covered in detail in chapter 13. There is also a complicated system in place that allows you to borrow against the assets in the RRSP which is usually done through a bank or trust company. This is generally not recommended because of the loss of tax-deferred compounding growth.

Safety of the RRSP

If your RRSP is with a bank or trust company, it can be insured up to $60,000 by the Canada Deposit Insurance Corporation (CDIC). The insurance companies themselves are in turn insured by the Canadian Life and Health Insurance Compensation Corporation. You can, therefore, have a maximum coverage of $120,000 at any one bank or trust company because there is another $60,000 coverage for any non-RRSP savings account. If you and your spouse have separate accounts, the amount is $240,000 in total coverage for the family. You cannot increase the coverage by having money in two different branches of the same institution.

If you are concerned about security for amounts over $60,000, it is best to deposit anything above that amount with another institution. The recent collapse of Confederation Life has some Canadians questioning the safety of these large "invincible" institutions and there may be good reason to think about "insurance on insurance."

Similarly, credit unions guarantee investments with insurance with different ceilings in each province. As a general rule, the coverage amount is larger with credit unions than with banks or trust companies. The insurance companies also provide coverage on guaranteed-type RRSPs (and RRIFs) up to $60,000, again provided by the Canadian Life and Health Insurance Compensation Corporation.

These insurance policies generally apply only to guaranteed-type investments and not toward mutual funds, bonds, or mortgages. If you have your RRSP with a broker or mutual fund dealer, you will not be covered by CDIC insurance, but I believe your greater return rate offsets this risk. Additionally, as you will see, by having a diversified portfolio with a proper asset mix allocation and by using the principles outlined in this book, you will mostly negate the need for this type of "expensive" low return insurance. This insurance is more important in the retirement years when the safety of the principal is everything, and it may then be worthwhile having some of your nest egg in these types of investments.

Foreign Content

You can invest up to 20% of your RRSP *book value* in foreign investments. The book value is the price at which you bought, which can be considerably less than the current market value if you have captured some of the phenomenal growth that has occurred elsewhere in the world in the past few years. Canadians are catching onto the golden opportunity of foreign investment; 28% of RRSP contributors took advantage of this in 1996 compared to only 12% in 1992.

Foreign content is important for both inside and outside the RRSP. The Canadian stock market accounts for only 2% to 3% of the world markets and it is very slanted toward certain sectors of the economy. If you look at returns over the last number of years from different markets throughout the world, you will see that the Canadian stock market is slightly below average in yearly returns. Additionally, countries perform differently each year depending on where they are in their own market cycle, which gives you the option of changing your country of interest each year if you wish.

Another reason for considering foreign content in your portfolio is because of the current poor financial status of Canada. The ongoing uncertainty of Quebec's status within Canada and the likelihood of another referendum in the near future could seriously dampen the economy .

There are many ways to obtain foreign content, but without a doubt the best way for the health care professional is through a good global mutual fund. Physicians reading this book will be happy to know that their own MD Growth Mutual Fund is one of the very best with an average return of 15% over the last 10 years as of early 1996.

The advantage to using mutual funds as your means of obtaining foreign exposure is that you can actually *increase your foreign content up to 36%*. Here is how: by choosing a 100% eligible mutual fund that has already included in its holdings 20% foreign content and then combining it with a foreign mutual fund that is not directly eligible but is under the foreign content rule, you can have up to 36% of your RRSP in foreign content. You will have to review the prospectus or ask the dealer which RRSP eligible mutual funds have this 20%.

As you will see in chapter 8, there are different types of foreign content mutual funds to choose from depending on whether you want to focus in one country or several. The experts are saying that areas of predicted growth for 1997 include India, Brazil, Korea, and Taiwan and that the United States is due for a correction especially after the presidential election.

There are other ways to obtain (and increase even more than 36%) foreign exposure such as buying foreign stocks, bonds, options, government and corporate bonds issued in foreign currency, and some mutual funds invested in futures contracts. But following the currency exchange as well as these foreign market investments can be quite tricky for the average and even experienced investor and for these reasons it is best just to stick with the mutual funds to obtain your foreign content.

However you plan to invest in foreign content, get started today! You need to then monitor your investment every six months in order to increase the content percentage if it drops below 20% and also to follow the performance. (It is expected that the 20% maximum allowance will increase in the near future.)

Name a Beneficiary

As soon as you open an RRSP you should name a beneficiary (and you should also repeat this information in your will). The mistake of not naming a beneficiary can be disastrous for your family. If there is no beneficiary and you die in an accident, the RRSP is cashed and paid to your estate which will be taxed at the estate's marginal rate. You can name anyone as your beneficiary, but if you name your spouse, the RRSP can simply be rolled into his or her own RRSP with no tax consequences if he or she is younger than 69 (or into a RRIF or annuity if over age 69).

It is also wise to name a contingent beneficiary in case you and your spouse are killed in an accident at the same time. In that case, the contingent beneficiary (e.g., a child or grandchild) can receive the assets through an "annuity" which may incur less of a tax bite than if it is channeled through the estate.

THE SELF-DIRECTED RRSP

Most investors buy their RRSPs directly from a particular institution which manages it for you. Banks, trust companies, insurance companies, and mutual fund companies all offer these types of managed RRSPs. The managed RRSP is the recommended way to start your RRSP investing, especially if you only have one or two financial institutions to deal with. (I strongly encourage using one or two mutual fund companies for the managed RRSP.)

But once your nest egg begins to grow, you may want to consider looking into self-directed RRSPs, which provides greater flexibility. I do not think you need a self-directed plan until you want to invest in something other than mutual funds, and this should not be an issue until you have at least $50,000 in the RRSP. I pick this figure because mutual funds are about the only investment vehicle that allows a good solid, diversified, and safe portfolio with assets less than $50,000. It would be very difficult to attempt this with stocks, for instance, because you would not be able to diversify enough. There are a lot of good mutual funds available that you can include in your investment portfolio without setting up a self-directed RRSP, but limit the number of institutions or mutual fund companies to two or three, otherwise the administrative fees start to add up. When your plan reaches $100,000, then you should definitely investigate the assisted self-directed plan with full service brokerage guidance.

The self-directed RRSP can be either *solo* or *assisted.* The former is arranged through a discount broker; the latter with the help of a full service broker or financial planner. As suggested by the name, you have more control over the investments in the self-directed RRSP and you pay just one administrative fee per year. There are many places where you can set up a self-directed plan, such as a bank, brokerage house, discount broker, or a mutual fund dealer. As a general rule I think most health care professionals should consider self-directed plans, but only after you have acquired a reasonable level of knowledge and comprehension of investing which this book provides.

One of the advantages to the self-directed plan is that it offers the highest "potential return" to the individual — if properly managed! Unfortunately, frequently it does not live up to this status because most people attempt to operate their plan on a solo basis, which is a big mistake. Most people, especially busy health care professionals, require the services of a knowledgeable broker or financial planner. They do not have the time (or inclination) to acquire the appropriate knowledge level required to successfully manage a solo self-directed plan, and unfortunately most of us do not realize this until we lose money.

The other advantage of having a self-directed plan is that you can avail yourself of other investment vehicles which are not available to the managed RRSP. Blue chip stocks, bonds and debentures, strip bonds, T-bills, high-yield mortgages, call options, warrants, etc. can be held in a self-directed plan, but not in a managed RRSP, which is restricted to term deposits, GICs, Canada Savings Bonds, cash, and mutual funds. Investments you *cannot* hold in a self-directed plan are real estate (but mutual fund real estate is okay), put options, futures, commodities, gold bullion, foreign currency (but you can as bonds), art, and most over-the-counter shares. (Some institutions are now offering "limited" self-directed plans that allow you to only invest in mutual funds & fixed income vehicles which charge cheaper annual fees.)

Additional flexibility is offered with a self-directed plan because you can change your investments as you wish and you can maximize your 20% foreign content and monitor that percentage much easier than if you had several managed RRSPs. I think foreign investing is a must for all health care professionals who have many years to retire and want good diversification in our ever-expanding global economy.

As mentioned, I encourage you to use the assisted type of self-directed plan and suggest that you engage the services of either a broker at one of the larger investment firms or a qualified financial planner (see chapter 10). If you use a bank or trust company, your self-directed plan can quickly become the "self-neglected plan" because the advice you receive is usually quite limited. (Although, to be fair, this is slowly improving.)

Most of the large brokerage firms are now controlled by one of the major banks. These larger firms have the expertise and research abilities (deep pockets) that can provide the guidance you will need to have a successful and diverse assisted self-directed plan. These larger firms also have quick access to all the different investment vehicles that a trust company or mutual fund dealer would not. I also think that health care professionals should consider the larger firms over the smaller independent brokerage houses simply because they have greater resources. This does not mean that you cannot get excellent service at the smaller firms, and if you are currently using a small firm and you are happy, then stay put.

Before you decide to set up your self-directed plan, make sure you compare the companies, fees for things such as annual administration ($75 to $150; "limited" plans range $25-$45), transaction fees for the common types of investments (zero to $70), and transfer and closing fees (zero to $100). The party line used to be that you required a minimum of $15,000 in your RRSP before setting up a self-directed plan because with the yearly fee of about $150 this would likely only decrease your return by 1%. With the recent federal budget change disallowing the annual fee to be tax deductible, then the amount should now be $30,000 by this logic. However, at the time of writing (Aug. '96), the government indicated that it may again reverse this, which has created some confusion?! Recently, the physician-owned MD Management announced that they may be opening their own self-directed plan, which will not charge any annual or set-up fees. This will save you about $300 per year after taxes. This will undoubtedly attract the attention of many health care professionals and a lot of the competition.

Selecting the individual broker or financial planner is probably more important than which firm you choose. I recommend meeting with several brokers or financial planners at different firms. The most important thing is to make sure the broker or financial planner knows what you expect in terms of your investment risks and return and how much feedback you want. If you do not tell them, they can and will only guess. Brokers, like all commissioned people, have acquired a bad reputation in the past and this stems in part from the potential excessive "churning" of assets in your account which results in more commissions. However, I believe that most brokers are reasonably reputable. In the bigger firms there is some internal monitoring as well, which isolates any above-average churner. Additionally, brokers recruit business on their reputation, so if they do not perform, they know that you are going to take your and your friends' business elsewhere. You can be sure though that if you are approaching your broker with a reasonable level of knowledge, the likelihood of churning decreases dramatically and the level of vigilance directed toward your account increases.

Beware of using a discount broker for a solo self-directed plan; I think for the average health care professional it is too risky. If you want to gain some experience with investing outside the RRSP, then using a discount broker can be fun and rewarding *providing you have done your homework.* In fact, if you have acquired enough investment knowledge, probably the best arrangement is to combine an assisted self-directed plan with a reputable broker and a discount broker for your non-RRSP investments. If you choose this route, don't hide the fact from your broker that you are also using a discount broker. By being up front, your broker may provide an opinion on your discount brokerage buys.

Most discount brokers are operated by the major banks. Even though all phone operators working with the discount brokerages have completed the Canadian Securities Course, allowing them to sell different types of investments, the amount of advice you will receive is minimal. If you do use the solo self-directed plan method, I recommend that you pay regular attention to financial newspapers such as the *Globe and Mail* and investment newsletters and books that I have listed in the Appendix.

One of the problems with the solo self-directed plan is that all too often the holder tries his or her hand at market timing by becoming a "frequent switcher," especially with mutual funds. If you are using a discount broker, than you can switch most of the holdings as frequently as you want depending on market conditions or your own personal whim. This frequent switching has the potential to make (or lose) a lot of money but is definitely not for the casual investor. Most financial planners do not recommend frequent switching for busy professionals such as health care professionals and instead recommend the well-proven "Warren Buffet approach" of buying quality investments and sticking with them: "buy and hold." (Warren Buffet is an American investor who has become one of the richest men in the world by using this strategy.)

Finally, if you are using a self-directed plan, it is crucial that you create the right asset mix allocation in order to optimize your return during different market conditions. This applies especially to those who are attempting a solo self-directed plan. The mix of assets and market conditions are discussed in some detail in chapter 12.

TYPES OF INVESTMENTS FOR THE RRSP

You can put several types of investments in your RRSP as long as they are Canadian (although there is a very useful "foreign content" percentage now allowed). But there are limitations, even if the investment is Canadian, and they are much more restrictive for the managed RRSP then for the self-directed plan. In this section I give an overview of the different types of RRSP investments; in later chapters I provide more details on each and the several variations that can be used both within and outside the RRSP.

It is useful to consider two categories of investments when referring to RRSPs: guaranteed investments and "non-guaranteed" or growth investments.

Some elect to put all their money into one category, while most spread their investments looking for higher returns and at the same time reducing the risk of substantial loss. As a rule, all health care professionals regardless of age, should have a combination of guaranteed investments and growth investments. The important question you should explore is what percentage of each should your portfolio have?

In a nutshell, the major differences between guaranteed investments and growth investments are the *level of risk, the net return, the level of steady income,* and *the tax implication.* The level of risk with the growth investment is higher on a day-to-day basis, but it is lowered significantly the longer you hold it.

The return difference can be substantial. If you invest $1,000 per year in a classical guaranteed investment, such as a GIC giving an annual 8% return, you would have $50,000 after 20 years. This pales in comparison to the growth investment equity mutual fund or blue chip stock giving a return of 12% resulting in $80,000 (14% would be $105,000) after 20 years!

The main attraction of the guaranteed investment is said to be a steady reliable income in the short term (and long term) compared to the growth investment which often has little or no immediate interest income but rather emphasizes capital gains and dividends. The interest income from the guaranteed investment is taxed higher than the capital gains income from the growth investment. This is of course of little importance within the RRSP because there are no taxes (until you withdraw) but has major implications for investments outside the RRSP. As you will see, it is the proper mixture of these two types of investments (or the asset mix allocation) that is important rather then any one individual investment.

As of 1995, 25% of all RRSPs were exclusively invested in guaranteed investments, which is a very poor investment technique and I hope the next few chapters will influence a change in any health care professional following this "safe" path.

Guaranteed RRSP Investments

Guaranteed investments are also referred to as fixed-income investments because they usually provide a pre-set fixed and steady income stream from the regular interest they pay. The guaranteed investments provide this income because you have *loaned* your money and, in return, the borrowing institution guarantees a set rate of return. The guarantee is only as good as the borrower but these are usually governments, banks, and trust companies.

Guaranteed investments are poor hedges against inflation especially over the long run. I think everybody needs some guaranteed investments in their RRSP, but I think the majority of health care professionals have too much exposure to them. As a rule of thumb, the younger you are, the less guaranteed investments you can afford to have because of the effect of inflation. Roughly, the percentage of guaranteed investments that your portfolio should have is equal to your age. That is, at age 40 you should have about 40% guaranteed investments and, therefore, 60% growth investments. But this is more complicated than just your age and depends on so many different factors that I have devoted all of chapter 12 to it.

The simplest guaranteed investment to understand and most frequently used for the RRSP is, unfortunately, the regular savings account. I would never recommend this for the RRSP because the return is often less than inflation itself! Other guaranteed investments include guaranteed investment certificates (GICs) and term deposits offered by banks, trust companies, credit unions, insurance companies, and mutual fund dealers. GICs are the most frequently used RRSP investment next to savings accounts and are very similar to term deposits except they are offered by different institutions.

These investment vehicles are great places for security and a place to put short-term money, but they should constitute a small percentage of your total portfolio unless you are in retirement. Most institutions that offer these RRSP vehicles do give you the flexibility to determine how much you contribute (or withdraw) on a monthly or yearly basis. But some plans (especially those with insurance companies) are contracts that lock you in for a set time and for regular payments. As a general rule, *stay away from these locked-in plans.* These are not the same as the PAC plan discussed earlier where default on payment has little if any financial cost.

With the GIC/term deposit, you have the option of locking in your RRSP to a certain rate for one to five years or agreeing to a variable interest rate which goes up and down with inflation. If inflation goes up and interest rates with it, then the locked-in type may not beat inflation which may make the variable type attractive. But if the interest rates drop and you are locked in at a good rate, then you will likely do better than the variable rate. The problem is that nobody knows where the interest rates will be next year.

If you do opt for a GIC, then you should use the "ladder" approach for maturity dates so that they do not all come up for renewal when the rates are rock bottom. The ladder approach minimizes your reinvestment risk with these interest-sensitive investments. You should shop around with the different institutions to see who is giving the best rate; there can be a 1/4% to 1/2% difference in the fixed guaranteed returns. Additionally you should find an institution that compounds the interest semiannually or even more frequently as this increases your actual final return. Finally, make sure that the guaranteed rate is on both the principal and the compounding interest. If you are giving serious consideration to the GIC or term deposit, you should review them in detail in chapter 6.

The other option that is considered "guaranteed" and is growing in leaps and bounds is the *money market mutual fund,* which is a mutual fund that invests in government-sponsored short-term treasury bills and bank deposits that are considered guaranteed because of who the issuer is. The fund can pay as much as 2% more then a term deposit or up to twice the return of a savings account RRSP. (These are covered in more detail under mutual funds in chapter 8.)

Until recently you required a self-directed RRSP to hold bonds of any sort, but recent changes allow you to hold Canada Savings Bonds in managed RRSPs. Bonds are intermediate between the GIC/term deposit and the growth investment in terms of average return, taxation, and safety. Bonds are an excellent investment vehicle for the RRSP because they have the capability of providing good income but also reasonable capital appreciation. They are covered in detail in chapter 8 along with strip bonds and mortgage-backed securities.

Growth RRSP Investments

Growth investments or "non-guaranteed" investments differ from guaranteed investments where you do not loan your money but you actually *buy* something with it (e.g., stocks, mutual funds). Growth investments are not guaranteed because they are investments that change in value from day to day and, therefore, a return value is not known up front. The advantage to them is that historically they have "proven" higher returns especially when invested for more than 5 to 10 years, which also makes them good hedges against inflation.

Health care professionals of all ages require exposure to these types of investments especially those younger than 55 to 60. How much of your total portfolio should be invested in growth investments depends on your investment objective, which in turn depends on several factors such as your age and risk level (discussed in chapter 12).

The most common type of growth investment is the mutual fund, which is a type of investment based on the principle that there is power in numbers and size. A mutual fund is created when a pool of savings from many different individuals is invested under the umbrella of a single professional company. Mutual funds offer the advantages of higher returns with relatively low risk, "cheap" professional management, an inexpensive means of diversification which lowers your risk, and many different types of investments and levels of risk to please the most conservative or the most aggressive investor. I think they are an excellent investment for the RRSP (and non-RRSP) and are especially tailored for busy people such as health care professionals.

Mutual funds can be invested in safe vehicles such as treasury bills (money market mutual funds) or the more risky vehicles such as the stock market (equity mutual funds). As mentioned earlier, you can hold up to 20% of foreign content investments in your RRSP, and mutual funds are an excellent safe way to capitalize on this option.

There are several other types of growth investments that you can put in your RRSP, but they require you to first set up a self-directed RRSP. In a self-directed plan, you can invest in individual stocks that historically have given the highest return on your investment. As you will see in the following chapters, I am a strong advocate of health care professionals holding blue chip stocks both within and outside the RRSP. Chapter 7 is dedicated to these types of investments.

A note of caution here: An investment vehicle that many health care professionals have invested in, in the past and continue to get solicited about is the Labour Sponsored Venture Capital Fund because of the great "tax savings." This is covered in more detail in chapters 8 and 11, but a word of early caution is to simply avoid these types of investments!

INVEST IN AN RRSP OR PAY OFF THE MORTGAGE?

What makes more financial sense: investing in an RRSP or putting money down on the mortgage?

The rule of thumb is that if you are in the 40% tax bracket or higher, you should maximize your RRSP and the tax savings should then go onto the mortgage. This is especially true for health care professionals in the higher tax brackets with the present day low mortgage rates.

If you are in the lower 27% tax bracket, you are usually better off putting it on the house. But the pros and cons of going either way can be worked through by knowing your present mortgage rate, "expected" rate of return on the RRSP, and your marginal tax rate.

However, because the trend for the yearly RRSP contribution is definitely going down and the rules are constantly changing, I recommend always putting the maximum money in the RRSP first before making the extra mortgage payment. The optimal course of action is to maximize the RRSP and put some extra payments on the mortgage.

HOME-BUYER'S PLAN

The Home-Buyer's Plan was introduced in 1992 to allow eligible home buyers and builders to withdraw up to $20,000 tax free from their RRSP and apply it toward their home. As of early 1996, almost 400,000 Canadians had taken advantage of this plan with the average amount borrowed being $9,500.

To qualify, you or your spouse cannot have owned a home in the last four years. A home can be a house, condo, townhouse, or mobile home. *Each* spouse can "borrow" from his or her RRSP up to $20,000 toward the home. The borrowed funds must be repaid within 15 years in equal annual installments and the minimum payment schedule is about $1,300 per year. The repayment has to commence by the end of the second year following the year of withdrawal. You cannot make an RRSP contribution that year, but can use the carry-forward rule to contribute the next year. If you do not abide by the repayment rules, then the missed payment will automatically be added to your income and taxed.

For most health care professionals, using this plan is not advisable because of the potential future above-average income (upon graduation) which will provide enough money or security to obtain funds in another manner. As well, using the plan will create a loss of the tax-deferred compounding gains from the RRSP. On the other hand, the plan provides a good opportunity to come up with your 25% down payment on your new home and avoid the CMHC fee, especially if you repay the amount borrowed quickly.

The plan may also be useful for the cash-strapped student who has some money in an RRSP and is considering buying a home while attending university. By borrowing from the RRSP, you get an interest-free loan which only generous parents can match. You would not lose out completely on the RRSP gains because of the carry-forward rule allowing you to make a bigger contribution after graduating when more cash is available. Then at the time of graduation, you can sell the home, hopefully reaping good tax-free capital appreciation which you can then put directly into your RRSP. If you do decide to use the Home-Buyer's Plan, you should try and repay the money as quickly as possible to minimize the loss of compound growth.

SHOULD I PUT MY MORTGAGE IN MY RRSP?

An RRSP-mortgage is created when you borrow money from your RRSP for the purpose of a mortgage: that is, you place your mortgage with your RRSP rather than with the bank. This is different than the Home-Buyer's Plan because there is no limit and the repayment rules are different. Only specific institutions will allow an RRSP-mortgage.

You will first need to set up a self-directed RRSP. The rules for putting your mortgage in your RRSP are strict and you would only consider this option if you have a substantial mortgage and the amount you are taking from the RRSP is in the range of $75,000 to $100,000 or more. Otherwise the interest savings would not likely offset the moderately expensive setup and maintenance fees ($1,500 to $3,000). When you use your RRSP in this fashion, you have to make regular payments to the RRSP, just like you would to a bank, and the interest you pay has to be compatible with present rates.

You can also borrow funds from the RRSP in the same manner for other investments (e.g., rental property), but again, you must secure the loan by placing a mortgage on your home. The benefit of this type of RRSP-mortgage is that you still pay the interest (plus principal) on a regular basis back to the RRSP, but now the interest payment into *your*

RRSP is deductible from your taxable income because it is being used for investment purposes!

As the benefits and rules regarding an RRSP-mortgage are complex, you should discuss them with your accountant if it interests you. Be sure to examine the potential risks.

SHOULD I BORROW FOR MY RRSP?

This question will be asked mostly by the students and professionals in those early years when the student loan, new mortgage, and costs of setting up a practice are draining you. The answer is usually yes for those in the 50%-plus tax bracket on the condition that you can pay it back within the next year. It is especially yes if you are out of university and already in a higher than 50% tax bracket and have access to a line of credit at a low rate.

For university students, borrowing is also worth considering because it will allow optimal compounding, and the earlier you start the better. But remember, you need to first earn income, which means earning money from a summer job or from rental income as discussed earlier. A lot of health care professionals do not graduate until their late twenties or early thirties, which when compared to other professionals, takes away five to ten tears of RRSP contributing years.

Finally, remember that the interest on a loan for an RRSP investment is not tax deductible, unlike other loans for non-RRSP investments.

DO I NEED PROFESSIONAL FINANCIAL ASSISTANCE?

There are so many "financial advisers" now soliciting the business of health care professionals that I dedicate a complete chapter to this increasingly complex matter (see chapter 10). As a simple rule, the less you have the less advice you need, and with the help of this book you will become your own personal financial planner allowing you to make more of these decisions yourself. I do not think you need to pay a professional adviser above and beyond any built-in commission if your RRSP is less than $50,000, especially if you stick to mutual funds as your sole investment type. This of course assumes that you are in your early years of building your RRSP (under 45) because if you are much older and have less than $50,000 in your RRSP then you will need to seek advice to see if your financial status and your retirement plan are on track (which they are likely not).

WHERE DO I BUY?

The list of institutions and people offering RRSPs continues to grow. We all know about the banks and trust companies, but you can also arrange an RRSP with credit unions, mutual fund dealers, financial planners, brokerage houses, and life insurance companies. The medical, dental, and pharmacy associations also offer their own investment plans and vehicles which are mostly in the form of mutual funds (or segregated funds).

Where you will buy your RRSP investments will be influenced by many factors such as the type of investment you require, your risk tolerance, your age, your expected number of years until retirement, as well as the number of years in retirement. Early in your career, you should consider sticking with two or three mutual fund companies to keep the administrative fees down. As your RRSP grows (more than $50,000) you may want to increase your return and diversity with things such as blue chip stocks. You will then have to decide where you will set up your self-directed RRSP, if you elect to go this path, as I advise.

Some, however, will not be able to tolerate the "risk" of mutual funds and will opt solely or mostly for the guaranteed investment. It is important to shop around when buying the guaranteed type of investments as the return can vary up to 1/2% and the registration, administrative, and management fees can also vary. The trust companies tend to give the best rates on the guaranteed types of RRSP vehicles but the best safe "guaranteed" return will likely be with the money market mutual fund.

For those who elect a self-directed plan, there are many questions you will need to ask your financial adviser (see chapter 10).

Life insurance companies offer different types of RRSP options. Most plans are set up under the umbrella of deferred annuities. Deferred annuities accumulate contribution funds on behalf of the policy owner until maturity or retirement. Some of these plans are offered at a fixed guaranteed rate of return until maturity, and others are invested in segregated funds. Segregated funds are similar to mutual funds in that they are a large collection of different investors' funds invested in different types of investments by a professional money manager; they are covered in chapter 8. Some life insurance companies also offer mutual funds.

KISS PRINCIPLE — RRSPs

1. *Start as early as possible and instead of buying that new car when you graduate buy a good secondhand one and put the difference into your RRSP.*
2. *Contribute early in the year or set up a PAC program and capitalize on dollar-cost averaging at a young age.*
3. *Early in your career stick with mutual funds (no-load).*
4. *Try and maximize your contributions early in life.*
5. *Consider an assisted self-directed plan when your RRSP accumulates $50,000 to $100,000.*
6. *Always maximize your foreign content using global mutual funds.*
7. *Name an RRSP beneficiary and contingent beneficiary in the contract and your will.*
8. *Keep the income-producing investments in the RRSP and the capital growth outside for better tax savings (see chapter 11).*
9. *Try not to switch your holdings (especially mutual funds) more frequently than every 12 to 18 months. Use a buy and hold strategy and give it time to perform.*
10. *Strongly consider blue chip stocks once your RRSP portfolio reaches the $75,000 to $100,000 range.*
11. *The difference between an 8% and 12% return (even 10%) is significant over time and this is the difference between investing in guaranteed investments and growth investments.*

Table 4
RRSP Growth at Different Contribution Levels (assuming annual return rate of 10%)

Annual contribution	$3,000	$5,000	$10,000	$14,500
Value at:				
Year 1	3,300	5,500	11,000	15,950
Year 5	20,150	33,580	67,160	97,376
Year 10	52,590	87,660	175,310	254,202
Year 15	104,850	174,750	349,500	506,771
Year 20	189,010	315,010	630,020	913,536
Year 25	324,550	540,901	1,081,820	1,568,636

Table 5
RRSP Growth with Different Rates of Return (assuming annual $5,000 contribution)

Compound Return	8%	10%	12%
Rate After Year:			
Year 1	$5,400	$5,500	$5,600
Year 5	31,680	33,580	35,580
Year 10	78,230	87,660	98,270
Year 15	146,620	174,750	208,770
Year 20	247,110	315,010	403,490
Year 25	394,770	540,910	746,670

NOTES:

5

INSURANCE AND WILLS

Some financial experts would argue that a chapter on insurance and wills should be right at the front of any good book on personal financial planning for the self-employed because it is generally considered the most boring and is frequently skipped over. But I am gambling that the intelligent nature of health care professionals will prevail and they will see the importance of making sure that their insurance and will are in proper order.

I hope that quoting just a few statistics will bring home the message for those who are tempted to go directly to the mutual fund chapter. It is estimated that 80% of Canadians have either the wrong type of life insurance or an inappropriate amount of coverage. The statistics show that if you are 30- to 40-years-old, there is a 25% chance that you will incur an injury significant enough to keep you away from work for more than six months in the next few years! Do you ski, cycle, play hockey, play soccer, drive a car, or encounter stress?

Health care professionals can save tremendous amounts of money — and headaches — by buying the correct type and priced insurance. There is only one thing worse than no insurance and that is the wrong insurance. The insurance business is big and complicated (this is the way they like it I'm sure), which allows for big profits from people like health care professionals who just can't get it right. We frequently get the wrong type and then underinsure (or less often overinsure) ourselves and families. Only by having a basic understanding of the different types of insurance available and the pros and cons of each can you make a reasonable choice on what you and your family require.

There are also potential tax shelters available with certain life insurance investments which most, if not all, health care professionals have been approached about and pressured into buying in the last couple of years. Are you able to properly assess whether these are good investments? This chapter will help you do so.

WHO NEEDS LIFE INSURANCE — AND WHEN?

Anybody whose death would cause financial hardship for his or her loved ones needs life insurance. If you are single and nobody is responsible for your debt then you probably do not need life insurance, but even in this case, remember that funeral costs can be $4,000 to $6,000 which somebody has to pay.

Most financial advisers would say that both parents in a family should have life insurance regardless of whether or not they both work outside the home because the at-home parent would likely have to be "replaced" by a nanny or homemaker, which would cost the surviving parent more money. However, if both spouses are working, and you could live comfortably on one salary, then you may want to insure only one of you — the one with the higher salary.

It used to be that the life insurance was recommended just for the first 10 to 20 years of a family raising children, but now most health care professionals will probably require some life insurance for most of their lives as it can play an important role in estate planning strategy. As you acquire assets throughout your life, you put your family at risk to pay the taxes on those assets when you die. If adequate insurance isn't in place, your family may find themselves cash strapped to meet the tax bill. (See chapters 11 and 14 for more on taxes and estate planning.)

When you need life insurance depends mostly on the age of your children and whether or not there is a mortgage or other debt. If you do not have dependent children, your assets can cover the funeral cost, and your spouse is able to support herself or himself, you may not need insurance. However, even in this case you may still want to carry some just to help out the other spouse or to simply leave something for other family members.

HOW MUCH LIFE INSURANCE?

The amount of insurance you need must be determined precisely for *you* as an individual. Also the amount required will change over time depending on income, number of children, and mortgage and other debt acquired along the way. A standard rule of thumb is to buy an amount equal to 5 to 10 times your annual net income, weighing into the calculation what you think future interest rates will be. That is, if you think they will be high, you need less insurance, and more if you think the rates will be low. However, this calculation is too rough for health care professionals with high incomes and large family assets.

Any insurance broker (and many of the health care professional associations) will provide you with a 20-page calculation booklet allowing you to calculate what you require. This is a useful but tedious exercise. We can do a reasonable and much quicker calculation right here.

Suppose your spouse is a homemaker and you have two dependent children. First calculate all present debt (mortgage + loans + any possible capital gains on other investments). Add funeral and legal expenses ($10,000 to $13,000) and children's future university education costs (currently $8,000 per year allowing for room and board). After paying this debt there should also be enough left over to invest at a conservative 8% to 9% that will support the family from day to day.

If you calculate that your family will need $50,000 per year, then you will need a minimum of $600,000 left after paying expenses invested at 8%. I say minimum because the inflation rate of 4% inflation drops the return to 4% to 5% and the money received from this investment will be taxed of course (the life insurance benefits themselves are, however, paid out tax free). Inflation will also affect education, which in 10 years will likely be $20,000 per year per child. Therefore, I would increase the amount you have calculated by 40% to 50% if your spouse is under 40 and you have children under age 10.

In this scenario, the amount required *after* paying off debt is $1.2 million in insurance. Now add this to your debt and you have a good estimate of your life insurance needs.

A potential debt that a lot of health care professionals are not aware of is the capital gains tax on death. At the time of death, the government deems that all assets of the deceased are sold with the result that the estate has to pay taxes on 75% of all gains. For example, suppose a cottage or stock bought for $25,000 in 1975 is now worth $200,000 in 1996 at the time of your spouse's death. The family or estate must pay taxes on the $175,000 capital gain (although real estate capital gains *may* be treated differently and will require an accountant's input). This should be planned for in your insurance calculation and is the reason that I have a chapter devoted to estate planning and protecting your families inheritance (see chapter 14).

There are many other considerations when doing your calculation. If your spouse can earn a good income, you can likely decrease the amount of coverage. If you have already accumulated a lot of assets outside your RRSP, then this will decrease the amount of coverage required. *Do not* include what is already in the RRSP as your spouse will be using this for retirement just like it was planned for.

Note that I have not deducted the possible Canada Pension Plan contribution that your spouse will receive as it is vanishing rapidly with the changes introduced in the 1996 budget, especially for anyone more than five years away from retirement. There are several more elaborate ways to come up with approximate figures but you can use this method as a starting point. If you wish to determine a more accurate figure, especially if you have young children and a dependent spouse, try contacting your professional association for information. Many of them have workbooks which you can work through to give you good approximations taking inflation in to account. Also ask your financial planner for an estimate, and finally ask a couple of potential insurance brokers to do the calculations for you. You will then have three or four opinions and estimates of the amount of coverage you will need, which will help you make your final decision.

TYPES OF LIFE INSURANCE

Although there are various bells and whistles attached to different life insurance policies, there are basically three types available:

1. *Term insurance, which provides insurance for a specified term or period*
2. *Whole life, a form of permanent insurance, which provides insurance for all of your life*
3. *Universal life, another form of permanent insurance*

We can make a few broad generalizations at the outset. Term insurance is for those under age 50 to 55; it provides your family with insurance in case the major income earner dies tomorrow. Almost every health care professional needs this type of insurance before the age of 50. It is the best bang for the buck.

Both types of permanent policies are mostly for those "older" health care professionals who already have their financial affairs by the tail and want to leave money to their family (estate) regardless of their age of death. These plans also offer the option of cash (as a loan or payout) to the purchaser before death and are, therefore, also referred to as "cash value" policies.

There are differences between the two types of permanent policies, which, by the way, are also called "sucker policies" because they are often sold inappropriately. Health care professionals in particular have been big suckers because they are buying these policies too early in their careers for the wrong reasons and frequently end up being underinsured.

The reason so many of these permanent policies are sold is because they pay a very handsome commission compared to term policies. Keep in mind that whenever you are dealing with a commission salesperson you have to know what you want in order to prevent being sold the wrong policy for you.

Term Life Insurance

Term life insurance provides coverage for a specific term (e.g., one year, five years, etc.). The term is up to you, but the shorter the term the cheaper the insurance and the longer the term, the more expensive it is. The best buy is for a median period of 5 to 10 years. The yearly premium remains constant for the term but increases upon renewal (unlike most permanent policies where the premium remains constant for the length of the policy).

Term life insurance is good value for younger health care professionals but becomes expensive for those over 50. It suits the young family where cash is tight but where good coverage is vital. If you cancel this policy at any time you get nothing back, which differs from the permanent.

You can and should pay more for the right to have the policy *guaranteed renewable* and for future *guaranteed premiums*. If you do not pay for these options early, then you risk either not being able to renew because of a change in the state of your health or having to pay outrageously high future premiums.

Most term insurance policies expire at a certain age (70 to 75) — which is usually before you do! — so they are not helpful in estate planning. However, most are convertible to a permanent policy prior to age 65 without proof of medical health. This can be a very important option to consider because it provides extra cash for estate planning.

Of course, all of these options come at a price, and you should compare various insurance companies. An insurance broker should be able to give you a computer printout comparing present *and* future rates of several companies. If you find that a broker is pushing you to buy a particular policy, it likely means that he or she is on commission and giving you a biased view, and you would be wise to move on to another broker.

KISS PRINCIPLE — Term Insurance

1. *Make sure you name a contingent beneficiary besides your spouse in case you are both killed in a car accident, for example, and the other party sues which can tie up the life insurance benefits in the estate settlement. It is best to name a parent or child in case of such an event.*
2. *Always pay the extra to ensure the policy is guaranteed renewable.*
3. *Always opt for guaranteed premiums so you know what your future premiums will be.*
4. *Consider the option to convert to permanent life insurance later in life as part of your estate planning if this is important to you (see the following section) but check the future premiums as well.*
5. *If you want coverage for more than 1 or 2 years, buy the 5- to 10-year term; it is much cheaper in the long run.*
6. *Compare the 5-, 10-, 15-, and 20-year guaranteed renewable rates when reviewing different policies.*
7. *Avoid the accidental death benefit.*
8. *Avoid the "wavier of premium" option because you will now have disability insurance.*
9. *Look at least five different policies before deciding on one.*

Permanent Life Insurance

Permanent life insurance provides opportunities for estate planning by freeing up cash (or other assets) for your family to cover the costs of your death such as paying the probate fees and estate capital gain taxes. It is also useful in the business world when buying out a business partner or to compensate a company in case of an important executive's death.

Permanent life insurance can also be used as a tax shelter and may be an option for those who have their RRSPs and mortgages under control. However, I think many health care professionals have been misguided on this topic and have inappropriately bought these types of policies solely as a tax shelter while losing sight of the real purpose of life insurance. Don't make the same mistake!

Permanent policies differ from term in that they are significantly more expensive, especially in the early years. Eventually, however, the cost evens out as term policies become more expensive past the age of 45 to 55 and permanent policies remain level. The permanent policy also gives you the option of getting cash back ("cash value") from the policy after a number of years, but remember that this is the option that snags the suckers! The cash value should *not* be the reason for buying this type of policy. You would be better off with a global Mutual Fund.

Having said that, it is worth understanding more about permanent policies because they may be useful in later life, especially for health care professionals with high incomes and, frequently, large asset collections.

As mentioned, there are two forms of permanent insurance, and they both allow tax-deferred growth within the policy and, like the term policy, benefits are paid to the preferred beneficiary tax free.

Whole Life Insurance

Whole life insurance provides insurance for life. The main feature in most forms of whole life insurance is that you build up a *cash value,* which you can use later or pass on to the estate upon death. You can choose either *participating,* which pays a dividend each year, or the less-common *non-participating,* which does not.

If you decide to cancel the policy, you can usually get cash back but this must be specified in the policy. There are several variations on the time you can cancel and the amount of cash you can claim. For example, the "term-to-100" policy is the cheapest form of permanent insurance because it has very few frills (e.g., it often has no cash value). The premium stays constant until age 100. You also have to pay taxes on any cash that you are considering taking out, but only on approximately 75%.

There are many variations on the number of years paying into the plan. You can pay a constant premium for the set amount of insurance over many years or pay higher amounts for a shorter period — similar to mortgage payments. The cash value in the plan grows at a preset tax-deferred rate.

Whole life was the backbone of the life insurance business in the past but is rapidly falling out of favour. You will likely see many new versions of it in upcoming years with more slants on tax deferral to attract the wealthy baby boomers. At present, very few whole life insurance policies are being sold; universal policies have basically stolen the show. In fact, many insurance brokers no longer even sell these policies.

KISS PRINCIPLE — Whole Life Insurance

1. *If you decide to cancel, look at putting the cash into an annuity which will give you a better tax break.*
2. *Consider borrowing from the policy before cancelling with rates similar to the bank.*
3. *Make sure you are aware whether or not your policy does give back cash if you cancel; those that do not are obviously cheaper.*
4. *"Term-to-100" policy is the cheapest type of whole life because you do not get anything back if you cancel.*
5. *Buy the insurance based on the coverage and premium price not on the cash value, especially if you are using it just for death or estate planning.*

Universal life insurance

Universal life insurance is something that all health care professionals should be aware of *if* (and maybe only if) estate planning is important to you. This type of insurance combines term insurance with a savings plan. The stated advantages of this type of insurance are a tax-free type of savings, a means of tax sheltering, an additional retirement source of funds, and tremendous flexibility compared to a whole life plan.

The premiums and the earnings they create can be invested as you wish, for example in GICs or mutual funds. You can borrow or take cash from the policy (although there is a penalty if you cash in the full policy before a certain time). The earnings from the investments you choose grow tax free until, if ever, you withdraw.

Another feature of universal life insurance is that you can alter the premiums and total coverage to suit your changing needs. During years of tight cash flow, you can just put in the minimum requirement and other years you can put in extra. In fact, you can pay some policies off in as quickly as six years or less if you have the cash.

Minimum and maximum yearly contributions are required with each plan. If you chose the *premium* payment plan, then the payments vary and require close attention, so it is probably best to choose a plan in which your minimum premium is fixed for a certain period and you are allowed to top it up to the maximum early in the life of the policy if you have the cash. As the amount of premium paid increases and the "investment" grows, you can use the funds already in the policy to pay for the future premiums, which is a big saving because these funds are being generated tax free.

Always make sure your plan has a *guaranteed premium* for life which will cost more but is worth it in the long run. You also want to have a *guaranteed minimum interest rate return* on your investment to cover you for those years when rates are extremely low.

A universal policy can also be used as a tax shelter, but this should not be the reason for purchasing one. While it can be a good investment if the purpose is for estate planning, it should be considered only by those health care professionals who have already maximized their yearly RRSP and paid off the mortgage. The other bells and whistles to such a plan, which a salesperson may try to convince you of, such as using it for extra cash, tax-free growth and tax deferral, savings for children's or grandchildren's education, are just window dressings and should not figure into your decision to buy in my opinion. However, it is best to review your decision with a professional broker as each person's case is different. (See chapters 11 to 16 for complete information on proper estate planning.)

I do recommend universal life over whole life insurance because of the flexibility in the type of investment options. I strongly encourage you to use investments in this policy similar to your RRSP. Always show the policy to your accountant before signing to see what the different tax implications are especially if you are considering buying this type of policy within your corporation. And, of course, when comparing policies you should look at the final cost of the plan. Compare the death benefit and cash value and the total possible cash input to pay for the policy, as well as the guaranteed renewable price.

Like the whole life policy you will see many new variations on this type of policy in upcoming years to attract the wealthy baby boomer business. Never lose site of the real purpose of life insurance; otherwise you may end up buying for the wrong reasons. As a rule, I believe that if it is too difficult to understand the "additional tax benefits" of various life insurance policies, you should probably stay away from the policy. Remember that the tax laws are constantly changing, so what works today may not work tomorrow, and you will also have the extra accounting costs attached to these "additional tax benefits."

KISS PRINCIPLE — Universal Life Insurance

1. *Because the commission paid to the seller is so high for this type of policy, remember that there is some conflict of interst.*
2. *Early cancellation usually means losing everything. Later cancellation may give cash but you will be taxed.*
3. *Never buy a plan without guaranteed future premiums.*
4. *Consider a policy similar to "term-to-100" to get low premiums and then any excess cash can go into the cash value account.*
5. *Consider "joint last-to-die" which minimizes the insurance company costs and maximizes your growth and cash value for the estate.*
6. *Maximize your contributions early for tax and compound growth purposes.*
7. *Be very careful in choosing the final plan and have your accountant look at it.*
8. *When comparing policies look at the death benefit, cash value, the total possible cash input to pay for the policy, and the guaranteed renewable price. Is the premium affected by your investment return? (i.e., Get guaranteed premium for life.)*
9. *Before you buy one plan compare it to at least four others because of the significant differences in premiums. A good broker will do this for you. Once you pick a company and policy you are basically stuck with them, so choose carefully.*
10. *Find out what the present and future administration fees are and make sure they are guaranteed fixed for the future.*
11. *Name a beneficiary rather then your estate to avoid paying probate fees (see chapter 14).*
12. *As a rule do not look at these policies until you have maximized your RRSP and paid off your mortgage.*

13. *Carrying a combination of term and permanent insurance can be useful if you have paid off your mortgage and maximized your yearly RRSP contribution.*
14. *Universal policies can provide better protection from creditors (although this should not be a major factor for health care professionals carrying liability insurance).*
15. *If it is important to your family that you leave your assets as part of your estate plan, consider having them pay the premiums for the universal policy.*

Match The Policy To Your Lifestyle

If you have a "low-risk" lifestyle, you will save money on your life insurance policy. For example, non-smokers pay 50% less, on average, than smokers! If you are a smoker, you must declare that to the insurance company or risk not being paid at claim time. (Non-smoking usually means no "cancer sticks" for at least a period of one year.)

If you take part in high-risk hobbies like skydiving, flying, or car racing, your premiums will be higher. Of course, you can ask to have a policy that excludes coverage for these activities, but that will negate the point of the insurance. If you take up a high-risk activity *after* you have taken out an insurance policy, then you are not obliged to reveal that information to the company and you will still be covered.

Be sure to carefully review the final policy before you sign as any mistakes are your responsibility to correct.

Do I Need Insurance On My Insurance?

The recent bankruptcy of Confederation Life Insurance Company made many consumers nervous about the stability of their life insurance policies. These fears should be alleviated somewhat by knowing that the Canadian Life and Health Insurance Compensation Corporation (CompCorp) provides some coverage. The problem is that it provides "insurance on the insurance" up to a maximum of $200,000 per person per company only. If you are worried about the security of the insurance companies, then you may want to have several plans with different companies, but keep in mind that there will be added administration fees for this scheme.

WHERE TO BUY FROM

Many of the provincial and national professional associations have their own life and disability insurance policies (e.g., the Ontario Pharmacists Association, Ontario Medical Association, and British Columbia Medical Association). You must be very careful in choosing these professional association plans because of the restrictions involved in some cases.

Many are very expensive; others are reasonably priced and even give annual refunds. Some policies can be canceled leaving you out to dry, and there is often no guaranteed renewable rates. There is frequently a low maximum coverage and the length of coverage is often a maximum of five years for disability insurance.

If you decide to go outside the professional associations, which most health care professionals do, then you will find that this is one area where being frugal and doing your homework can save you a lot of money.

The insurance industry sets its prices (premiums) based on their calculation of average risks of death and life expectancy. Built into that price is a cushion or reserve that they invest (in bonds, money market, stock market, GICs, etc.) with an expected 8% to 10% return. A poor year with lower returns for the company results in higher future premiums for those individuals who did not get a guarantee. Each company has its own specialists and advisers on future inflation and interest, which means they all have different opinions regarding potential returns and, therefore, the premiums they should charge.

The other major influence on premiums is the number of claims made, lapse rates, etc. The companies that are more optimistic in their estimate of claim rates, for example, will have better rates than those who are more pessimistic. All this means that you must make sure you shop around and *compare both future and present prices.*

If you are too busy to do your own insurance shopping, you can rely on an insurance broker. Brokers are licensed and can be found in abundance by looking through the Yellow Pages. Approach two or three so you can compare their experience and rates. Use these guidelines:

1. *The broker should have a minimum of five years' experience in selling life insurance.*
2. *He or she should be a member of the Life Underwriters Association of Canada and, ideally, have either a*

Chartered Life Underwriter (CLU) or the Chartered Financial Consultant (CHFC) designation.

3. *He or she should be using a computerized database with recent price comparisons. The good ones will do a comparative analysis for you on at least five different plans.*

If you can get a broker who is recommended by a friend, that is even better. Remember that there are definite conflicts of interest when it comes to selling life insurance. The broker can sell you virtually identical plans, but the commission from one company to another can be different, creating an obvious bias. Even within the same company there are conflicts of interest. For example, the commission for selling a whole life or universal plan can be five to eight times higher than for term insurance.

Finally, you can use the Internet to do your homework. You will find Web sites that offer information on every type of insurance. Within 24 hours you can have many quotes at your fingertips without even having to leave your home.

DISABILITY INSURANCE

You need disability insurance the minute you start earning an income. It is even more important once you start a family and have accumulated debt such as a mortgage or car payments. The statistics show that 30% of 35-year-olds will be disabled for at least six months before the age of 65, and close to half of those people will still be partially disabled five years later. This risk is greater than five times the risk of death! But less than 50% of working adults carry disability insurance.

Health care professionals are not immune from these statistics. The number of claims from health care professionals has been steadily and rapidly increasing with the biggest jump being in the area of "psychological" claims which includes stress, depression, and substance abuse. Insurance companies were not prepared for the subsequent hike in payouts and a lot have had to revamp their policies making it even more important that you, as a buyer, be aware of the terms in the fine print. Some of the recent changes have unknowingly left a lot of health care professionals with very inadequate policies.

Group disability or private disability plans?

There are basically two types of coverage that most health care professionals will have available to them: group disability insurance and private disability insurance. Group disability insurance is often referred to as the "professional association's" disability insurance and the private disability insurance is referred to as "individual." Most opt for a combination of both types, using the private disability insurance to supplement the often meager and declining group plans.

Group disability insurance is very popular among medical doctors and other health care professionals because the policies are usually cheap (40% to 50% less than the private insurance), but as a rule they have several serious holes and the holes keep getting bigger as the number of claims increase.

The group disability plans can decline renewal at any time, increase premiums any time, and even decrease the benefits if the till gets too low. As well, the ceiling offered often falls far short of the health care professional's income (usually a maximum of 60% to 65% of gross income or a low set ceiling), which means you will require additional coverage. You can't expect 100% coverage, of course, because then there would be no incentive to go back to work, but you will usually need about 70%.

Currently, through the British Columbia Medical Association, the group insurance maximum benefit is $5,200 per month for six months and $4,845 per month after that. These amounts would leave some physicians very short on their monthly budgets.

There is also a ceiling on the amount of payout with the private plans, but it is much higher. The maximum income from the combination of group and private is usually less than 70% to 75% of your gross income up to a certain ceiling.

For those health care professionals who are employed by hospitals or schools and have their premiums paid by the employer, be aware that you will pay taxes on the benefits. If you are self-employed and paying the premiums yourself, you do not pay tax on the benefits. You may not want your corporation to pay the disability insurance because you will often get a better tax break by paying it personally (but this differs from person to person). If you also get the office overhead coverage, it should be purchased by the corporation.

Following is a checklist of options for disability insurance rated by "must-have," "preferred options," and "nice but not necessary." Use this checklist when investigating both group plans and private disability insurance plans.

DISABILITY INSURANCE POLICY CHECKLIST
Must-have

- ☐ *Covers disability from accidents and illnesses (such as stress and alcoholism).*
- ☐ *Is "guaranteed renewable" without a medical exam or regardless of your state of health.*
- ☐ *Guarantees future premiums.*
- ☐ *Is "non-cancelable" for any reason except failed payment.*
- ☐ *Has a cost-of-living allowance for anyone under age 50 to keep inflation in check.*
- ☐ *Definition of disabled is for "own occupation" so that, for example, if a surgeon gets a slight tremor and cannot operate, but can do family practice or any other job, he or she can still collect. (This definition should remain in place for the life of the policy; some convert to "any occupation" after one or two years.)*
- ☐ *Benefits last until age 60 to 65 or for life, but this is dependent on your present financial situation.*
- ☐ *Waiting period longer than 60 days that decreases the premiums by 25% to 50%. (For those with group insurance which kicks in after 15 to 30 days you may even want a longer waiting period on the private plan because of the savings, but only if you think you can afford the wait.)*
- ☐ *Has "residual disability" to allow continued top-up payments if, upon returning to work, you are not able to make the same income as before the disability (e.g., stress allows only two days work per week).*

Preferred options

- ☐ *A "recovery benefit" allowing you to continue to collect payment for three to four months after you return to work if your income is 20% less than pre-disability.*
- ☐ *Contains a "guaranteed annual future increase benefit" to anticipate increases in your income or to keep inflation in check. (If you are already at or near your maximum income then avoid this option. This should be available regardless of your health.)*
- ☐ *A "retirement protector" that contributes to a retirement fund to offset the RRSP contribution that you may not be able to make while disabled.*

Nice but not necessary

- ☐ *An HIV and hepatitis policy (especially to be considered by surgeons).*
- ☐ *A refund payable to you if you do not make a claim after a certain number of years.*

There are a maze of other options available which will cost you more; whether or not you need any of them is an individual decisions. Always ask your broker why you might need any particular option and what the alternatives are, if any.

Whom to Buy From

There are very few companies who sell private disability insurance plan, so your choices are limited. The two leaders by far are Paul Revere Life Insurance Company and Great-West Life Assurance Co. There are other players such as Aetna Life and Canada Life, so shop around and compare when the time arises to buy. Make sure you review your policy every couple of years as you will probably require less with age as your portfolio builds and your debt decreases. If you are interested in further reading on disability insurance, see *Russian Roulette: Gambling with Disability,* by Dr. J Paterson.

Other Sources of Disability Insurance Income

There are other potential sources of income available to Canadians when they become disabled but they provide meager payments for most. Nevertheless, you should be aware of them. All "employed" health care professionals pay workers' compensation which provides coverage if you are injured on the job. Benefits are available from the day after the injury. The maximum benefit available varies among provinces, but is in the neighbourhood of $2,500 to $3,000 per month. This is non-taxable income and will be deducted from your group or private insurance plan. Unfortunately, most health care professionals are or will be self-employed and are therefore not eligible for workers' compensation payments.

Self-employed health care professionals are not eligible for disability claims through unemployment insurance (UIC) because they do not contribute to the plan. However they can benefit from the Canada Pension Plan if the disability is "severe and prolonged" and prevents gainful employment of any kind. This is up to an approximate maximum of $815 per month until the age of 65. It is not taxed and does not usually reduce your personal disability insurance plan amount, but likely will reduce your group plan payment.

CompCorp provides insurance on disability insurance up to a maximum of $2,000 per month with each company. Again, if you want security on your disability insurance and require more than $2,000 per month, than you will have to have more than one policy.

OTHER TYPES OF INSURANCE

House Insurance

Unlike car insurance, house insurance remains relatively unregulated which means there are substantial differences in pricing. By shopping around you could save hundreds of dollars.

The are two main forms of house insurance: *limited* and *comprehensive*. Most health care professionals will likely opt for the comprehensive where everything is covered except what is stated as being excluded. The limited type covers only what is listed in the contract. It is generally wise to opt for a high deductible which will substantially decrease the cost.

You need to ensure that there is enough coverage to replace the home and its contents at present cost. It is, therefore, paramount that you do an inventory (preferably on video) of the house and its contents. Keep the video placed in your safety deposit box or some other safe place away from the house.

Be sure your coverage is for *replacement* cost and not market value as your 1975 David Blackwood or Christopher Pratt print that cost you $200 then would now cost you $3,000 to $10,000 to replace. Areas that are notorious for conflicts come claim time are sewage backups, computer coverage, cameras, expensive bikes, boats, and damage from your own fireplace. Find out what the policy is for these items before you sign anything.

Here is a list of ways that reportedly decrease your premium:

1. *Install a burglar and fire alarm with central monitoring and save 15% per year. (Even non-monitored alarms will save you 5%.)*
2. *The non-smoker gets 5% off.*
3. *Dump the wood burning stove and save 10%.*
4. *Neighbourhood Watch saves you 5%.*
5. *Add your car insurance and save 5% to 10%.*
6. *Increase your deductible.*

Travel Insurance

It is imperative to have appropriate travel insurance when you travel outside Canada. Hospital costs in the United States, for instance, are on average $6,000 per day, and medicare will cover very little of that.

Insurance companies tend to divide travellers into two groups when it comes to insurance: those under 65 and those over 65. The cost for the under-65s is very reasonable; not so for the over-65s. There are more than 50 companies offering close to 100 different travel insurance plans, so once again, your motto before buying should be "shop and compare."

I think one of the best plans available, if you leave the country (or your province) more than twice per year, is that offered by the Canadian Automobile Association (CAA) especially if you are already a member. They have fantastic rates as low as $80 per year for a family of four covering as many trips as you wish. Coverage is for medical expenses, death expenses, lost luggage, and delay or cancellation of trips.

Some Gold Visa and MasterCards also have travel insurance coverage but, many are now opting out of this area. If you have one of these credit cards, check that you are still covered before you go on a trip. You need to find out what the restrictions are concerning duration of the trip, length of coverage, and any age limitations.

As a rule avoid the banks and local airport vendors as they are very expensive.

When shopping for travel insurance use this checklist as a guide to compare different companies (and credit card coverage):

1. *Are all hospital costs covered?*
2. *What is the length (maximum) of coverage?*
3. *Will it cover family members to come visit?*
4. *Do they have a toll-free number?.*
5. *Is an air-ambulance covered?*
6. *Is there coverage for returning your vehicle to Canada?*
7. *What pre-existing medical conditions are excluded?*
8. *Do they pay the hospital directly? If not, find out what type of receipts are needed.*
9. *What sport-related injuries are not covered?*
10. *Are all destinations covered (e.g., Cuba)?*
11. *Are you covered for trip cancellation and lost luggage?*
12. *Are there any changes in coverage with age (e.g., over 75)?*
13. *What does the policy not cover?*

Once you have made your choice, be sure to opt for the yearly rate over the individual trip rate, and if you are over 65, choose a larger deductible ($500 or over) to save on costs.

A good starting place for your research is the Canada Life and Health Insurance Association. They will provide you with a booklet listing important things to consider when buying travel insurance as well as a list of over 25 different companies. You can call the association toll free at 1-800-268-8099.

Another excellent resource for retired "snowbirds" is the book, *The Canadian Snowbird Guide,* by Douglas Gray. This book covers insurance and many other aspects of travelling and has helpful hints such as reminding you that travel insurance is eligible for a tax credit!

Auto Insurance

A detailed discussion of automobile insurance is impossible because of the variations between provinces, some having public insurance plans and others relying on the private sector. Some generalizations can be made, however.

First, *liability coverage* is mandatory, both because of our increasingly litigious society and because it provides coverage for the other person (body or car). The recommended amount for the health care professionals is at least $2 million.

Collision coverage insures your car in the case of a collision only. If you want more coverage for theft, vandalism, etc., you will require *comprehensive coverage.* The easiest way to save on these premiums is to again go for a large deductible ($500 and up).

YOUR WILL

When you are thinking about insurance is a good time to also think about your will. If you haven't prepared a will yet, now is the time to do it. If you do have a will, you should regularly review it.

Both you and your spouse should have separate wills, especially if there are children from a previous marriage. The purpose of the will is to see to it that your final wishes are attended to and that your estate is divided as you want and covers all your assets. If you don't have a will, there will be delays in processing your estate that may cause hardship for your family. As well, your estate will be distributed according to the law, not according to your wishes.

Your will forms the foundation of estate planning, which is covered in more detail in chapter 14.

You can buy "do-it-yourself" wills and guide books on the topic to save yourself lawyer's fees, but I recommend that health care professionals spend the money on a lawyer (usually around $300 to $500, but negotiable) because their estates are larger than average and so much is usually at stake. However, you can save money by preparing properly. Use the following list to prepare and make decisions before the lawyer's time clock starts ticking:

1. *You must name an executor in the will who will be responsible for administering the estate as outlined in the will after you have died. Most people name their spouse, but you should also consider naming an alternate executor in case you both die at the same time. A good choice is a friend with some financial knowledge or your accountant or lawyer. You could name your child if he or she is old enough, but if you have more than one child you may want to avoid any potential conflict between siblings.*

   If you appoint a lawyer or other professional, ask what fee will be charged and then put it in the will. Executor's fees can be expensive: up to 5% of the value of the estate. The job entitles arranging the funeral, preparing your final tax return, selling any assets, settling any debts, and distributing the estate. You should make sure the executor understands your will and know that he or she can and should call on the help of professionals too if necessary.

2. *You also have to name a guardian and trustee for your children in case both parents die. The guardian and trustee can be the same or two different persons. They would be responsible for raising the children and assisting in allocating the means by which the estate is paid to the children. The funds left in an estate for those under 18 would normally be held in a trust. The trust can be set up in many ways (e.g., the children to receive it in a lump sum at age 18 or divided payments over several years). If you are leaving investments in trust for children or grandchildren, then the types of allowable investments should be clearly stated in the will.*

3. *Make sure you name a beneficiary for your RRSP/RRIF and any life insurance policies in addition to any other assets. If you do not name a beneficiary for your RRSP, the plan will be cashed and included in your final tax bill. This would then increase your probate bills.*

4. *Name a contingent beneficiary for your life insurance (and other assets) in case you and your spouse are killed at the same time. If there is a minor involved, consider setting up a testamentary trust for each child plus a trustee.*

5. *At the time you are thinking about your will, you should also designate somebody as a power of attorney by signing a power or attorney form (which is separate from your will). A power of attorney allows your appointed person to take control, make decisions, and sign legal documents concerning your financial affairs if you become medically or mentally unfit (e.g., you are in an extended coma, mentally ill, or simply cannot be somewhere to sign your name). Give a copy of your power of attorney to your lawyer so that it can be readily accessed if necessary. If you leave the only copy in your safety deposit box, it won't help anyone because it won't be found until your death.*

Most people name their spouse as power of attorney, but you should also consider naming a contingent power of attorney in case both of you are disabled or killed at the same time.

A power of attorney takes effect only during your lifetime; once you die your will takes over. You can change the power of attorney at any time and can even have more than one for different aspects.

You can also name someone who will make decisions about your health and medical treatment, often referred to as your "personal care power of attorney." This is best achieved by preparing a *living will.* Although the legal force of living wills is still evolving, it can help by ensuring that you have expressed your wishes about your health care choices regarding being kept alive by artificial means if you have a terminal or "indignant" disease.

You should update your will every couple of years, especially if there is a change in your financial affairs, you have a child, or you separate or divorce. Make sure you have a couple of copies made and put at least one in your safety deposit box.

SAFETY DEPOSIT BOX

As a final comment in this chapter, I want to remind you that all of the documents discussed are highly valuable and should be kept safely. The simple act of renting a safety deposit box and using it to store valuable documents is a neglected and often forgotten part of personal financial planning. Here is a list of the documents that should be held in your deposit box today:

1. *Insurance policies*
2. *Copy of the will (other copy at home, with lawyer, and executor)*
3. *Videotape of your household contents for insurance*
4. *Bank account numbers*
5. *Birth and marriage certificates*
6. *Real estate ownership documents and other investments such as stock certificates*

NOTES:

- mortgage
- loans (+ other debts)
- children's education
- capital gains taxes
- spousal/family support
- tax shelter
- "cash back" option
- "retirement funds" option

6

THE "GUARANTEED" INVESTMENTS

INTRODUCTION

So far, we've covered the basics of personal financial planning for areas in which all health care professionals are or will be exposed. This chapter, and the next few following, emphasize additional means of creating and sheltering greater wealth. With this information any health care professional can easily increase his or her mediocre investment return by 2% to 5%. This difference can mean retiring at age 55 rather than 65.

Unfortunately, this is where a lot of people, and health care professionals in particular, get lead astray and incur great financial losses because of poor investing strategies. You probably know at least one colleague who has ventured down this slippery path. This chapter and the next two provide you with a good road map to the different types of investments that health care professionals may want to invest in. Later in the book, the information in chapter 12 will help you decide which type of investments are appropriate for you at this point in your life. Most of the information provided applies for investments both inside and outside RRSPs, but there are specific differences that will be mentioned where appropriate.

You will recall from earlier chapters that a guaranteed investment refers to a type of investment where you "lend" money to an institution, and in return they "guarantee" you a regular return in the form of interest payments. Unlike with growth investments, the interest income earned on guaranteed investments is taxed "normally," not as capital gains. Nothing of course is 100% guaranteed, but the government and Canadian banks are about as safe as you can get and they and trust companies are the major issuers of guaranteed investments.

Many of these investments have the additional safety of being covered by the Canada Deposit Insurance Corporation (CDIC). At banks and trust companies, your deposit is insured up to $60,000 for investments maturing in less than five years. This covers up to $60,000 for both an RRSP investment and non-RRSP, and both spouses accounts are covered as well as joint accounts. That means that the overall potential coverage at any one institution can be up to $240,000. The credit unions also have similar insurance, but with higher coverage amounts.

There are several guaranteed vehicles that you should be aware of: regular savings accounts, term deposits and GICs, treasury bills, bonds, and "safe" mutual funds that invest in treasury bills or money market funds. Each has its own merits depending on how long you wish to invest for and what inflation is doing. Most are basically "risk-free," but this safety factor is offset by lower returns. As a general rule, guaranteed investments are best suited for money that will be required in less than five years and when you absolutely need the security of knowing that it will be there such as during the retirement years. Table 6 at the end of this chapter compares different rates of return for various guaranteed investments.

It is worth repeating here that *the two best guaranteed investments are making extra payments on your mortgage (easily giving you 18% gross return) and paying off personal debt like credit cards (giving you more than 20% return). The beauty of these "investments" is that they are also no risk.*

INTEREST RATES

This is a good place to give an introduction to interest rates as the guaranteed investment returns are so closely linked to the rates. There are several factors which influence our interest rates, some of which the government controls and others it does not. The external interest rates of other countries, particularly the United States, has a very big influence on our rates.

The Bank of Canada is the "central bank" and is one of the major players that influences our interest rates. The Bank of Canada sets a central *bank rate* which is what it charges the major chartered banks and they in return add approximately 1% to establish the *prime rate.* The central bank rate is set 25 basis points above the average yield on the 91-day T-bill where a basis point is 1/100th of a percentage point. Every Tuesday the Bank of Canada sells T-bills to the banks, trust companies, investment companies, etc. which then establish the going rate for these T-bills. The Bank of Canada itself can influence the price of these T-bills by buying them themselves and pushing the price up (or down) depending on where it thinks interest rates should be going.

This decision of where the rates should be going is very complicated and is based on many external factors as well as the state of the Canadian economy and inflation. An important and predictable feature that does influence interest rates the number of people looking for money. In the past two decades we had the 10 million baby boomers at their peak spending. The next decade will be one of saving for the boomers and the demand for money will be lower, which is one of the reasons that some experts predict that we will have lower interest rates.

As a general rule, interest rates are 3% to 4% above inflation. The T-bill and the bank rate are constantly changing, but the charter banks' prime rate, (and hence mortgage rates) usually do not change until there has been a significant change in the central bank rate.

The T-bill rate can be an early warning to the savvy investor for a possible mortgage rate hike. You will frequently see the Canadian interest rates increasing when the Canadian dollar falls, which is caused by the central bank trying to keep foreign investors interested in our T-bills and bonds by giving them a better return.

Many types of investments are interest sensitive. Generally, GICs and T-bills are good investments during high interest rate times when the returns will be high and stocks and real estate are poorer investments. This is because borrowing during high interest rate times is expensive for contractors and companies trying to expand.

SAVINGS ACCOUNTS

The first and "worst" type of guaranteed investment is the regular savings account. The average return on the regular savings account for 1995 was 2% to 3%. This type of "investment" can create poverty because it often does not even match inflation.

The major institutions will try to draw you into investing in their savings account plans by offering higher returns in accounts with fancy names such as "premier." These offer returns of 4% to 5% if you leave thousands of dollars in them.

I would stay clear of these accounts as there are so many other options, even for the short term. A lot of health care professionals keep a

$2,000 to $3,000 emergency fund in a "premier account" to have access to ready money. My advice is to close the account and instead use a line of credit for emergency cash. Invest this cash elsewhere or at least keep it in one of the other investments discussed below.

TERM DEPOSITS AND GUARANTEED INVESTMENT CERTIFICATES

Term deposits and guaranteed investment certificates (GICs) are basically the same except term deposits are for shorter periods: 30 to 270 days versus one to seven years for GICs. They are offered by banks, trust companies, and credit unions. Insurance companies also offer GICs and term deposits under the name "deferred annuities."

Term deposits and GICs offer a preset interest return for a predetermined period. Both can now be bought in cashable or locked-in forms, and as a rule the cashable type offer a lower return.

Before you invest in these vehicles, you must consider inflation rates, especially for the long-term investments. For example, if you are in the top tax bracket and lock in at 8% and inflation floats up to 5% (as it did in 1991) then your after-tax return outside the RRSP is only 4%. But your *real* return is -1% — because of inflation! A rule of thumb is to invest in long-term GICs only if the spread between inflation and the return is more than 3%. If it is less, wait until it improves.

Of course, the problem is that nobody knows exactly where inflation is heading in the long term. However, the rate of GICs is a reasonable indicator of what the experts expect. That is, if the return rate is less than 3% above inflation, the seller is expecting a decline in inflation; if it more than 3%, the seller is expecting an increase in inflation. GICs can be bought at any time but are most heavily advertised in September and October to compete with the annual sale of Canada Savings Bonds.

A frequently asked question is whether it is better to invest in a GIC for a year or in a short-term deposit that you can renew frequently. The answer is that if the interest rate is dropping, invest in the GIC; if it is on the way up, then take the short-term deposit and capture the increasing rate and interest with each renewal. The other alternative is to purchase a cashable GIC and if the interest rate goes up, cash it and buy another at the higher rate.

If you are investing more than $5,000 over a period longer than four years, then it is wise to divide the investment amount and stagger the maturity dates and possibly the investment dates. For example, if you have $10,000 to invest, divide it into five GICs of $2,000 each and arrange for five different maturity dates. If rates are poor and are expected to rise (but you need the income) then wait and invest $2,000 every six months with different maturity dates (while waiting you can use a T-bill or term deposit).

This technique is referred to as the *ladder approach* and it allows you to get an average GIC rate over the years. When the nearest "rung on the ladder" matures, you then replace it with a more distant rung (another five- to seven-year term) which usually gives you the highest yield. This system also provides you with cash every year (nearest rung) to spend or reinvest as you please.

The other advantage of the ladder approach is that it avoids the problem of having all your GICs maturing at a time when interest rates may be low, which is important if you are going to reinvest (such as when you are retired and you are relying on the interest income to live). Of course, if the interest rates are good on the initial buy, then by all means invest all at once, but still consider staggering the maturity dates.

When shopping for a GIC, you want to look for the best rates and for a seller who is offering interest on the principal *plus* the accumulating interest. Although not advertised, most banks and trust companies will give you an extra 1/4% to 1/2% *above* the advertised rate for the RRSP/RRIF GIC if you simply ask and if your investment is for $5,000 or more.

Additionally, watch out for the frequency of the compounding of interest. For example, $1,000 invested at 12% for 10 years will give you $3,106 with annual interest accumulation versus $3,300 with monthly compounded interest. This difference is considerable if you look at larger amounts: with a $100,000 investment over 10 years, the gain is more than $20,000.

Also make sure you ask about all the potential penalties that can be charged for premature cashing, and before you incur penalties look at the option of borrowing the money that is needed or using your line of credit.

If you will not need the funds before the maturity date, then choose the non-cashable plan because the return will be higher. If there is a possibility that you will require the funds before maturity, then get the redeemable/cashable plan which will lower your return by about 1/2%. Alternatively, you can use the ladder approach as described above to get the higher-paying non-cashable investments and still have cash available at regular dates. And don't forget to discuss the maturity date when you make your investment, because if you do not give specific instructions, it will simply be reinvested by the institution with the same term, which may not be your best choice at that time.

TREASURY BILLS

Treasury bills (T-bills) are unlike most GICs in that most are *not* cashable on demand without a significant penalty. The T-bill term can be as short as 30 days or as long as 364. T-bills are meant to be short-term investment vehicles and the best time to invest in them is when interest rates are high.

You can buy T-bills through the bank or an investment dealer. The broker will allow you to buy them with almost any maturity date up to 364 days and the minimum investment is $5,000. The banks require much more and are not as flexible with the maturity dates. They sell T-bills in multiples of $1,000.

T-bills are issued at a discount rate and repaid at full face value upon maturity without interest. Therefore your net return is the difference between the discount price paid and the redemption face value. For example, you might buy a 90-day $10,000 T-bill in February for $9,840 giving you a 6.7% return when you get the full $10,000 back in May.

T-bills are a good place to park excess cash that you may want to use in the near future and they give you a much better return then your regular savings account. Additionally if the interest rates start to go up, so will the return on the T-bill, which is not the case with regular savings account.

T-bills and bonds have been touted in the past as a better option then GICs for short term cash because of the greater flexibility, but now "cashable GICs" are available, they are all quite competitive. Before buying any T-bill you should look into the money market mutual fund, which is covered in chapter 8.

BONDS

A bond is a promissory note given to you by an institution in exchange for cash that you loan to that institution. In return, you will be paid a fixed or guaranteed rate of return semiannually for the term of the bond.

The term on a bond can run anywhere from 1 to 30 years with higher yields being offered on the longer terms. Some people define short-terms bonds as meaning 1- to 5-year terms, medium-term bonds as 5- to 10-year terms, and long-term bonds as 10- to 30-year terms.

Features of Bonds

There are two basic types of bonds: government bonds (federal and provincial) and corporate bonds. For individual investors like health care professionals it is best to initially stick to the government bonds. They are safer and more marketable than the corporate bonds although some may lose this advantage soon if they do not clean up their debt/deficit problem.

The government bonds are offered as Canada Savings Bonds (CSBs) or as Government of Canada Bonds. Government bonds are virtually risk free; corporate bonds generally are not as safe as GICs but are usually safer than stocks. They have the advantage over locked-in GICs of being able to be sold before maturity if you need the cash quickly.

Corporate bonds usually give higher returns and the company is obliged to bond holders before stockholders, but they are still not as safe as the government. There are many variations on the types of corporate bonds which are reflected in the higher returns but lower safety; some of these are covered later.

A bond has three features: the *face value,* which is what you pay for it; a predetermined rate of interest or the *coupon rate,* and the *maturity date,* which is when you get your face value back. The *net return* (or yield to maturity) depends on what happens to the interest rates, the stated interest on the bond, and the maturity date. The net return is, of course, fixed if the bond is held until maturity.

The last few years have given unprecedented double digit returns on bonds, mainly because of the low inflation and lowering interest rates. It is unlikely that this performance will be repeated in the next few years because interest rates are cyclical and, therefore, will likely head back up.

The "net return" depends on whether you decide to sell it prematurely or hold it to maturity. If you hold it to maturity then the net return is simple; it is the sum of the semi-annual interest payments plus the face value at maturity. However, if you decide to sell prematurely then your net return may be more or less depending on what has happened to the interest rates. The general rule to remember is the *seesaw principle.* That is, the return on bonds is inversely related to the direction of interest rates: as one goes up the other goes down. This relationship can create lucrative additional returns in the form of capital gains (or losses) for the bond holder if the bonds are sold before maturity under these optimal circumstances.

Let's look at an example. Suppose you buy a $1,000 bond with an 8% guaranteed interest return per year and then the interest rates go up, allowing somebody to buy another $1,000 bond with a 10% interest return. This would make your bond unattractive if you were trying to sell it prematurely. If you needed to sell because of a cash crunch, then your bond would have to compete with this 10% bond, and you would have to sell at a lower price (say, $800). At maturity, the holder would still get the original face value of $1,000 back.

The opposite scenario could happen if the interest rates go down so now the new $1,000 bond would be offered at a lower interest rate of, say, 6%, making your 8% very attractive. Buyers would then be willing to pay more than the face value for your bond, say, $1,200, which is $200 of capital appreciation for you.

Bonds are rated by the Dominion Bond Rating Service and the Canadian Bond Rating Service on a regular basis. These systems use an alphabetical rating scheme where AAA is better than A- which is better than BB, etc. The American rating services of Moody's and Standard & Poors also rate Canadian bonds. It is wise for health care professionals to stick to bonds with ratings of a single A and up even though the lower-rated bonds offer higher returns.

You can buy bonds through the government, banks, trust companies, and brokerage houses. The commission is less than for buying stocks, and it increases with the term of the maturity. When using a broker ask if his or her company has underwritten the bond (i.e., bought the whole issue) because there is probably more incentive to sell you this bond over another which is still okay if it meets your standards.

Most individual bonds require a minimum of $5,000 and to get good diversification (staggered maturity dates) requires investing a minimum of $25,000.

Who Should Buy Bonds?

If you are under 40, then bonds will probably play a minor role as the yield is relatively low over the long term, especially when inflation is considered. However the last few years have been excellent for bonds and they have outperformed stocks in the past 15 years. Anyone with a good asset mix allocation of different investments would have capitalized on these good bond times. Many financial experts are predicting that 1997 will see a reversal of this with a slow rise in interest rates and inflation and, therefore, it may not be a good year to overexpose yourself. In the long run, however, most are predicting good returns on bonds as interest rates and inflation will likely remain relatively low.

If you are older or retired and holding bonds in your portfolio for regular guaranteed interest income, you will be less concerned about selling prematurely for capital appreciation. You still need to consider the seesaw relationship between interest rates and return on bonds. If rates are going down, then you should look at longer-term bonds so you will not have to renew at lower rates in one or two years. Conversely, if the rates are going up, you should look at shorter-term bonds so you can renew every year at a higher rate rather than being locked in at the lower rate for many years. This technique should be used in addition to the ladder approach of buying, discussed earlier under GICs. Bonds also do well, of course, if interest rates are already high and stable, and this would be another time to lock in longer terms.

You should always check to see if there is "call provision" on a bond which allows the issuer to call the bond in prematurely. Usually this is because interest rates have dropped making the bonds expensive for the issuer. For these reasons, seeking the assistance of a broker or a financial adviser with expertise is important if you are planning to hold a lot of bonds in your portfolio.

Generally, bonds are better for the older health care professional who is looking for safety of capital, a better return than the GIC, good potential flexibility, and some potential capital appreciation. Other investors (frequently younger) try to specialize in predicting what will happen to interest rates and then aggressively buy different bonds accordingly in order to capitalize on the capital gains.

Investment Options in Bonds

Canada Savings Bonds (CSBs) are the gold standard when it comes to bonds. They are different from other bonds because you cannot sell them to a third party and the face value is constant despite interest rate changes. The advantages are that there is no commission to buy or sell, they can be sold back to the government at any time for quick cash, and they are risk free.

CSBs are offered only in the last two weeks of October. They usually have terms of seven years and the rate depends on present and future predicted inflation and interest rates. They can be cashed at any time at full face value plus interest earned and are just as flexible as a term deposits. They are, therefore, a good place to park short-term cash, and they provide a secure place to obtain regular guaranteed income if you are in or nearing retirement.

Recent changes make it easier to put CSBs into your RRSP (you no longer require a self-directed RRSP). I would be leery about doing so, however, if you are under 55 because the main advantage to CSBs is their liquidity which goes against the long-term plan of the RRSP. As well, the price for this quick cash accessibility is a lower return. However, some younger investors may want to use CSBs within their RRSPs as a means of building up cash to avail of a later buying opportunity (e.g., fall in stock or mutual fund prices).

On average, the CSB gives returns about the same (or even lower) as a GIC or term deposit. They should make up only 5% to 10% of your portfolio, which can then later be used to take advantage of market changes that occur. While they are reasonable investments because of their safety, their low return makes them an unattractive option for a major part of your portfolio. You can do better with other types of bonds, especially strip bonds (see below).

More information is available on CSBs by calling the government toll-free number: 1-800-575-5151.

OTHER TYPES OF BONDS

There are many variations on the conventional bond and because some of these are excellent both inside and outside the RRSP, I review some of them here.

A *debenture* is a type of corporate bond. It is very similar to a conventional bond except the guarantee is not a specific asset. The guarantee is an "IOU" from the company and, therefore, is only as good as the financial stability and reputation of the company. Therefore you should only consider debentures offered by the larger solid blue chip companies.

Convertible bonds are similar to conventional bonds except you can exchange the bond for a certain number of shares before a certain date. You should consider buying a convertible bond only if the company is solid and is in for a period of growth. If the price of the company shares goes up, then you benefit from the conversion and also the value of the bond goes up plus you have received guaranteed interest income in the interim. This interest income, however, is less than the normal conventional bond because of the convertible feature.

These types of bonds are generally good buys if interest rates are falling and the stock price is rising. Make sure that the time period for conversion into a stock is five years or more. Overall, when chosen properly, convertible bonds are good investments for inside and outside an RRSP because of the safety factor, the guaranteed yield, and the potential gain if the stock price goes up.

Strip bonds are one of the best types of guaranteed investment available to health care professionals over the age of 45 for use in their RRSP portfolio. Strips (also called "zero coupons") differ from conventional bonds in that they do not pay semiannual interest. You buy them at a discount and then receive the full face value at maturity (similar to T-bills).

Strip bonds divide the bond (government or corporate) into the semi-annual *coupon,* which is the guaranteed interest, and the *residual bond,* which has potential capital gains like the conventional bond. You have the option of buying either the strip coupon or residual bond, although usually individual investors buy the former and institutional investors buy the latter.

You buy the residual bond at a discount so that a $10,000 bond would be bought, for example, for $4,600 and at maturity in 10 years you get the full $10,000. This method then allows you to afford to buy more bonds now with less cash because of the discounted price.

When you buy the strip coupons you are purchasing the semi-annual interest coupons. The strip coupons are also sold at a discount and you get the full value at maturity. No regular interest is paid in the interim; instead you get it all at the end. This is a great way to maximize on compounding interest because you can lock in at a good rate for 20 to 25 years, which is all tax deferred if inside an RRSP. It also avoids the problems and hassles of having to reinvest every two to five years as with many of the conventional bonds.

The longer the term the cheaper it costs you and the higher the final yield. You can hold the strip until maturity ignoring interest rate fluctuations or you can sell the strip prematurely and capture the capital gains if rates drop. This is a type of leveraging because now you can afford to buy three of these strip bonds, because they are discounted, whereas with the conventional bond you would be able to afford just one.

If you hold strip bonds outside an RRSP, the government requires you to pay tax on the "inherent interest" or on paper interest. This makes strip bonds attractive *only* within an RRSP (or RRIF).

With strip bonds, you have the option of buying a single maturity date which could be match to a year you require the cash (e.g., the year you retire). The other option is a staggered maturity using the ladder approach replacing the closest and top rung with a more distant maturity and higher-yielding bottom rung, which will provide a regular cash flow for you in retirement if needed. Most institutions are now offering strip bonds as package with staggered maturity dates to make life easier for the buyer.

Overall, strip bonds are excellent investments for the RRSP because they are safe (created mostly from government bonds), the RRSP allows full tax advantages of compounding growth, they are cashable at any time, they have potential capital gains, and if the commission on the buy is kept low, the return is much higher then a GIC. Strip bonds are meant to be for long-term investing and should, therefore, have terms of at least 10 years and preferably 15 or more. Because they do not pay any regular income, they are best for those 45- to 55-year-olds who do not require this investment for regular income. Some people, however, buy them aggressively for short-term investing especially when interest rates are dropping or already high. I would not recommend this for the average health care professional.

The commission on strip bonds has been a sore point for some buyers recently because of gouging by the brokers. Be sure to ask what the commission is for buying and selling as the range can be quite variable (2% to 10%). This again points to the simple fact that people like health care professionals are regularly taken advantage of because of poor financial knowledge.

You can buy strips through any of the discount brokerage houses or full service brokers.

Real return bonds are bonds offered by the government with the return being based on the inflation rate. They are excellent investments only if inflation is rising and if it is above 5% to 6%. Like strip bonds, real return bonds are best suited within the RRSP so you avoid paying taxes on the inherent annual interest.

Junk bonds are often issued by companies that are desperate for cash and that frequently do not have a good financial sheet or track record. To compensate for this they offer "great" returns. Stay away from these even though some "good" companies sell them (e.g., Air Canada, Noranda, Inco). If you are holding stock in these "good" companies, their junk bonds are supposedly safer.

It is nice to know that Canadian bonds are also issued in *foreign currency* and these are 100% RRSP eligible. They are offered by the government and some large corporations. The coupon rate is often less than the Canadian bonds, but you can have a good net gain because of currency fluctuations. This is an option to know about if you thought that the Canadian dollar was ever going to take a tumble.

Finally, you might want to take advantage of a *bond mutual fund* where you get safety, good return, good flexibility, and professional advice all in one simple package. For a small amount of cash ($500), you can have diversification and safety in your portfolio.The only criticism about the mutual funds is that the fees can be more expensive then buying your own bonds but then you (or your financial adviser) must follow the bond market which is time consuming or will cost you the financial adviser's fees.

KISS PRINCIPLE — Bonds

1. *Bonds are safe and liquidable, but inflation can again eat up your gains so your exposure as a percentage of your total portfolio should be appropriate (see chapter 12). The main aim is safety and income but there can also be some capital gain.*
2. *Try and buy bonds when interest rates are going down, keeping in mind the seesaw principle. This is more important for the younger investor who is thinking about selling prematurely for capital gains. For the older investor the more important issue is the rate that you lock in at and the use of the "ladder approach."*
3. *Early in your career (age 25 to 40) use just the bond mutual funds when your nest egg is small (less than $50,000).*
4. *Later in your career (age 40 and over) use both bond mutual funds and individual bonds, especially strip bonds. Individual bond buying allows for higher returns (less commission) and should be bought using the ladder approach (more than $100,000).*
5. *Strip bonds are an excellent choice for the RRSP after the age of 40, but check the commission.*
6. *Bonds generally give higher returns than GICs and T-bills.*

7. *The percentage of your portfolio exposed to bonds should be adjusted from time to time to reflect present and expected interest rate changes.*

OTHER "SAFE" VEHICLES

Another type of investment that has been gaining popularity in recent years, especially as part of retirement investment plans both inside and outside RRSPs, is the *mortgage-backed security.* These investments are guaranteed by the Canada Mortgage and Housing Corporation making them virtually risk-free and the return is usually higher than GIC and government bonds.

Mortgage-backed securities investments are pools of insured residential first mortgages that are issued by banks and trust companies. The minimum investment is $5,000 and the term is usually 5 years but can vary from six months to 20 years. These investments almost always give 1/2% to 3/4% higher returns than bonds with the same term.

The investment pays a monthly income along with a small part of the principal (hence the benefit in retirement) for 5 to 10 years. At maturity you get about 94% of the original investment back. You can opt for the higher paying but fluctuating "open" type or the slightly lower interest paying "closed" type. The closed mortgage-backed security has the advantage of steady monthly payments.

You can sell your mortgage-backed security before it matures, but remember that the price you get is influenced by current interest rates as are bonds. They can also have some capital gains. They are slightly less liquidable than bonds especially if interest rates are increasing. You can purchase them through your broker or most chartered banks.

Mortgage-backed securities are ideal investments for the nearly retired or the retired investor because of their safety (there is no limit on their insurance), they provide excellent returns, are liquidable, and they provide monthly income.

Finally, the other safe or "guaranteed" investment vehicle is a money market mutual fund, which is covered under mutual funds in chapter 8.

Table 6
Different Guaranteed Investment Return Rates for June 1996

	1 year	3 year	5 year	10 year
GIC	5.00%	6.30%	7.05%	—
T-bill ($100,000)	5.12%			
Federal bond	5.16%	6.06%	6.82%	7.64%
Provincial bond	5.03%	6.14%	6.98%	7.77%
Corporate bond	5.42%	6.38%	7.05%	7.81%
Strip bond	5.16%	6.40%	6.95%	8.01%

(Remember that many factors influence these rates such as whether they are cashable or non-cashable.)

NOTES:

7

GROWTH INVESTMENT #1 — THE STOCK MARKET

This chapter and the next two deal with growth-type investments, which are investments that emphasize growth in terms of capital appreciation (gains) with less emphasis on income.

THE GROWTH INVESTMENT MARKET

The growth investment market has been gaining momentum because baby boomers have been pouring cash into the RRSP market which has driven the North American stock markets to all-time record highs (at the time of writing). This trend of saving and investing rather then spending is expected to continue at record levels for the next 10 to 15 years and will create great investment opportunities for those who participate. Unfortunately, only 35-40% of Canadians invest in anything other than guaranteed investments offered by banks, trust companies, or credit unions and by excluding growth investments, health care professionals — and all Canadians — have deprived themselves of significant growth.

Growth investments are riskier because the returns are not guaranteed but historically (over the last 60 to 70 years) they have netted a higher return over the long term because of capital appreciation (i.e., the gain your investment has made and is *realized* or pocketed when you sell).

All health care professionals should have some growth investments in their portfolio, including the early retiree, if for nothing else but as a hedge against inflation. The exact percentage of growth investments that you hold in your portfolio is influenced by several factors, which is covered in chapter 12.

The main difference, for me, between a guaranteed investment and a growth investment is retirement at age 48 to 50 rather than 60 to 65! A reasonable return on a guaranteed investment is 8% versus 12% for a growth investment. This difference when applied over 20 to 30 years is staggering. If you were to sock away $5,000 per year in your RRSP at 8%, you would have approximately $395,000 in 25 years. If you were to instead put the same cash in a growth investment with a return of 12%, you would have $747,000 in the same time.

One of the most important features about growth investments is the fluctuation in return that can occur (stock market ups and downs), but this can be minimized by putting time to work for you. The more time you have (or the younger you are), then the more you can afford to expose yourself to growth investments. Even if you are 60 years old now, you still have 25 to 30 years ahead of you, which is more than ample time to ride out the growth investment fluctuations.

Most experts are very positive about the general outlook of growth investments over the next 10 to 15 years. It is felt that the elderly boom that is approaching has already switched gears from spending to saving, and this has been reflected in the enormous amount of money that has been pouring into the stock market directly and via the mutual funds over the last couple of years. And remember that this is just the beginning. There are 10 million boomers in Canada and they are just starting to turn 50 which is the peak saving years.

Henry Dent, in his excellent book, *The Great Boom Ahead,* shows that the stock market's performance closely correlates with the number of North Americans who are in the 45 to 50 age group, which will sky rocket to 80 million in the next 5 to 10 years. And what happens to the U.S. market is strongly reflected in our Canadian stock market. Most believe that these baby boomers will do to the stock market in the next 5 to 15 years what they did to the real estate market in the 1970s and 1980s. This may also be combined with record low inflation rates which is again more fuel for the stock market.

Finally, you need to remember that this elderly boom is also occurring in many other industrialized countries at a time when computers and telecommunications are creating an easily accessible global market. This ever-expanding global market will transfer the growth from the older economic engines into the "new engines" of the next decade, according to Nuala Beck in her book *Shifting Gears.* Beck sees the future engines as telecommunications, computers, semiconductors, and health care, all of which currently puts North America (especially Canada and its health care professionals) on the cutting edge for future growth.

A STOCK MARKET PRIMER

There are five different stock markets in Canada: Montreal, Toronto, Winnipeg, Alberta, and Vancouver. The stock market is the place where different companies can raise capital by going "public" which means that they offer the public a chance to purchase a piece of their company pie. The piece of pie is bought in the form of a stock (or share) and the size of the pie depends on the number of stocks that the company is offering and how many you are willing to buy. The quality of the pie (stock) depends on the financial wellbeing of the company both now and in the near future.

The Toronto Stock Exchange (TSE) is the largest in Canada listing over 1,200 companies and accounting for over 75% of the Canadian exchange business. The Montreal Exchange (ME) handles about 15% followed by the Vancouver Stock Exchange (VSE) and the even smaller Alberta and Winnipeg exchanges. Overall, the Canadian stock exchanges are very resource oriented (mines, oil, and gas) but the VSE is where many of these resource companies reside. The larger companies such as BCE and Northern Telecom will be traded on more than one exchange to give them optimal exposure.

The largest and best known stock exchange is the Wall Street, New York Stock Exchange (NYSE) which catches the attention of investors from around the world. Most have also heard of Nasdaq which is an electronic computerized stock market without a trading floor.

Types of Stocks: Preferred and Common

A stock or a share is a certificate showing part ownership in a company. It is through the sale of these stocks that the company raises capital allowing it to expand and compete. You will own part of any company for which you hold stocks and the more you own (common stocks) the louder your voice will be in that company.

There are two basic types of stock that you can buy: preferred and common. As you will see later, there are many variations of these two types.

A *preferred stock* is so called because it has preference over the common stock in terms of receiving dividend payments and assets in the possible scenario of bankruptcy. This last point is moot as usually neither the preferred or common stockholder receives anything with a company liquidation. The preferred stockholder is paid a quarterly dividend before the common stockholder gets any returns. Preferred stocks do not give you any voting rights unlike common stocks. Preferred stockholders still come after bond holders and other creditors in the pecking order of who gets paid first at the end of the day.

People buy preferred stocks because they generally give a better return than GICs and bonds and the dividend income they receive is taxed at a lower rate if it is a Canadian company. Remember, the bond holder is paid interest income while the preferred stockholder is paid a dividend income, but both should receive steady income as long as the company is doing well. Therefore even though your pre-tax return may appear mediocre compared to the GIC or bond, dividends frequently still out perform them when the taxes are paid because of the favourable taxation(see chapter 11). You, therefore, would not usually hold Canadian preferred stocks in an RRSP because you cannot take advantage of this tax benefit (because no taxes are paid in an RRSP).

The one possible exception is the *convertible preferred stock*. It has properties similar to the convertible bond discussed earlier. This stock can be converted into a common stock at a later date which is quite attractive if the price of the common stock increases or if interest rates decline. The convertible offers you good income (although less than the regular preferred), good safety, and potential capital gains. It can be suitable for the RRSP because of this last feature.

The preferred dividend per stock is usually prefixed upon the purchase. If a company has a poor year, then you may not get your dividend but usually the next year any unpaid dividends are paid if the financial picture has improved. Conversely, if the company has an excellent year, you do not reap any more benefits then previous years.

Most people buy preferred stocks for ongoing yearly income, which is usually higher than guaranteed investment income. They are good investments for the retirement years but only if outside the RRSP/RRIF. The dividend is usually paid quarterly, so if you are relying on it for income, you have to be able to budget accordingly.

Preferred stocks are similar to bonds in that they usually move in the opposite direction of the interest rates. It is best to sell them when interest rates are lower than when you bought and then you will accrue a capital gain in addition to the dividend. Similarly it is wise to buy when you think interest rates are on the way down.

The most important thing to remember about preferred stocks is that they are only as good as the company that sells them. Health care professionals are advised to stick to large, well-established companies with stock ratings of P1 or P2 (in a range of P1 to P5). Ratings are listed through the same agencies that rate bonds.

There are many complicated ways of reviewing the safety and value of different preferred stocks but the best way for the health care professional, besides looking at the ratings, is to ask your broker for assistance. At the same time you should have your broker advise you on the variables attached to your stock. For example, is the stock "redeemable" (call feature) which means it can be called in at a preset price after a certain date. Is the stock "retractable," which means you can cash it at a certain time at a preset price.

You can purchase preferred stocks through your broker or discount broker or, alternatively, you could buy them as a mutual fund which would save you some hassles. Preferred stocks, as a general rule, do not rate highly on my list of investments for those health care professionals under age 55 to 60. I think they should be used only outside the RRSP in retirement years for the regular income and relative safety and then the convertible stock should be looked at closely as well.

Common stocks are riskier than preferred stocks and, therefore, the gains and falls are also potentially greater. You have probably heard many horror stories about people who have lost money by "gambling" in the stock market. But as you will learn, when the stock market is "played prudently" (this means investing rather than gambling) you can expect returns several percentage points higher than guaranteed investments over the long run.

Common stocks give you part ownership in the company and a voting right in company decisions. You usually have one vote per share, so the more shares the more votes and influence you can have. Some companies have more than one class of common stocks which are denoted by letters such as "A" or "B." These different classes have different features (voting rights, dividend payments, etc.) which is reflected in the stock's price. Like the preferred stock, common stocks are listed on the various stock exchanges and can be reviewed on a daily basis in the business section of most newspapers.

The price of these stocks changes from hour to hour being influenced by everything under the sun. Like bonds and preferred shares, common stocks are also interest sensitive but to a lesser degree. It is important to recognize that a stock price can drop even though the company is solid and is making money because of the very complex market cycles (see below).

Common stocks may or may not pay quarterly dividends. Many people purchase common stock for the capital growth income rather than the dividend income although certain stocks do provide a steady income as well as some capital appreciation (e.g., utility and bank stocks). The capital growth on common stocks can be enormous, as was exemplified in the recent gold sensation Bre-X which went from 12 cents per share in 1993 to a high of $170 in February 1996!

Common stocks are quite appropriate for the RRSP because of the emphasis on growth, but they are also ideal outside the RRSP because of the favourable taxation that capital gains receive. If there is a dividend it will not see the tax benefit within the RRSP. (See chapter 11 for more on tax implications.)

Options

The *options* market is another market unto itself and requires great experience and knowledge and an awareness that you can easily lose money. But when invested in properly, it can be a source of great wealth.

An option basically gives the buyer the option to buy or sell a stock at a fixed price for a specific time period from another investor. The two different types are *call options* and *put options.* A call option is the right to buy a share at a specified price (strike price) before a specific date regardless to what has happened in the market (and with interest rates). You only have to put down a fraction of the cost of the share and your hope is that the share price will go up before you have to pay the full price.

A put option works in reverse. It allows you the right to sell a stock on or before a specific date at a specific price. Options are highly leveraged because you only pay a small percentage of the actual price and a single option contract is equal to 100 shares. If you do not act on the option before the expiry date, then you will lose the amount invested plus the commission and the option is said to have expired. Hence, there is some safety in knowing what your maximum loss can be.

There are many different ways to play the options game. The easiest to understand is simply buying call options on a good stock that you feel will increase in price. If the standard common stock is $10 per share, then $10,000 will buy you 1,000 shares. But if you go the options route, then for $1,000 you can buy 10 call options for $1. Remember that each call represents 100 shares and, therefore, you are still playing with the same number of shares (1,000) but for 1/10th the price.

If the strike price is $11, then the stock must go to at least $12 for you to break even (to cover the strike price plus the $1 premium that you paid). So at this point you have only paid $1 per stock and if it goes above $12 by the expiry date, you are a winner. You will be further ahead than the person who invested the $10,000 as well because you had leveraging working for you which amplifies your percentage gain.

Options are listed in most business sections of newspapers and you can buy them through your broker or discount broker. As already mentioned, they are for seasoned investors because of the potential losses that can be associated with leveraging. Only call options are eligible for RRSPs. For those who are interested in learning more about options, see the references to the books for this chapter in the Appendix.

Futures

Futures are contracts that require the buying or selling of a specified commodity (e.g., wheat, corn), security (e.g., T-bill), or currency (e.g., gold) at a specific price on a certain date. Again there is major leveraging as you initially only put down a small proportion of the overall investment. A futures contract *obliges* the buyer or seller versus the option contract which gives the right but not the obligation to buy or sell. The potential loss with futures is great and something that most health care professionals should avoid — it is a dangerous use of leveraging.

Rights

A right allows the shareholder to purchase (or the right to) more company stocks in the future and usually at a discount (strike price). It is another way that companies raise capital. A right is often offered at the same time as the common stock is sold and usually you are allowed one right for every stock you own or buy. There is a time restriction attached to the right which is usually within two months (the strike date) and if this expires without your exercising the right, you lose whatever you paid for the right.

Longer terms make the right a *warrant,* which means you can exercise the right to buy or sell more stocks. These are also RRSP eligible. Some bonds also have warrants attached to them and often they are free to make the bond more attractive. Warrants and rights differ from options in that they are offered by the company itself, whereas options are sold by investors.

Derivatives

Derivative refers collectively to any of the above-mentioned types of investments (options, rights, futures, warrants) where the financial tool being sold is directly related to the price of something else.

Over-the-counter Stocks

Over-the-counter stocks (OTC) or *unlisted stocks* are not traded on the major exchanges but through dealers and should not be touched by health care professionals unless they have a "definite" tip or knowledge of an up-and-coming stock such as a pharmaceutical company with a new product. Over-the-counter stocks are listed in the business section of the paper just after or before the other stocks.

Initial Public Offerings

Initial public offerings (IPOs) are common stocks being sold "before the store opens." They present an opportunity to get in on a new company at the ground level. The price is usually less than the expected stock price and most often it is your broker who approaches you because his/her company has underwritten a large block of these stocks. It is very hard to generalize about IPOs because each company is different, but if you trust your broker's research and the stock fits your investment plan, then you might consider them. You will also read about *secondary issues,* which are additional common stocks being offered by a company that already has publicly trading stocks. These are usually offered to raise further capital.

DRIPs

Dividend reinvestment investment plans (DRIPs) are something that all health care professionals should be aware of. DRIPs allow you to reinvest the stock dividend back into buying more stocks without having to use a broker, saving you a commission fee. You first have to buy the initial stock through a broker or discount broker and register it in your name. You then write to the company asking them to set you up with their DRIP program. You can then buy shares in that company directly. Some companies give you a 5% discount on the stocks, which is another saving. Some also allow you to purchase additional stocks above and beyond those bought with the reinvested dividend (these are potentially the best). The person who benefits the most from a DRIP is the investor who is only making small regular contributions because otherwise the minimal broker or discount broker fee would eat up your investment.

More and more companies are jumping on the DRIP bandwagon, but don't jump on without thinking. Make sure that the company still meets your purchasing criteria. Stocks should not be bought simply for the discounted commission fee. You should also always check what the selling restrictions are in the event that you wish to sell in the near future. If you want to buy within your RRSP, you will need a self-directed program.

To find out who offers DRIPs you can write to the local stock exchange. As well, you can get the information from many investment newsletters such as the *Investment Reporter* (March 1996) and The *Canadian Shareowners Association* (CSA) investment letter (see Appendix). The CSA has even set up a low-cost investment program that allows the process to occur even easier. You will also hear about using DRIPs to create an investment for your children which is one of the ways to save for education, but there are other/better options as you will see in chapter 15.

Index Funds

There are many stock market indexes, but the one you will hear about most frequent is the Toronto 35 Index Participation Units (TIPs index fund or TSE 35 index). This index follows the activity of the 35 largest Canadian companies listed on the stock market. But TIPs is also listed on the stock market itself, allowing people to invest directly in it.

The index is similar to a mutual fund in that it represents shares from a group of different companies (35) that are sold to the public as a single unit through the Toronto Stock Exchange (TSE). Unlike a regular load mutual fund, however, there is no commission fee or registration fee, but there is the broker's fee for buying and selling shares.

The HIPs index fund is a collection of the 100 largest companies traded on the TSE (TSE 100 Index). Like the TIPs, the HIPs allows you to have immediate diversification in the top 100 TSE companies for a very small price. You can use both of these in your RRSP/RRIF.

The advantage to investing in these index funds is that they usually do not under perform the market average (because they are the average), but they also do not often over perform the market average. For this reason I do not recommend them for health care professionals because you can do better by building your own investment fund or by using a mutual fund.

Short Selling

Short selling is the practice of profiting from a stock that is dropping in price. Short sellers make their money by "selling stock before actually buying it." The idea is based on the fact that you "borrow" the stocks from your broker and then sell them to another person (at say $10). The profit comes when the stock price drops and you buy back the stock (at say $6). You then return the stock to the "rightful" owner from whom you originally borrowed them from and you get to pocket the $4 difference minus commission fees.

There are several potential problems with short selling however. For example, if the stock price goes up or if the original owner wants them back, you have to buy at that price and any price increase is your loss. Short selling requires a good understanding of the market and its influences and is not for the average health care professional. One area, however, where some health care professionals could profit is if you heard through the grapevine that a certain drug study (usually phase 3) is negative and will cause the stock to plummet. You would have to be cautious, however,that this was not a form of insider trading which is illegal. Short selling should be done with the assistance of a knowledgeable broker.

Foreign Markets

Investing in stocks of foreign markets is best done through a good mutual fund. That way you get affordable instant diversification with professional management. Remember that there are no dividend tax breaks for these foreign companies but any capital gains are still treated favourably similar to the Canadian companies.

Even if you don't invest in the foreign markets, it is important to follow them — especially the U.S. market — as there is a very close correlation between what happens on Wall Street and what happens on Bay Street. Methods of following the markets are discussed later.

THE MARKET CYCLES

Market cycles are the ups and downs of the market which occur over the short and long term. The market's longer sequential phases are known as the expansion phase, followed by the peak, then the recession phase, and finally the trough and recovery.

A more simplified classification divides the cycles into either the *bull* or *bear* phase. A bull market is an active market where the demand and, consequently, stock prices are going up. Everybody is happy because the value of stocks are increasing. The bear market is the reverse with the most recent serious setbacks being in the early 1980s and 1990s. The now-famous October 1987 Black Monday was the worst one-day stock disaster in history.

In the last seven decades, there have being eight major bull periods and seven bear periods in North America. The average bear market duration has been 13 months in the last 30 years and they have always been followed by bull markets. More important, the succeeding bull markets have always more than recovered from the previous bear losses in less than 12 months in all but two cycles dating back over the last 50 years. (The average North American stock market return has been 11% to 12% over the last 70 years.)

Bull markets last, on average, three times longer than bear markets, but in recent years the bulls have been lasting even longer such as the one that we are presently experiencing(Oct. 96). If we look just at the TSE 300 index over the last 25 years, there have been 11 bull markets where the index has advanced more than 30% with the average being 55%. Each Canadian bull market lasted on average 19 months and was then followed by a bear market which lasted on average 8 months.

The question, of course, is will past performance predict future performance? The prevailing belief is that this stock market trend is likely to continue upward, especially over the next 10 to 15 years, but again with cycles of bulls and bears. Therefore a more appropriate question might be how long this present bull or the next bear market will last? With this information you could theoretically jump into the early bull market and then pull out before the bear market hits. Even better, you could buy in the pit of the bear market and sell at the peak of the bull market (buy low, sell high).

Of course, this ideal is next to impossible to achieve because of the endless variables that influence these cycles. If the next bear market is unusually protracted like the crash of 1929, then those portfolios that were overexposed to stocks and mutual funds could be seriously damaged. But as mentioned in an earlier chapter, the present elderly boom and globalization will likely push the stock market to unprecedented levels over the next 10 to 15 years allowing for major gains for those who choose to participate. Additionally, by having an appropriate asset mix allocation that takes into account your present age and number of years until retirement, the likelihood of failure in the stock market is significantly reduced.

The statistics show that your chances of winning are much greater for those who are in for the long run. If you invest in the stock market for 1 year, your average chance of winning is 73%; this increases to 90% to 95% if you stay in for 5 years, and 10 years pushes the likelihood of not losing money up to 96% to 98%. If you stay in the market for 12 or more years, there is a 99.9% chance that you will come out ahead. Coming out ahead of course is only "real" if the return is at least 3% to 4% above inflation.

As a rule, the stock market has outperformed any other type of investment over the long run. But there have been periods where bonds have outperformed stocks such as in the 1930s and 1940s and more recently from 1981 up to 1995 where stocks gave an average return of 9.5% and bonds 12%. This was due to low interest rates and inflation. These are averages only and the exact individual return depends on your specific choice of stocks and bonds. As you will see in chapter 12, choosing the right portfolio is the key to safety if using the stock market as a means of building your nest egg. Later you will learn about diversification and asset mix allocation which are methods of providing protection against these market cycles no matter what age you are.

The basic influences on market cycles are interest rates, inflation, exchange rates, the economic picture of other countries, and a variety of other factors. All markets go through these cycles and each country's market is at its own phase in that cycle at any one time. For example, the average stock market return for Canada in 1995 was +13.5%, but for the United States it was +33.7% and Britain was +20.4%. However, other countries were going through rough bear markets at the same time such as France with a -0.8% return and China -13.3%.

There are ways to safeguard against these "unpredictable" market swings. The simplest but basic rule is to pick good stocks and stick with them through the ups and downs (buy and hold) and complement this strategy with a diversified portfolio of different investment types (i.e., stocks, mutual funds, bonds, cash, real estate, and gold). The buy and hold strategy ignores the market fluctuations and is dependent on the belief that the final market direction and stock price is upward.

THE MARKET JARGON

Blue chip generally refers to stock from a large company with a solid track record. Many of the best blue chippers also make it a rule to pay regular dividends on common stock which I think is a good measure of their credibility. Some examples of good blue chippers are Northern Telecom, Magna International, Bombardier, Imasco, BCE, and BC Gas.

Large cap refers to a company with market capitalization over $500 million. Market capitalization is the value of the number of outstanding stocks multiplied by the stock price. All blue chip companies are large cap, but the reverse is not true.

Mid cap refers to companies with market capitalization between $200 million to $500 million and *small cap* companies refer to those that have less than $100 million to $150 million. These are the new and possibly upcoming companies where very few, if any, dividends are paid, but significant capital appreciation may occur.

A *penny stock* refers to a very small and often risky or "speculative" stock and these are frequently small-scale mining companies. The stocks are usually priced under $1; hence the name. A penny stock could also be a new innovative or "venture" company that is on the cutting edge of some new computer or other high-tech advance. This is where the quick fortunes can be made because a penny stock of 25 cents can easily go to $1, which gives you a fourfold return and which is a much larger percentage gain that a 75-cent increase on a blue chip valued at $25.

A *stock split* is basically done to reduce the price of expensive stocks to make them more affordable. If a stock's price was $60 and there was a 2-for-1 split, then the new value would be $30 but holders would have twice as many stocks. As a general rule this is usually a good thing to happen to a stock and frequently the value of the stock goes up slightly after the split.

There are a number of *indexes* that will help guide your investing. The index number is often compiled through complicated calculations meant to reflect market activity. Indexes are listed daily in most newspaper business sections; you will also hear them mentioned on most evening newscasts. The most important for the Canadian market is the Toronto Stock Exchange 300 index or just simply the TSE-300 index, which is a daily indicator of market activity for the 300 largest companies listed on the TSE. The direction is up in a bull market and down in a bear market. There are many other indexes such as the TSE-100 and the TSE-35. Each market has its own multitude of indexes and sub-indexes which reflect different sector activities and measure many different variables.

The most widely referred to and used index is the Dow Jones Industrial Average, or simply just the DOW, which reflects activity on the New York Stock Exchange (NYSE). Interestingly, this follows only 30 large blue chip companies. The other frequently referred to index is the Standard & Poors index (S & P 500) which covers the activities of 500 U.S. companies. The TSE 300 is weighted more in cyclical industries (mining, gas, gold) then the S & P 500 which is a more diversified index. You can use these indexes to compare how your portfolio's performance (and your broker) is doing as compared to the average.

Buy orders and *sell orders* are made over the phone with the discount broker or full-service broker. All orders should be for the number of stocks and not the amount you wish to invest as you could end up with many more stock then you wanted if there is a misunderstanding. You simply ask to buy or sell a certain number of stocks at the market price, which means they will be bought or sold at the best price that can be found at that moment.

A *limited order* sets restrictions on the buy or sell price for that day. Or you can specify a price and make it a *good until canceled* order which continues beyond that business day but which can be dangerous if you forget about the order down the road.

A *stop loss order* does just what it says. It tells your broker to sell if the stock falls to a certain level to minimize loss. It is probably best to stick with a market order, which is usually assumed to be a "day" order. You should try for an "all or none" order where the order is filled in one transaction. If there is more than one transaction required to fill your order, you could end up paying more commission fees.

Before you place your order you will ask the broker what the *bid* and *asking* price is for the day so you can make your mind up about purchasing today or waiting until later to see if the price is more favourable. As a rule, the lower the "spread" between the bid and the ask the easier it is to sell or unload that stock. Some people also put an upper limit on the price they are willing to pay which is not a bad idea. As a general rule, however, once the stock meets your criteria, you should just buy it regardless of the day-to-day fluctuations because you will be buying for the long run.

EVALUATING STOCKS

The basic principle for the health care professional when evaluating and considering buying stocks is to stick mostly to quality stocks. This will limit your buying to mostly large companies (but not exclusively) with blue chip stocks.

There are several yardsticks available to measure a company's stock value, but the easiest and probably best is *a track record of paying regular (increasing) dividends.* Any company that can do this and appears to have a good future meets the criteria of a quality stock. Once your portfolio grows to a substantial size (over $100,000) and is well diversified, then you could consider some smaller companies if you are willing to constantly monitor their performance.

But how do you choose between the many blue chip companies? The easiest way is to simply ask your broker whose job it is to know which are good stocks and which are not. Brokers working at the big five brokerage houses base their stock choices for their clients on the vast amount of research that their company does behind the scenes. But if you would like to know some practical ways that allow for the individual investor to choose proper stocks (for the long-term hold) besides asking your broker, then read on.

Like most things in life, it starts with common sense. As has been said, pick only quality blue chip companies that seem to have a reasonable future. You will want to look at and buy stocks from different companies within each of the different sectors (e.g., financial sector, utilities, etc.) in order to diversify your portfolio, so you will need a method to evaluate which company is the best in each sector.

There are many formulas and ratios that you can refer to, and here I have tried to cover the basic comprehensible ones. The first thing you need to establish is the existing *capital per stock.* To derive this, find the number of issued or outstanding stocks and divide this into the net worth of the company. The figure will give you a rough figure of the amount of capital present for each stock which you can compare to other stocks within the same sector. The more capital, the better the buy (usually).

Next you want to know the *yield per stock* (dividend yield) which can be found in the business section of most newspapers, or you can calculate it by dividing the stock price into the annual dividend (e.g., a stock trading at $20 and paying a dividend of $1 has a yield of 1/20 or 5%). This is useful to know when comparing two different companies in the same sector. It also gives you an idea of what your before tax-return is on the investment.

Your total return would also have to include any capital gains in addition to the dividend yield, so in the example above, if the stock price moved up to $22 then this would be a 10% capital gain giving you an annual 15% total return.

The *P/E ratio* is the price-to-earnings ratio and is an indicator of a stock's value. It is also listed in the stock section of most papers. If a company's stock cost $20 and it earns $2 per common stock year, than the PE= 20/2 = 10. The higher the earnings, the lower the PE. One of the best uses of the P/E is to compare with other stocks in the same sector and the best buy is often the one with the lowest P/E. This is not always true, however, because different sectors have different P/E ratios and some like the cyclical sectors are better buys when the P/E is high than when it is low. Rapidly expanding high technology companies can also have a very high P/E because they may be putting all the money back into the company for research, but they may still be excellent buys because of the potential capital gains.

The *price to book value ratio* (or book value) is another indicator of a stock's value. Generally, the lower this ratio the better the buy. This ratio is calculated as follows: If a company has a net value (which is assets–debts) of $10 million and has one million stocks, then the book value is 10 million/1 million = $10 per stock. You should stick to stocks that trade close to their book value or, even better, less than their book value. Book values can be altered, but they are good indicators especially when comparing within a specific sector of industry.

The *intrinsic value* of a stock is really the inside word on the real value of the stock. Only a company accountant or a good broker would know this. If the intrinsic value is more than the price of the stock then it is a buy.

You can get most of the above information from your broker or from the numerous investment letters such as *Investor's Digest* and *Investment Reporter*.

FOLLOWING STOCKS

Following the market requires you to monitor the stocks in your newspaper's business section where they are listed daily. The frequency of this monitoring depends on the type of stock you buy. If you invest in blue chip stocks and are holding them within your RRSP, then every 6 to 12 months is sufficient because of your buy and hold strategy. If they are held outside your RRSP, then you should monitor them a little more frequently because you may want to move them around a little more depending on your cash needs at any one time. If you invest in mid- or small-cap companies, you will have to monitor them more frequently because of the higher volatility. If you are "gambling" in the stock market (penny stocks), then you should follow the market daily.

The prices of the stocks were until recently most listed as the dollar value plus a fraction: 7-1/8 is $7 and 1/8 of a dollar. The T.S.E. and V.S.E. have now switched to a decimal system, i.e. $13.25 rather than $13 1/4. Penny stocks are simply listed as the penny value. The paper's listings of all stocks are quite simple to interpret and most have an explanatory box listing the different meanings behind each row. The tabulation is similar in each paper and I have included an example from the *Globe and Mail* as well as its interpretation which is self-explanatory. [see below]

The other way to follow stocks (besides asking your broker) is to subscribe to one of the hundreds of investment newsletters. From time to time these investment letters are evaluated, but there is no good continuous evaluation and a lot are fly-by-night operations. Choose a newsletter that has been around for more than 10 years; its track record should speak for itself. The ones that I like from my own personal experience are the *Investment Reporter, Investor's Digest, The Money Letter,* and *The Canadian Shareowners Association* newsletter which are all listed in the Appendix. The advice given in these newsletters should play only part of the role in making your decision about which stock to pick. The final decision should rest on the ideas discussed in this chapter as well as considering what your overall investment plan is.

You can also research stocks on the Internet. Using the Internet as a means to monitor, buy, and sell stock will continue to boom as the number of users increase. I have listed some recommended sites in the Appendix that are worth having a look at.

How to read the stock tables

1	2	3	4	5	6	7	8	9	10	11	12
↓	↓	↓	↓	↓	↓	↓	↓	↓	↓	↓	↓
▼	52-week high low	Stock	Sym	Div	High	Low	Close	Chg	Vol (100s)	Yield	P/E ratio

Bold-faced stocks closed yesterday at least 5 per cent higher or lower in price than the previous close. Stocks must close at a minimum $1.
Underlined stocks traded yesterday 500 per cent or more above their 13-week average daily volume (on Canadian exchanges only).
1. **(Arrow up or down)** – New 52-week high or low in day's trading.
2. **52-week high/low** – Highest and lowest intra-day price in past 52 weeks.
3. **Stock** – Abbreviated company name.
4. **Sym** – Ticker symbol assigned to issue by exchange; .PR is preferred share, .WT is warrant, .UN is unit, .S means stocks are subject to regulation of the SEC Act, .W means when issued.
5. **Div** – Indicated annual dividend (excluding special dividends).
6. **High** – Highest intra-day trading price.
7. **Low** – Lowest intra-day trading price.
8. **Close** – Closing price.
9. **Chg** – Change between closing price and previous closing board lot price.
10. **Vol** – Number of shares traded in 100s; z preceding figure indicated sales are reported in full.
11. **Yield** – Expressed as percentage, calculated by dividing the dividend by current market price.
12. **P/E ratio** – Price/earnings ratio; current stock price divided by the company's earnings per share from continuing operations for the latest 12 months. The P/E ratio is not shown if greater than 100.

Data supplied by Dow Jones Telerate Canada Inc.
To comment or make suggestions about our stock or commodity quotations, please call 416-585-5500.
You can also reach us on the Internet at stock@GlobeAndMail.ca.

	52-week high	low	Stock	Sym	Div	High	Low	Close	Chg	Vol (100s)	Yield	P/E ratio
			A-B									
	3.50	1.20	ABL Cda	ABL		1.28	1.28	1.28	-0.02	15		
	21.60	3.80	♣ACC Tele	ACL		21.10	21.10	21.10	+0.10	1		24.3
↑	30.25	17¾	AGF Ma	AGF.B	0.60	30.25	29.80	30.00	+0.05	202	2.0	22.2
	11.00	10.00	♣AGRA	AGR		11.00	11.00	11.00		147		
	0.16	.035	AJ Perron	AJP		0.08	0.08	0.08	+.005	355		
	0.85	0.35	AQM Auto	AQV		0.38	0.38	0.38		265		
	1.15	0.80	ARC Resin	ASR		1.00	0.96	1.00	·0.05	170		
	14.85	11¼	♣AT Plasti	ATP	0.18	14.50	13.80	14.50	·0.70	137	1.2	11.2
↑	14.65	8¾	♣ATI Techs	ATY		14.65	14.00	14.60	+0.60	2094		25.2
	47.00	19⅝	ATS Autom	ATA		44.00	43.00	44.00	+0.25	335		30.8
	11.40	2.62	♣Abacan	ABC		10.75	10.45	10.45	-0.15	2221		
	24.35	8	Aber j	ABZ		19.85	19.50	19.50	-0.25	2906		
	23⅝	16.50	Abitibi-Price	A	0.40	19.70	19.40	19.70	+0.20	5997	2.0	8.4
↓	4.55	0.51	Accugra	ACU.A		0.75	0.51	0.65	-0.10	467		
	16.15	13.00	♣Acetex	ATX		13.75	13.75	13.75		11		13.0
↑	17.65	9¾	Acklands	ACK		17.65	17.50	17.50	+0.10	20		17.2
	1.70	0.64	Adex Mini	AMG	0.11	0.72	0.66	0.67	-0.03	273	15.9	
	7⅜	3.20	♣Adrian Rs	ADL		4.25	4.05	4.10	+0.01	190		
	1.30	.325	Advancd G j	AED		0.44	0.44	0.44		90		
	0.95	0.50	Advancd M	AMR		0.73	0.73	0.73		315		13.7
	0.84	0.27	Advantex	ADX		0.43	0.40	0.40		65		
	4.80	1.50	Advntre	AVN		1.80	1.80	1.80		15		

SOURCE: Globe & Mail

STOCK MARKET DIVERSIFICATION

Diversification simply refers to the principle of not putting all your eggs in one basket. Diversification is more important with stock investing then any other form of investment vehicle because of the higher volatility and risk. For example, in the early '90's, IBM took a tumble which would have seriously hurt the investor who had most of his or her portfolio invested in this "good" blue chip company had they needed their money during this period. But the diversified investor who had stock in 9 or 10 other blue chip companies would have been all right because they could have sold one of the better performing srocks.

Diversification should be considered at several different levels. First, you should diversify the type of investments chosen for your portfolio (i.e., stocks, bonds, cash, real estate, gold), all of which respond differently to the market cycles. You also need to diversify within that specific type of investment; that is several different types of stocks respond differently to the market cycles. You must spread your stock risk around to absorb a setback if one of your stocks tumbles. Finally, you must also diversify by country. Different countries are at different places in their market cycle at any one time, so optimal gain will be achieved only by being exposed to different ones at different times.

When diversifying in stocks, you ideally want to try and have at least 5, but preferably 10, different stocks spread out over the different economic sectors so that you will experience an average of the ups and downs of the individual stock price but also the ups and downs of the market cycle as a whole. For investors using stocks outside the RRSP, having stocks in different sectors will enable you to sell those that are doing well with present market conditions when you need the cash rather than selling a stock when it is down.

There are basically five different stock sectors to invest in: manufacturing, resources, finance, utilities, and consumer. Each of these perform differently depending on where in the market cycle we are. Some companies span across more than one sector and with company takeovers at an all time high we will likely see more of this in the future. There are many other sub-classifications of stocks that you will see under sub-indexes in the business section, but for purposes of creating a portfolio we only need to concern ourselves with these five major ones.

The type and mix of stocks that you buy will depend on your age, risk level, and investment plan, all of which will create a specific asset mix allocation for you. From this asset mix allocation, the stock percentage in your portfolio can range anywhere from 10% to 80% with the remaining being invested in other types of investment vehicles such as bonds, cash equivalents, real estate, gold, etc. As a general rule, the younger you are then the more you will be looking at capital gain stocks, and the closer to retirement the more you will want income-producing stocks.

Some stocks, especially those emphasizing capital gain, are very much influenced by market cycles and are referred to as *cyclical stocks* and include the resource and manufacturing stocks. These stocks do exceptionally well in peak bull market times (large capital growth) but tend to do poorly in bear markets (recessions). They tend to perform well with rising interest rates. Examples include stocks in mining, oil, gas, forestry, and manufacturing of all types (automobiles and steel). Gold stocks also fit into this category.

Cyclical stocks are generally not considered for income, but more for growth or capital appreciation. The "ideal" time to buy these stocks is at the end of a recession when they are cheap, and then you would want to sell when they are at the peak of the bull market. Health care professionals should consider cyclical stocks only as a large percentage of their portfolio if they have age on their side and only after they had a solid base of other safer stocks.

The two relatively "safer" income-sector stocks are the utility and financial ones. Here the emphasis is on a steady supply of income in the form of dividends and, as a result, the volatility of the stock prices is much less. The utility stocks always remain in need even through recessionary times because of their basic product (heat and light). The net return from these stocks is mostly from the income with lesser emphasis on capital growth, but you will still see some steady growth with these stocks. These companies do very well in recessions and when interest rates are dropping, and it is at these times you would want to increase your percentage holding, especially outside the RRSP. In the RRSP you would likely do less trading and stick with the buy and hold strategy, although you can make some minor year-to-year adjustments. These stocks do not do as well when rates are rising but still provide a steady income. Remember that dividend income is optimal outside the RRSP if possible because of the favourable tax treatment.

The financial institutions are the other excellent form of income stocks. All of the big six banks will give you a good net return and most experts would consider these a "safe" investment.

There are many other excellent stocks outside the Canadian market. International stocks can offer major gains (or losses), but it is very difficult for the average person to make knowledgeable investments. The best way to take advantage of international markets is through a broker who specializes in foreign investing or preferably through an international or global mutual fund (discussed in the next chapter).

STRATEGY FOR BUYING STOCKS

The strategy that you use for buying stocks is very important. You can opt to leave this totally up to your broker, but even if you do I recommend that you know at least the basics. Even if you are a small player, as most health care professionals will be, you need to have a strategy for the market.

There are generally two ways to play the stock market: the correct way is by investing and the incorrect way is by "gambling." The investor is willing to leave money in the market for at least three years, but the gambler is always running in and out of the market chasing "the hot one."

The latter method is *not* recommended. Usually these "hot tips" are from somebody who knows less than you do about stock investing. As a rule these tips rarely pan out. However, being in the medical profession allows some of us to be close to the phase 2 and 3 research studies, which can provide early information about an up-and-coming drug or company which can sometimes work to our advantage. Be sure to avoid "insider trading", however.

Almost as dangerous as following "hot tips" is the "market timing strategy." This is also gambling and most often occurs with the penny stocks. It is a difficult form of gambling because you have to roll the dice twice: when you buy the stock and when you sell it. Any money played on these strategies should be money you can afford to lose; this type of market "play" is not part of personal financial planning.

The one strategy that has time and time again outperformed any other is "buy and hold", which has made some people very rich. This is the best approach for health care professionals because it focuses on quality, which means safety, and it is the least annoying strategy from a monitoring perspective. This strategy is optimal for anyone who will not need the invested principal for four to five years or longer. You can then ignore day-to-day fluctuations (which will occur) and instead pick 10 or more good companies and invest equal amounts in each. This strategy almost guarantees good returns even if one or two do very poorly over the long term. You will also save on commission fees because of the lack of trading.

The more time you hold stocks the more likely you will override the market cycles simply because the market direction has *always* been up over the long term. Several studies have shown that most of the major gains over the last 15 to 20 years were made just a few days (less than 1%) out of the many, many trading days. If you are not using the buy and hold strategy, then you can easily miss out on these few days where most of the gains have occurred.

You will hear many people referring to *demographic investing,* which still emphasizes the buy and hold strategy but the focus of the stocks is based on expected future needs of the baby boomers. The two authors who are most often quoted on this approach to stock buying are David Foot and David Cook. Cook is a broker with Scotia Mcleod in Ottawa and is co-author with Susan Highstone of a new book called *The Pig and the Python* which focuses on demographic investing.

The major areas touted as future growth secondary to the demographic demands include health care, pharmaceuticals, telecommunications, and the financial services industry. The financial services industry, for example, has done extremely well over the last few years because of the baby boomers switching to savings over spending. Trimark Financial has had an increase of 60% per year when compounded since its introduction in 1992. So far this year (1996), its stock value is up 90%! Mackenzie Financial Corp. is up 18% and AGF Management is up 25%.

The "contrarian strategy" is, in theory, the best approach to market investing. But because nobody knows where the market cycle is today or where it will be tomorrow, this approach fails prospectively but is great retrospectively. It also goes against human nature to sell when things are great and buy when things are poor (buy low and sell high). This is why the buy and hold strategy is best. However, you will note that most mutual fund managers will always have some cash on hand to take advantage of buying opportunities that occur when there is a market setback. Once you have a sizable portfolio, it is worth having some cash on hand (T-bills, money market mutual funds, or CSBs) to take advantage of the contrarian strategy.

Other strategies you will read about include "top-down" and "bottom-up". The top-down strategy tries to predict what is up and coming for the next part of the economic cycle; the bottom-up strategy sticks to present good performers in the cycle. "Value investing" strategy looks for companies that have value not yet recognized and can be very rewarding when combined with the "buy and hold" strategy.

SAMPLE STOCK PORTFOLIO FOR THE HEALTH CARE PROFESSIONAL

Most health care professionals should initiate their portfolio investing in mutual funds because of the instant diversification and excellent returns that are available both inside and outside the RRSP. But once your assets reach the range of $50,000 to $75,000, you should give strong consideration to investing in individual stocks because of higher potential gains. There are endless combinations of stocks that would suffice any individual health care professional, but you need to tailor your selection to your present investment plan, which depends on many factors.

Initially, stick to blue chip stocks that have a record of regular dividends. After you have at least five of these safe income stocks, you can start adding on more aggressive growth stocks (cyclical stocks) with less emphasis on regular dividends.

By taking just age into consideration, it is reasonable that the younger you are, the more aggressive you can be with emphasis on growth stocks over income stocks. A typical sample portfolio taken from a recent May, 1996 issue of the *Investment Reporter* would be a combination of CAE Industries, Caldwell Partners, Loblaw Co., Newalta Corp., and Nova Corp. All of these are priced under $15 and three of them offer DRIP programs. This portfolio is aggressive with three growth stocks (CAE, Caldwell, Newalta) but also has Nova and Loblaw's as stable income stocks which will also have some appreciation. The *Investment Reporter* called this their "growth portfolio," which would be appropriate for the under-40 investors who have time on their side.

For the 40- to 60-year-old investor, the *Investment Reporter* recommended their "income portfolio" which still contains growth stocks but ones that also provide higher dividends to provide more safety and cash if needed (especially if outside the RRSP). Their picks were Bombardier, Imasco, MDS Health, SNC-Lavalin, and Septre Inv. You will recognize more of these companies because they are mostly big blue chip companies.

For the investor over 60, the emphasis is on preservation of capital and steady income, so very conservative blue chip companies were recommended: Bank of Montreal, BCE Inc., Thomson Corp., Imperal Oil, and IPL Energy. All of these offer the DRIP program, allowing you to increase your net return even more. The over-60 health care professionals will be focusing mostly on less volatile stocks such as those offered by the finance, utilities, pipeline industries, and maybe some consumer stocks.

You may want to buy your stocks on a monthly basis or every three to four months if you are using a PAC program with your broker. If you are using $1,000 per month, I recommend buying just one type of stock at a time. You should aim for the relatively safer stocks initially and in the first year of acquiring stock just stick with these three to four if your total contribution is in the range of $9,000 to $13,000. In the following year add 3 more different stocks in the same fashion so that after three years you will have 9 to 12 diversified stocks in your RRSP (or outside) portfolio. I recommend adding the more aggressive growth stocks after you have acquired your safe stock in case there is a market downturn during your buying.

The following stocks have been recently (mid-1996) highly recommended by various experts. This is by no means a complete list (and some may not be recommended by the time of printing), but it will give you an idea of the different types of stocks in the different sectors. Another way to determine the "good" stocks is to look at the next prospectus issued from your favourite mutual fund manager and see what has been chosen in his or her portfolio.

1. *UTILITY: IPL Energy Inc, Fortis Inc., Canadian Utilities Ltd., BCE Inc., BC Telecom, Northern Tel., Northern Gas, Westcoast Energy, TransCanada PipeLines Ltd.*
2. *FINANCE: Bank of Montreal, TD Bank, First Marathon, Trimark Financial, Mackenzie Financial Corp.*
3. *MANUFACTURING: Merck & Co., Bombardier, Imasco*
4. *CONSUMER: Thomson Corp., Gillette Co., MDS Health, Loblaw Co., Dynacare Health Group, Extendicare*
5. *RESOURCES: Imperial Oil, Noranda, Petro-Canada, Potash Corp.*
6. *MULTISECTOR: BCE, Canadian Pacific, Laidlaw, Seagram*

Remember that when you are deciphering the return on these blue chip stocks to include *both* the dividend and the capital gain. Fortis Inc., for example, currently gives a 6.1% dividend yield, but when you add in the 10-year average capital gain of 4.8%, you end up with a tidy 11% return on a very, very conservative stock. This is one of the lower returns for the above-mentioned group because it is considered an income stock. The banks give even higher net returns. Imagine what you can do with some growth stocks!

Finally, remember that your stock selection should always be based on what you think will do well in the future. Most people are emphasizing the global economy as well as the elderly boom in directing their stock selection, and these factors are expected to create enormous growth in telecommunications, software companies, computer companies, and health care orientated companies. This logic was followed by Stephen Northfield in his *Globe and Mail* article (May 30, 1996) when he developed a "boomer portfolio." Eight Canadian and eight U.S. stocks were chosen to take advantage of the coming wave of aging baby boomers. The Canadian stocks were Trimark Fin., Transit AT, Canadian Tire, MDS Health Group, Extendicare, Loewen Group, White Rose Crafts, and Upper Canada Brewing. The U.S. stocks were Neiman-Marcus, Winnebago, Harley Davidson, Charles Schwab, Callaway Golf, Helen of Troy, Living Centers of America, and Brunswick Corp. The performance of this portfolio as of Aug. '96 was significantly higher than any of the indexes.

This list is provided just to give you an idea of the sort of future planning you or your broker or financial planner should be thinking about; it is not an exhaustive list of excellent future companies.

SOME "TIPS" FOR BUYING STOCKS

1. *Good days to buy stocks include the day before a holiday, last day of the month, and the first three to four days of the month. Monday is a good day to buy and Tuesday through Friday are selling days.*
2. *December is a good month to buy stocks, especially mines and resources, as prices often drop and then increase in January.*
3. *If the market has been on the way up for five to six weeks, wait before buying as there will likely be a small settling or setback soon.*
4. *In general, buy stocks with a lower P/E ratio in any one sector.*
5. *A general trend is that when interest rates go down the stock market goes up and vice versa (important to know if you want to buy low and sell high).*
6. *Most experts say that the more money you have to invest the less need for growth stocks.*
7. *If a stock falls 20%, consider selling. (Mainly refers to small cap or speculative stock.)*
8. *If a stock's price soars and is volatile, consider selling half to recoup your initial investment and leave the rest for icing (again this is for speculative stock).*
9. *Health care professionals should strongly consider the health care and biotech stocks because they are our business and we understand them. Most of these stocks will do well in the future.*
10. *Small-cap companies have generally outperformed large-cap.*

11. *The "January effect" says that if the markets are positive in January then they likely will be for the rest of the year.*
12. *The "U.S. presidential cycle" states that in a pre-election year the stock market will be good and post-election year will be poor. What happens in the United States is always reflected in our market.*
13. *I do not encourage any health care professional to use these 12 "Folklore" tips, but they are interesting to know about.*

KISS PRINCIPLE — Buying Stocks

1. *Most health care professionals are underexposed to growth investments (stocks and mutual funds). Most experts believe that the stock market will give unprecedented returns over the next 10 to 15 years.*
2. *Stick to blue chip stocks that have a record of increasing dividends both for inside and outside the RRSP.*
3. *The majority of your assets should be in a buy and hold strategy for at least four to five years.*
4. *Diversification across the different sectors is a must.*
5. *The easiest way to hold stocks is with a mutual fund, but you can earn more if you hold individual stocks. These should be considered after your portfolio has reached the range of $50,000 to $75,000.*
6. *A knowledgeable, trustworthy, full service broker or financial planner is recommended for most health care professionals once you start considering stocks. (see chapter 10)*

8

GROWTH INVESTMENT #2 — MUTUAL FUNDS

A mutual fund is a large pool of money from different investors, invested and managed by a professional manager. There are several different types of mutual funds that range from high risk (e.g., resource mutual funds) to being virtually risk free (e.g., money market mutual funds) that will satisfy any investor's risk level.

Mutual funds should be the foundation of the portfolio of all health care professionals, especially in the early career years. They are definitely one of the best, if not the best, investment vehicle. They should be used both within and outside the RRSP. In fact, I believe that if you invest the majority of your portfolio in nothing but diversified mutual funds, you could do as well as any other investment and likely better than most. But having said this, I would still consider adding blue chip stocks as an additional investment vehicles once your portfolio reaches $50,000 to $75,000.

As good as mutual funds are, there are several "traps" you need to be aware of, such as the inappropriate practice of "frequent switching" and excessive commission fees. It is also important to not fall into the trap of "chasing the hot ones." The buy and hold strategy discussed in chapter 7 applies to mutual funds as well. You should be looking at mutual funds only if you plan to leave the funds in the account for *at least* three to four years (although there are some exceptions such as the money market mutual fund).

The mutual fund industry is booming and will likely continue at the same pace for several more years as the baby boomers focus on saving for retirement. While there are occasional stories written about the "upcoming mutual fund crash," many experts believe this is very unlikely. Even with the all-time one-day record 1987 market crash, the average drop was actually less than for individual stocks and only 2% to

3% of total assets were withdrawn by mutual fund investors. Additionally, we did not see any significant sell off with the market setbacks of 1990 and 1994. This reflects that the average mutual fund investor is in for the long run and is willing to ride out even big fluctuations.

If there is a mutual fund crash, it will be no worse than the general stock market which will not harm the health care professional because after reading this book you will have a diversified portfolio with a proper asset mix allocation to get you through such times. And even more diversified and further protected against an individual market crash are those international mutual funds; several presently (mid 1996) have annual 10- to 15-year average returns of 15%! This allows for doubling of your money every 4.8 years and is "relatively" safe. Most indicators point to strong economic times over the next few years and the markets will likely soon reap the benefits of the corporate belt tightening that has occurred over the last couple of years.

I agree with the critics of mutual funds who point out that the "average" fund performance pales compared to the TSE 300, but through the help of this chapter, health care professionals will be investing only in the top third performers.

Mutual funds are ideal for the health care professional because they —

1. *Offer affordable professional advice (the fund manager and team)*
2. *Offer a very safe way to invest in the stock market (instant diversification) and get big returns*
3. *Offer a broad choice of funds with different objectives that can match anyone's investment need*
4. *Are easy to understand, follow, and keep score*
5. *Are easy to purchase and sell (have good liquidity)*
6. *Allow an easy means to change or adjust your portfolio*
7. *Offer an excellent way to invest in some of the global and emerging economies with expert advice (This is the best way to obtain your RRSP 20% foreign content and your non-RRSP foreign exposure.)*

TYPES OF MUTUAL FUNDS

A mutual fund is an investment in which many different people's funds are pooled and invested by an expert investor or fund manager. The investor buys units (or shares) from the mutual fund company which has a dollar value called the *net asset value* (NAV). The NAV is equal to the total value of the mutual fund divided by the number of units. Both the value of the unit and the number of units will change from day to day similar to stocks.

A mutual fund holds anywhere from 10 to 70 different companies' stocks (or bonds) which gives you instant diversification for a very low cost. The optimal number of stocks within a mutual fund is said to be 50 for diversification and return, but this depends greatly on what type of mutual fund it is.

The majority are open-end mutual funds where there is no limit to who or how many invest, but you can also buy closed-end mutual funds which have a fixed number of shares and which trade on the stock exchange. The majority of health care professionals hold open-end funds and this is where my discussion centres.

There are two types of mutual funds: *growth mutual funds* and *income mutual funds* but now you can get any mix of these two with what is called a *balanced mutual fund.* Generally speaking, the growth mutual funds are "risky" with capital appreciation being the game; the income mutual funds are "safe" and more appropriate when a steady stream of income is the priority. But there is much variability depending on which company and fund manager you are investing with. The investment vehicles used in mutual funds are exactly the same as those covered in previous chapters only now there is an expert making the day-to-day decisions and providing constant monitoring.

A general rule of thumb to determine the ratio of growth funds in your portfolio is to subtract your age from 100. For example, if you are 35, you should have at least 65% (100 – 35 = 65) in growth mutual funds and the remainder in income mutual funds. This is a very broad generalization and does not take into account several important variables such as your expected years of retirement.

For a mutual fund to be eligible for an RRSP, it must have at least 80% of its investments in Canadian securities with the remaining 20% being allowed in foreign investments if the fund manager wishes. As was mentioned in an earlier chapter, it is strongly recommended that you utilize your 20% foreign allowance within your RRSP in order to spread your risk outside of Canada. These foreign investments often bring in big returns, and the best way to access your 20% is through a foreign international/ global mutual fund. In fact, by choosing your mutual funds properly, you can achieve up to 36% foreign content by choosing an RRSP eligible fund that has 20% foreign content and then combining that with a non-eligible RRSP mutual fund up to your allowable 20%.

THE GROWTH MUTUAL FUND

Historically, growth mutual funds give the best returns over the long run (five years or more) because the emphasis is more on capital appreciation and less on interest income bearing vehicles. Because they are invested in mostly stocks, they do experience day-to-day fluctuations, but the long-term return is usually very positive. The amount of fluctuation depends on the type of stocks that are held — some fluctuate much more than others.

The mutual funds discussed below are categorized into headings following those published in the *Globe and Mail.* These "types" or headings are generally standard. There are several different types of growth funds with some being 100% RRSP eligible and others only eligible as though the 20% foreign content rule.

Canadian Equity Mutual Fund

This mutual fund category is one of the more popular and larger ones emphasizing capital appreciation with investment in the Canadian stock market, especially common stocks. It accounts for about 25% of all Canadian mutual funds. There is approximately $45 billion invested in Canadian Equity mutual funds at the time of writing.

Some funds stick with nothing but blue chip stock and others hold a mixture including mid- and small-cap companies. Most companies also add up to 20% foreign content which still allows them to be eligible for RRSPs.

The mutual fund usually has stocks from 30 to 50 different companies, which minimizes the risk. This mutual fund is for long-term investment (more than five years) and can give you 10% to 15% return over this period if properly chosen.

The return for the average broad-based Canadian mutual fund should be similar to the TSE-300 composite index, but in fact, a lot of these mutual funds have under performed this mark. Many new mutual fund companies are forming and "folding" (they do not actually fold but instead merge with another mutual fund) each year, so it is important for you to go through the proper evaluation process when making your choices.

Consistent above-average good picks for the RRSP are the following: Altamira Equity, Altamira Capital Growth, Trimark Canadian Fund, Trimark RSP Equity Fund, University Avenue Canadian Fund,

I would have also included the MD Equity Fund in this list, but over the last two years it has under performed the group average. Because of this poorer performance and declining sales, MD Management is in the process of changing managers which may bring them back in favour with physicians in the future.

Note: My selection of different mutual funds throughout this chapter is based on my own personal biases. If you would like further guidance on a yearly mutual fund selection, I recommend an excellent annual mutual fund review book by Gordon Pape, *Buyer's Guide to Mutual Funds.* There is also a good newsletter published monthly, the *Canadian Mutual Fund Advisor.* Both publications rate individual mutual funds and indicate what the aim of the fund is so the investor can see if this matches his or her own investment plan. Remember, though, that what might be a good choice today may not be by the time of publication, so it is up to you to investigate. You should be able to find and select your own mutual funds that suit your needs after reading this chapter.

Canadian Small- to Mid-Cap Equity Mutual Fund

This is also a Canadian equity mutual fund category but the stocks are in smaller companies with a market capitalization less than $500 million. This fund is also 100% RRSP eligible.

The track record for small- to mid-cap companies shows that they have outperformed the TSE 300 in the past 10 to 15 years. I encourage using this mutual fund only in your portfolio if your asset mix allocation or age permits. A lot of these are roller coaster rides, so you do need time on your side. The fund drawing most attention is the Marathon Equity Fund, which has just become closed to any new investors. A good "stable" fund is the Bullock Growth Fund D; slightly more aggressive with good returns is the ABC Fundamental Value Fund.

Dividend Mutual Fund

This is also a Canadian equity mutual fund, but it invests only in companies that pay dividends, both in the form of preferred stock and common stock. The companies are mostly blue chip whose securities are highly rated by the Canadian Bond Rating Service and the Dominion Bond Rating Service.

You may recall that preferred stock takes priority over common stock in terms of dividend return and is, therefore, a safer vehicle than the common stock equity mutual fund. Most of these mutual funds also hold common shares from these same companies but generally less than 25% of the whole mutual fund. You *would not* use this mutual fund in your RRSP because you would lose the advantage of using the federal dividend tax credit (which lowers your tax bite) simply because you do not pay taxes within the RRSP.

The best use of this mutual fund is for those close to retirement or in retirement who have cash outside their RRSP and want stability, good returns, and a lower tax bite.

For physicians, the MD Dividend mutual fund is a good performer with an average to slightly above-average return. Another consistent above-average performer has been the Prudential Dividend Fund of Canada and Phillips, Hager and North Dividend Income fund.

International Equity Mutual Fund

Every professional investor gets nervous when talking about international stock investing because of the many variables involved that will affect your *final* return (e.g., currency fluctuations, local economic factors, differing accounting practices, etc.). But it is these reasons that make international mutual funds so attractive to average investors and especially to the health care professional. These worries are taken care of by top professionals from around the world.

Many of these funds have had outstanding gains over the last 10 to 15 years because of their stock and country diversification. The average economic growth of many countries outside North America has been much higher then the industrialized countries over the last few years, and this trend is sure to continue into the next decade.

There are many types of international mutual funds, some being "global" and others being "regional specific" such as many of the Emerging Mutual Fund. The regional specific ones are very risky, but the global ones are relatively safe because of diversity. These international mutual funds account for 20% of total Canadian mutual fund assets at present, which will definitely increase over the next few years. *Every health care professional needs exposure to these mutual funds at all ages of life.* I think they are currently the best bang for the buck. They are not RRSP eligible, but you can use them to make up your 20% foreign content. They should also form a major portion of your non-RRSP portfolio because of their relative safety, high returns, and favourable taxation.

Some examples of excellent global mutual funds are C.I. Global Fund, Fidelity International Portfolio, MD Growth Fund, Templeton Growth Fund, Templeton International Stock Fund, Trimark Fund, and Trimark Select Growth Fund. According to the *Globe and Mail,* the average performance for these few mutual funds as a group (for the period ending June 30, 1996) over the last year has been 19.7%, over 3 years 17.1%, 5 years 17.3%, and 10 years 12.4%. The MD Growth Fund has been one of the best, if not the best, because of its excellent performance under the guidance of the Templeton group as well as the very low management fee.

U.S. Equity mutual funds are regional specific forms of international mutual funds and many have been weighted heavily in U.S. markets in recent years because of the good performance. These may provide a good hedge against the Canadian dollar. Investing in these funds is also a good alternative to owning individual U.S. stocks, which could be subject to U.S. estate taxes.

The riskiest international mutual funds are the emerging funds, which include countries mostly in Asia, eastern European, and Latin America. These countries have 80% to 85% of the world's five billion people but only produce (and consume) 20% to 23% of the goods and services. With globalization and declining birth rates in the industrialized countries, there is expected to be large economic growth in these countries. In fact, most global mutual funds have these regional markets as a large percentage of their fund's holding, but the emerging mutual funds have mostly stocks specifically from these countries.

These funds are very volatile and risky because of the lack of geographical diversification, but they can bring in big rewards. Although the last couple of years have been poor, the gains in 1991 to 1993 were outstanding. The countries expected to do well over the next couple of years include Brazil, Chile, China, India, and Mexico. I would not generally recommend focusing specifically on emerging mutual funds because of their volatility; concentrate instead on the above-mentioned global mutual funds. If you do wish to invest directly, be prepared to leave the money in for at least five years to cover the market swings, and do not invest more than 5% of your portfolio.

Real Estate Mutual Funds

These are quite different than the other mutual funds because the fund managers borrow money in addition to your money to invest in real estate. As well, their net fund value is "approximated" because a realtor must "approximate" the value of the property holdings, which can fluctuate quite a bit. The difference between the evaluation and what you actually get can be quite different. More important, the funds are not easy to access as most medical doctors know after their MD Reality Fund temporarily suspended redemptions because of the nose dive the real estate market took in Ontario in 1990 to 1994. I think these funds have had their day and I would now stay clear of them.

Specialty Mutual Funds (Sector Mutual Fund, Precious Metals and Natural Resources Mutual Fund)

As the name implies, these are sector specific investments such as oil and gas, gold, technology, precious metals, and health. Some of these are totally RRSP eligible but most are not. The ride is often a roller coaster but over time a lot of money can be made. For example, Royal Precious Metal Fund has a one-year return of 131% and a five-year return of 31% as of May 1996. They are sector weighted and, therefore, not diversified and should not be a major player in any health care professional's portfolio. If you do partake, keep the exposure less than 5% of your total portfolio.

LABOUR-SPONSORED VENTURE CAPITAL FUNDS (LSVFS)

Labour-Sponsored Venture Capital Funds (LSVFs) are very much like mutual funds in that they hold many companies' stocks (albeit speculative) under one managing company and they are listed with the mutual funds in the weekly business section of the *Globe and Mail* and other newspapers. Health care professionals are currently being bombarded with LSVFs because of the potential "tax savings." Stay away from them — even if they are "medically" orientated!

LSVFs did provide a good tax break up until the 1996 federal budget, but now they are even less attractive for the health care professional. Even before the budget, I would not have recommended them because their emphasis is on tax sheltering and not investing. These funds exist to raise cash for companies that cannot get the cash anywhere else! Because the government would like to give some of these newer companies a break, they have allowed Canadians to invest their RRSP money with them if they wish. And because of the high risk involved, the government has also provided big tax breaks.

You cannot access these funds for five years (soon to be eight) and then there may be nothing to access if the company goes broke (of which the majority do). You still get the tax break, but who cares if your RRSP has nothing to show for it after five to eight years?

One LSVF that is getting a lot of attention is the medically orientated Canadian Medical Discoveries Fund which is managed by a physician and has close ties with the Medical Research Council. Its short track record so far has provided good returns and the merits of the fund are good. Unfortunately the matching provincial tax credits in Newfoundland, Quebec, Manitoba, Alberta, and British Columbia do not exist making them very unattractive in these provinces.

BALANCED MUTUAL FUNDS

If you are too conservative to invest in an equity mutual fund or are just happy with your present financial portfolio but want safety and a good hedge against inflation, then balanced mutual funds are for you. These are a hybrid of the growth and income-type mutual funds both in terms of safety and performance. These mutual funds hold stocks, bonds, mortgages, and money market vehicles but with a usual maximum of 40% to 60% in stocks, which is, incidentally, the same as most of the large pension retirement funds.

The "balance" of each individual mutual fund is, however, variable. The best funds are able to monitor the current market situation and successfully make small adjustments to capitalize on the particular part of the cycle that they are presently in. The idea is to provide safety and income but also some capital appreciation to hedge against inflation. They will on average give better long-term returns than a pure bond fund and be less volatile than a pure equity fund. They are mostly RRSP eligible.

There are significant differences between the different balanced mutual funds and this is one area where the "volatility measure" can be very useful; it is best to stick to the low volatility funds. The balanced mutual fund is generally slanted more toward the older health care professional.

Some of the mutual fund companies are now offering *asset mix allocation* (AMA) funds that are on the surface similar to balanced mutual funds but their performance records are much poorer. The AMA funds rely on frequent switching to optimize fund value depending on short-term market changes. Some programs that offer AMA funds are the Midland Walwyn's Compass and Royal Trust Personal Asset Management Service. I strongly discourage you from investing in these funds; instead, I favour the more traditional balanced mutual fund if that is what your age, risk, and portfolio plan calls for at present.

You will also read about *index mutual funds* being offered by the mutual fund companies. These are similar to the TIPs and HIPs indexes discussed in chapter 7, except there are the additional fees. I advise against investing in these mutual funds.

Some excellent balanced mutual funds are the Altamira Growth and Income mutual fund, CI Canadian Balanced, MD Balanced Fund, Trimark Income Growth Fund, and Trimark Select Balanced. There are plenty of good picks among this group and the returns have been excellent, averaging 17.5% for one year, 12.5% for three years, and 12.8% for five years for the period ending June 30, 1996. The Canadian Dental Association's CDA Balanced Fund has been putting in slightly above-average returns in this group as well, but like the MD Management mutual funds it has restricted enrolment (for dentists and their family).

THE INCOME MUTUAL FUNDS

The objective of income mutual funds is to safeguard the investment and provide consistent income. There are several types of income mutual funds. These use a variety of "income" investment vehicles, so the risk factor is quite variable within this group.

The most common type of investment are bonds, mortgages, preferred stocks, and treasury bills which would all fit under the umbrella of guaranteed or relatively safe forms of investments (although some also rely on common shares to a small degree). Some funds concentrate in one area only (e.g., just mortgages or just bonds) and others use a mixture of these investments to create their fund.

Adding to the diversity and volatility within this group is the option for the fund manager to use nothing but corporate bonds or nothing but government bonds which will affect the return and also the volatility and safety. This factor is reflected in the "volatility measure" published in most newspapers.

Bond Mutual Funds

The income mutual funds that invest in nothing but bonds are not surprisingly referred to as *bond mutual funds.* These funds invest in government, bank, or large corporate bonds. Their average return is less than the growth mutual fund but they usually have less fluctuation and volatility, which means more safety and peace of mind. The bond mutual funds did give unprecedented double digit returns recently because of the very low interest rates.

The fund manager has to sell and buy different bonds frequently while trying to predict what will happen to the interest rates. Some trade more frequently than others, which is indicated in the "volatility measure." However, these fluctuations should not affect you if you invest in the bond mutual funds mainly for interest income because you will still be getting the regular income. The problem is that people panic and sell during these market declines and this is when losses occur. If you want to decrease the volatility of your bond mutual fund, stick to those that invest in government-only bonds and only those with short-term maturity dates.

You can have capital appreciation with a bond fund but the usual emphasis is on preservation of capital and generating income. Most of the Canadian bond mutual funds have as a major holding government-guaranteed bonds and major bank bonds. But many also have corporate bonds which give higher returns but are, of course, more risky. Some bond mutual funds invest in specialty bonds such as strip bonds and others in foreign government bonds which are more volatile. You will have to ask or check the prospectus to see what you are investing in.

Bond mutual funds are excellent alternatives to the guaranteed type of investments discussed in chapter 6. Although you may be able to do better by investing directly in individual bonds, until you have the knowledge and time to follow them, nothing beats the bond mutual fund for safety and good income. They are not guaranteed by deposit insurance, but because most of the bonds are government offerings they are very stable. The return is mostly in the form of interest but some funds do have bonds that have good capital appreciation as well as dividend income. Interest income is taxed at a higher rate outside the RRSP than a growth mutual fund where the income is taxed as capital appreciation.

Bond funds are generally more suitable for investors nearing retirement, although young health care professionals should have some exposure to bonds as dictated by a suitable asset mix allocation. This exposure can be increased during times of dropping interest rates because of capital appreciation (seesaw principle).

Bond mutual funds provide a good guarantee on the principal plus a return that can be 1% to 3% higher than GICs. The hedge against inflation is not as good as the growth mutual fund but remember that inflation plays a much bigger role in the long run. The average return on all the Canadian Bond mutual funds as of May 1996 was 9.6% for 1 year, 7% for 3 years, 9.1% for 5 years, and 9.2% for the last 10 years (source: *Globe and Mail*).

Three bond mutual funds that have excellent above-average track records to date (and managers) are the Altamira Income Fund, Dynamic Income Fund, and the Philips Hager & North Bond Fund. The dentists' CDA Bond and Mortgage and the physicians' MD Bond Fund have slightly above-average returns as well and are also recommended. You should try and keep your picks to those funds with a management expense ratio (MER) of less than 1.5 (see explanation below).

Canadian Bond Mutual Funds in Foreign Currency

These types of bonds provide an excellent hedge against drops in the Canadian dollar. Investing in them is one method of allowing for a larger then 20% foreign exposure in your RRSP if a dropping Canadian dollar is of concern to you.

Mortgage Mutual Funds

These funds concentrate on mortgages and are very safe because they invest mostly in residential first mortgages. Generally, bond mutual funds give higher long-term returns than mortgage funds because of their guaranteed income plus capital appreciation, but for any given year the current income from the mortgage mutual fund is usually slightly higher, and hence a great choice for the retiree. Mortgage mutual funds are generally less volatile then bond mutual funds as well because their investment (the mortgages) terms average three to four years. If the market itself is volatile with falling interest rates, then the edge in performance usually goes to bond mutual funds.

Some funds invest in a mixture of mortgages and bonds. Mortgage mutual funds are probably the safest income fund after the money market mutual fund and make for a great conservative place to put money in the later retirement years. They have no capital appreciation, however, so remember that they are not a good hedge against inflation. Probably the safest mortgage mutual funds are those offered by the banks because if there is a default on a mortgage the bank will likely take the hit rather than the mutual fund!

Money Market Mutual Funds

Money market mutual funds are the best type of mutual fund for absolute guaranteed current income as well as preserving your initial investment. They are your cash-equivalent investment using mutual funds. There is virtually no risk because they invest in short-term vehicles such as government treasury bills, bank certificates of deposit, and high-quality commercial paper. As with all mutual funds, there is some variability which is reflected in the "volatility measure."

They can give you 1% to 3% greater return than other guaranteed-type investments, such as savings accounts. (Make sure you compare the *indicated* return (or current yield) between funds, as the *effective return* (or compound return) is often artificially high.) As well, money market mutual funds can be liquidated in less than 24 hours and some mutual fund companies even allow chequing privileges on them.

The main purpose of investing in money market mutual funds is using them as a very safe place to park your money until you decide what to do with it. They are a good place to put cash in your RRSP while awaiting a buying opportunity as in a pending market downturn. They are also a good investments in times of rising interest rates and will then outperform the bond mutual funds. Because of their short-term nature, they best reflect current interest rates and are, therefore, strongest when rates are high or increasing. In declining interest rates the bond mutual funds outperform them because of the capital appreciation.

The physicians' and dentists' professional associations both have good money market mutual funds which I recommend. The other suggested one that does not charge a load is the Green Line Canadian Money Market Fund and Canada Trust Everest Money Market mutual fund.

SEGREGATED FUNDS

Life insurance companies are also in the profitable mutual fund business, and about 20 different companies now offer over 100 different segregated funds that can be held inside or outside RRSPs. Segregated funds are quite similar to mutual funds, but there are differences. (see below) There are only a few insurance companies that also offer mutual funds in addition to segregated funds (e.g., Vistafunds offered by Manufacturers Life Insurance Co. and managed by Altamira Management Ltd.).

A selling feature for segregated funds is that 75% to 100% of the *initial* investment or principal is guaranteed, but this guarantee does not cover the investment gains made through compounding which is where the majority of your money will come from after several years. The other selling feature is said to be that segregated funds are better for your estate planning because of reduced probate fees, but as you will see in chapter 14 there are equally effective ways to protect your estate. They also are supposed to be creditor-proof in the case of lawsuits, which is a bonus, but as most health care professionals carry liability coverage, that may be an unnecessary factor.

The segregated funds have traditionally been difficult for the consumer to follow because of less stringent government regulations: no or infrequent financial statements and nonspecific fees and commissions. Recently this has been changing which may make segregated funds more attractive in the future, but for now, the average mutual funds still win out. (The exception may be the older health care professional who wants the added protection on the principal investment.)

The Canadian Dental Association has a Retirement Savings Plan (CDA RSP) in place for Canadian dentists which is administered by the Canadian Dental Service Plan Inc. (CDSPI). The CDA RSP has been servicing dentists for the last 38 years. There are no direct sales or service fees and the management fees are below the industry average. The savings plan offered is in the form of segregated funds and is offered through Imperial Life Assurance Company. The individual different funds are managed by different investment companies similar to the mutual funds offered by MD Management. You can follow the individual segregated performances in the mutual fund section in most Canadian newspapers.

Overall, segregated funds are more conservative and have had "average" returns only when compared to mutual funds as a whole. But like everything in life there are exceptions such as Canada Life's International Equity Fund which had a return of 15.8% in the five years up to March 1996. Some of the CDA RSP segregated funds have above average records as well.

FEES AND CHARGES

Knowing about the many different fees attached to mutual funds is an essential part of personal financial planning and can mean the difference between choosing a winner and a loser. There is a wide range of fee structures offered and you can save yourself thousands of dollars over the years by shopping wisely. Just as the 1/2% reduction on your mortgage can save you a bundle (and all you have to do is ask for it), the savings on the negotiable commissions with load funds can also save you a fortune in the long run. This is especially true for the well paid health care professional who will be investing hundreds of thousands of dollars over his or her lifetime.

Sales Commission

The sales commission is what the seller is rewarded with for selling you the mutual fund. There are two basic forms of commissions: the *load* and the *trailer fee.* At one time, mutual funds were mostly load funds which meant there was always a commission fee that you paid up front with the purchase. The banks however were instrumental in changing this. They introduced no-load mutual funds which meant no commission when you bought their funds. No-load mutual funds are sold directly to the public from the company's main offices (similar to buying a Coke right from the factory rather than the corner store). You just have to get the toll free number from the business section of any newspaper and call. No-load funds are still in the minority but their numbers are growing. The MD Management Mutual Fund or the CDA RSP SF are considered no-loads (but are restricted) as well as all of the bank mutual funds. If you buy a no-load from a broker he or she will not likely receive a commission or even a trailer fee and is, therefore, often not keen on selling them.

Load funds

The load refers to the cost you pay to the seller for buying that mutual fund. It is a percentage of the total purchase and differs for different mutual funds.

There are two types of load mutual funds: *front-end* and *rear-end*. The front-end requires that you pay the commission up front. The load is usually based on a declining scale, so the more you put in the less you pay. This acquisition fee or commission fee is paid mostly to the person who sold you the mutual fund. It is negotiable and should *always* be discussed before the purchase because it can range from 1% to 9%! Because most health care professionals are excellent clients, you should use this to your advantage to barter a lower front-end load.

The rear-end load mutual funds are becoming more popular and are now the most common type of load fund sold. With rear-end funds, you pay a fee only when you cash in the mutual fund. Some rear-end fees apply to the initial investment only; less preferable structures are those that apply to the market value at the time of cashing, which would likely cost you more. The best are those that charge no fee at all as long as you leave the mutual fund longer then seven years. This arrangement is referred to as a *declining deferred redemption fee* and it is the best type of rear-end load mutual fund.

An example of such a fund is one that would cost you 4% if you cashed your mutual fund after one year, declining to 2% at the fifth year, and then 0.5% or zero after seven years.

The story does not end there though. The management fees, or the management expense ratio, on the rear-end mutual funds are slightly higher than the front-end so there can be a "break even" period after about three years if both mutual funds have similar annual returns. But if you are in for the long run, as a rule the rear-end funds are the better bet. If you may need the funds before five to seven years, then you are better off negotiating a front-end fee. Do not worry about the sales person when you buy a rear-end mutual fund; the commission is paid immediately by the mutual fund company and averages about 5%, which is often more profitble than the front-end loads.

There are many variations of these fee structures such as flat redemption fees and combination loads with front and rear charges, etc. An important factor to determine with rear-end fees is whether they apply to the initial investment only or to the market value at the time of cashing. The latter would likely cost you more: for example, 3% on the original investment of $20,000 is much better than 3% on the present market value of $30,000.

Repeated studies have shown that the average overall net performance of both no-load and load funds has been the same. You will likely end up using both types of mutual funds with the percentage slant in favour of the no-loads because they cost you less and allow more of your money to go to work for you right away.

What really counts at the end of the day is what gives you the best overall return. The front-end load can be all right if it is an excellent mutual fund and you can negotiate a low acquisition fee, say 2% or less. The rear-end mutual funds usually have slightly higher annual management fees (0.5%) which must be considered.

More and more mutual fund companies are now giving you the option of choosing between front-end and rear-end loads. Some advisers like the front-end loads because if you decide to switch mutual funds then "you will not feel obligated" to stay versus the rear-end where early departure from the fund triggers a price to pay. Others would say the exact opposite: the rear-end load is better because it "prevents" you from early and frequent switching.

Because you should be investing for the long run within your RRSP, I recommend the rear-end load over the front-load. If you are investing outside the RRSP, then it may make more sense to go with the no-load or the front-end load so you will be able to move the cash around. But remember that when you switch out of an equity mutual fund, the capital gain is realized and you pay tax on it when it is outside the RRSP. This is another reason to buy the right mutual fund and stick with it.

Trailer Fees

Trailer fees are paid to the seller by the mutual fund company. This fee, or commission, encourages sellers to sell particular funds and to convince you, the buyer, to hold onto those funds. If you sell that specific mutual fund or change dealers then the original seller/dealer loses the trailer fee and your new dealer then gets it.

Trailer fees are paid to the dealer on a yearly basis as long as you continue to hold the fund and usually accounts for about 1/4% of the overall management expense ratio (see below). Not all mutual funds pay trailer fees but most of the loads do and a few of the no-loads. Trailer fees are a win-win situation for the mutual fund company. If they can keep you in their fund then the funds net assets will be larger which means a higher net dollar value for the management expense ratio (MER), which means more personal income for the managers. And this is where the mutual fund companies make most of their money — from the management fee.

Different mutual fund companies offer different percentage trailer fees which may encourage dealers to sell you one type of mutual fund over another. This is another of the many conflicts in this "investment" business of which the ignorant health care professional can fall prey to. Some examples of the different trailer fees on front-end load equity mutual funds: AGF pays 0.5%, C.I. pays 1%, Templeton pays 0.5%, and Trimark 1%. Don't be afraid to ask your mutual fund dealer questions from time to time because from the $50,000 in mutual funds that they are investing for you they are getting $500 *every year* for just sending you a couple of reports.

Management Expense Ratio

The management expense ratio (MER) or operating cost is the ratio or percentage of the total mutual fund assets that go toward managing the mutual fund and includes managers' fees/salaries, managers' overhead, advertising, research, postage, printing, etc. There has been a steady rise in the management fees over the past few years which is in part due to the gradual switch from front-end loads (which is paid by you) to the declining redemption fee (which is paid by the fund out of the management fees).

Comparing MERs is important when investigating different mutual funds, because they remains fairly constant versus the returns which can fluctuate. In a market downturn, the difference of 1% is important. The range is anywhere from 1% to 3% with the lower rates being charged on the income-type mutual funds and the higher fees on the growth-type mutual funds. One would assume that as the fund size increases, the MER should decline, but such is not human nature.

The mutual fund percentage return listed in the *Globe and Mail* and other newspapers is *after* the MER has been removed. *This is where the savvy and knowledgeable investor can earn 1% to 3% more by investing in stocks directly rather than in mutual funds.* But stocks are not for everybody, especially the busy health care professional and therefore mutual funds run a close second despite these management expenses.

Trustee Fees

Annual trustee fees are charged on just about all mutual funds held inside RRSPs and run about $25 to $45 per year. There is only one charge per company regardless of how many of their mutual funds you hold. Depending on how many funds you have with different companies, this fee can make a difference in your overall return.

Registration Fees

Some companies charge a one-time registration fee of $40 to $50 on no-load funds.

Switching Fees

Switching fees differ from company to company and it is extremely important to know about them when choosing between two funds. This consideration is more important for the non-RRSP mutual fund because you will likely do more switching with it than with a fund within your RRSP.

Switching fees are the cost the company charges you for switching from one mutual fund to another within the company. The best type is *no charge,* which most of the banks and a lot of the no-load mutual funds offer, although even they are now limiting the number of switches per year because of recent abuses. The second best type of switching fee arrangement is a simple flat fee. The worst type is one that charges a percentage of the fund's assets.

It is worth mentioning again that frequent switchers almost always lose. The studies show that you can lose between 30% to 50% of the gains against the buy and hold strategy! It is a good rule that once you decide on a mutual fund, especially the growth ones, to hold for at least

16 to 24 months before switching (and preferably three years or longer). Of course, if there is a major change in the fund's principles or the fund manager, then you should switch if it is not in line with your plan.

KISS PRINCIPLE — Annual Fees on Mutual Funds

1. *The annual fee you pay to hold mutual funds is one of the biggest disadvantages of them. You will pay somebody 1% to 3% per year for mutual funds, compared to an initial one-time 1% to 2% charge to buy blue chip stocks!*

EVALUATING AND FOLLOWING MUTUAL FUND PERFORMANCE

When evaluating a mutual fund before buying it — and while holding it — there are three factors you should look at: past performance, volatility, and the fund manager.

While past performance does not predict future performance, it is the best indicator we have. Future returns are very likely to be similar if the fund manager is the same. You should compare the 1-, 2-, 3-, 5-, and 10-year average returns to others within that group. These are listed regularly in most business papers. More important, you need to look at and compare the year-to-year returns. Some mutual funds have great average returns based on one excellent year of 100% return, for example, but 0% for the next three years, giving an "excellent" average return of 25%! If you do not check year-to-year, you could be picking a poor mutual fund.

A fund's volatility is a measure of the variability in the month-to-month returns and should ideally be low or low within that group. The lower the volatility the more likely the fund's performance will be consistent. Generally, money market mutual funds have the lowest volatility followed by mortgage funds, bonds funds, and preferred-dividend funds. The growth mutual funds have the highest volatility and among them resource and gold funds (sector mutual funds) are the most volatile with equity funds that invest in mostly large blue chip companies the least volatile.

The fund manager is also very important. If there has been a recent change in the manager, you musn't rely on the fund's past figures as the new manager may have a different strategy and hence different future returns. The different types of investment strategies used by the fund managers are similar to those covered in chapter 7 and you may want to pick a manager whose investment style fits yours (e.g., buy and hold). Although there is no "rating system" for mutual fund managers, you will learn from reading the business section of the newspaper which have the good track records.

To follow all of these factors, you should familiarize yourself with the mutual fund tables provided in the business section of the newspaper of your choice. (Remember, the subscription is tax deductible for most health care professionals.) Each column gives you important information about the mutual fund, and at the bottom is listed the *average* performance for the group. You should make sure that most of your mutual funds are at least average if not above average; if not, consider switching.

Most of the above information is published once a month in the *Globe and Mail* in a special section called "Report on Mutual Funds." The *Financial Post* also provides excellent coverage. Southam publishers offer two useful products: the *Mutual Fund Source* is a monthly updated computer disk that provides the above information and more, and the *Mutual Fund Sourcebook* is a publication with the same type of information. There are also now plenty of software programs available as well as the Internet that provide guidance and day-to-day monitoring of the different mutual funds (see the Appendix).

STRATEGIES FOR BUYING MUTUAL FUNDS

There are several strategies that can be used for buying mutual funds some of which are similar to those used to buying stocks. The strategies can be broken down into *how, what, when,* and *where*. First, however, we need to review the buy and hold strategy for mutual funds. I encourage the buy and hold strategy as the best path to success, and there is some fine tuning that can be done along the way that will help optimize your return.

As a rule, increase your percentage of annual/monthly buys of equity mutual funds when interest rates are dropping or low and decrease this percentage when rates are increasing. The same rule applies to the bond mutual funds. So in a time of increasing interest rates, you might want to consider increasing your money market mutual fund holding or other investments, such as GICs, T-bills, or mortgage-backed securities. As a rule, the amount of change should be no more than 5% to 15% (depending on your age).

The *how* of buying mutual funds is straightforward. The *Globe and Mail* and many other newspapers list the toll-free numbers for mutual funds sold in Canada. Call these numbers and they will tell you who in your local area is selling their mutual funds or whether it can be done directly over the phone as with most no-load mutual funds. If you already have a financial planner or broker (or discount broker) than you can purchase the funds through him or her.

You will need to fill out an initial application and make your first purchase with a cheque through the mail or with your credit card. I strongly encourage using the PAC program discussed in chapter 2 to impose a forced savings pattern and to take advantage of dollar-cost averaging. This will require you sending a voided cheque to the company or your broker/financial planner.

Initially just limit yourself to one or two funds within one company to keep the administrative fees low. Once you are above $10,000, then open a plan with another company and again use one or two funds to allow for some diversification. Stick with the no-loads initially if you can.

At this stage there is really no need for a self-directed RRSP and no need for a financial planner. Once your RRSP reaches the range of $40,000 to $50,000, you have to make some decisions. If you are comfortable with just mutual funds, then limit the number of companies to three with a total of seven to nine funds. This number allows diversification of fund managers' investment styles as well as diversification within the market. Remember, if you hold mutual funds from too many companies (more than three or four), you may be spreading yourself too thin and the different fees will start to add up, decreasing your final net return.

What type of mutual fund you invest in will depend on your asset mix allocation (see chapter 12). Your age, risk tolerance, years to retirement, years of retirement, and your overall investment plan are all factors. The theory is that you should always have a mixture of stocks, bonds, and cash equivalents to allow for an optimal return in a variety of different market conditions. The typical combination would be an equity mutual fund, an income (bond) mutual fund, and global mutual fund in varying percentages depending on your investment plan. A more conservative combination would be a balanced mutual fund plus the income and global mutual fund.

Mutual funds allow you to have an excellent asset mix allocation, but it is important to chose the right ones. Statistics show that over 50% of equity mutual funds have under performed the TSE-300! The banks sold 50% of the RRSP mutual funds in 1995 which is very unfortunate because they are frequently among the worst performers, especially in the equity mutual funds sector. Before you buy, you may want to check out a good source such as Gordon Pape's book *Buyer's Guide to Mutual Funds* or the *Canadian Mutual Fund Advisor* newsletter.

There is much debate over whether you should buy into the large mutual funds or go with the smaller ones. Some recent editorials have stated that the larger mutual funds (net assets) are less likely to out perform the TSE-300 simply because their holdings are so large that they mirror the index by virtue of their enormous size. Although I think there is some truth to this, there are several very large mutual funds that still outperform the pack including the Altamira Equity fund (over $2 billion) and the Trimark Canadian ($1.5 billion). I recommend holding a combination of these larger mutual funds as well as some smaller ones: once again, diversify.

When you buy mutual funds depends on whether they are in or outside your RRSP. If inside, the beginning of the season is a good time if prices are cheap. Alternatively, you can buy on a regular basis using a PAC program. If you are buying outside your RRSP with a lump sum, you should purchase after any capital gains are distributed; otherwise you will end up paying more taxes than necessary with the equity mutual funds. These distributions usually occur annually in December, but some differ.

Where you buy partly depends on what type of mutual fund you wish to buy. Any bank or trust company will sell you no-load funds at the counter. However, I would stay away from many of these places. You can buy other no-load mutual funds directly through the company; the phone numbers are listed each week in the *Globe and Mail.* Some no-loads can also be bought through an independent sales person, almost all brokers and discount brokers.

The other place to buy no-load mutual funds and segregated funds is through the professional associations. The physicians have available the MD Management and the dentists have the Canadian Dental Service Plan Inc. Both of these associations have average to above-average performers for some of their funds. I recommend some of the funds offered by both of these associations as part of your portfolio. These associations have many different financial companies running the different mutual funds and so the performance of each reflects this. You have to pick and choose your mutual fund with attention to who the individual fund manager is. There are other smaller professional associations that some health care professionals can look into such as the anesthetists and the pharmacists. (More is said about these professional associations in chapter 10.)

If you are buying load-funds, you will not have any problem finding a seller. The best person to buy mutual funds from is your financial planner if you have one or through a stockbroker or a discount broker which you can find listed in the Yellow Pages. As a rule, if you are buying load funds of value less than $5,000, then a discount broker will give you the best value, above this they are about even if you barter a little with your broker to bring the front-end commission down to 2%.

The real competition for where to buy your load mutual funds is just starting to heat up. A new group of mutual fund dealers has just started in Ontario calling themselves the zero-fee brokers. The two most active so far are Mutual Fund Direct (1-800-268-1066) and Wayne H. Levine & Co. (1-416-494-7100). They receive their commission only through the trailer fees. They, of course, will be selling front-end load mutual funds only and there will be no advice, so you will have to know what you are buying. But for the informed buyer, this option can be a money saver. Expect to see zero-fee brokers in all provinces in the near future.

KISS PRINCIPLE — Mutual Funds

1. *A good no-load is the best choice for a mutual fund, both inside and outside the RRSP.*
2. *No-loads do not come with advice but you should not be relying on the salesperson for advice anyway. (The MD Management (and the CDA RSP segregated funds) no-load mutual funds are the exception in that they do provide reasonable advice.)*
3. *Rear-end mutual funds with a declining fee are the next best type of mutual fund for inside the RRSP.*
4. *Front-end mutual funds should also be looked at but try and negotiate a low load.*
5. *The compound average return and the annual return should be looked at before choosing a mutual fund.*
6. *When comparing any two mutual funds pick the one with the lower volatility and MER.*
7. *The same fund manager is crucial for continued performance.*
8. *The maximum number of mutual funds you should hold is seven to nine with two to three different companies.*
9. *Diversify your mutual funds between large and small funds and between growth and income according to your specific asset mix allocation.*
10. *Use the buy and hold strategy for 80% to 90% of your portfolio but make minor adjustments every six months depending on the direction of the interest rates.*
11. *Mutual funds are the best way to hold foreign content both inside and outside the RRSP.*
12. *Do not attempt frequent switching of your mutual funds.*
13. *Insurance company segregated funds may be worth looking at in retirement years because of their extra built-in safety.*
14. *A good financial adviser is recommended for any health care professional buying mutual funds who is too busy to investigate and monitor them.*

NOTES:

9

GROWTH INVESTMENT #3 — REAL ESTATE

Many health care professionals are already invested in real estate in various forms, and many will likely continue to be in the future. Often, the real estate investment is in the form of office space for personal practice (e.g., a renovated downtown house). As more health care professionals are forced out of their employee positions and into self-employed private practices, buying office real estate may become a very practical financial option. If you can afford it, buying your own office is often more advantageous then paying rent for 25-plus years and the sooner you do it the better.

Another common form of real estate investment for health care professionals is the small rental property (house or condo rental) used solely for the purpose of investing. This chapter focuses mostly on these two forms of investment real estate. Most of the principles, however, that apply to the smaller forms of real estate also apply to larger investments such as commercial and apartment complexes if that is what interests you.

REAL ESTATE — THE GREAT CANADIAN INVESTMENT

Real estate has traditionally been one of the best investments in Canadian history as well as being an excellent hedge against inflation. The market has been greatly influenced by the baby boomers who have had their peak house buying spree in the last 15 to 20 years, creating great demands. From 1975 to 1985 the average Canadian home price jumped 145%; from 1985 to 1993 there was another 100% increase. These figures work out to an annual average return of about 11% to

13% over the last 15 to 20 years and do not take into account the favourable taxation that real estate encounters.

In certain areas, such as Toronto and Vancouver, the gains have been double and triple these numbers. Many people have become millionaires by simply living in their own homes. The smart ones have now downsized and realized their gains, but many others remain "house rich and cash poor." The capital gains were even more impressive for those savvy individuals who, in addition to owning their own homes, also invested in real estate using the leverage principle.

Despite this recent boom, many investors believe that real estate may not have a rosy future. Many feel that real estate will no longer give the returns that it has over the past 15 to 20 years. Others disagree, but emphasize that the type of real estate and the location will be much more critical. The statistics show that the past few years have been poor for the real estate market, especially for homes with values greater than $200,000 to $400,000 (depending on location).

Over the next five to eight years, we will see the final generalized real estate boom of house buying as the final wave of young boomers buy their first homes and the middle-aged boomers make their final "buy-up." There will still be good investment opportunities, but they will be in more selective types of homes reflecting who will be doing the buying in the future.

The next boom in real estate will be slanted toward smaller homes and condos, especially in smaller towns that are within one to three hours of major centres. This will be driven by the retiring baby boomers or the "elderly boomers" who will be drifting back to rural living (with modem, computer, and fax in tow). The downsizing will create a glut of the "monster homes" and a possible rapid decline in their prices because there will be no buyers. Garth Turner, author of *2015 — After the Boom,* recommends that now is the time to unload these types of homes as their value will likely drop significantly over the next few years.

Economist and author David Foot also believes that there will be a significant drop in the general real estate market simply based on demographics. Foot stresses that most of the boomers have bought their homes and the succeeding generation ("baby bust") is so small in numbers that there will be a glut of homes in the next 10 years. He believes that real estate sales will not pick up until the year 2010 because this is the age that the boomers' children will start buying. But first they will want to rent, creating a demand for rental properties in specific regions of Canada: Alberta, British Columbia, and Ontario.

There will be other areas of future real estate demand such as the "resort-vacation" properties where skiing, golfing, boating, etc. are readily accessible. A good analogy is that the boomers will do to these resort homes what they did to the principal residence market from 1970 to 1990. There may be a lull for a couple of years while the boomers top up their RRSPs (we are currently seeing this boom in the stock markets) but then the resort-vacation property demand will take off.

Homes with in-law suites may also be attractive in the future as I think that more baby boomers are going to have to help out their aging parents especially if we see further cuts in health care facilities for the elderly.

As well, the high divorce rate may keep real estate alive as "split" couples each look for homes. This market will generally be looking for small to average-size homes. The turnover of homes may not be as great in the future as well (therefore less supply) with people residing in their homes longer thanks to advancing health care. This of course brings us to the final area of future real estate demand, which will be the retirement communities, seniors' complexes, and nursing homes. Unfortunately, these types of real estate are financially out of reach for most individual health care professionals but will certainly be a place of great future growth.

Before you decide to invest in real estate, you need to take a hard look at the specific location. It is impossible to make blanket statements about real estate because there are drastic differences between provinces (compare, for example, Prince Edward Island and British Columbia) and even within each province there are significant variations. Two simple guides (but not foolproof) to help you decide if real estate has a future in your area is to check the local vacancy rates for rentals and check the direction of housing prices over the last four years. There was a nationwide drop in prices four to five years ago; is your region starting to recover? This information can be obtained free in a quarterly report put out by Royal LePage, which covers house prices and rents across Canada.

If the vacancy rate is less than 5% and the housing price trend has been up over the last few years, then you are probably in a reasonably good area to invest in real estate rental properties. If there is a migration of young people away from your area then this would make real estate a poor future investment. Similarly, if your community's retirees are moving away, then real estate is likely not a good investment as these people are the future small home and condo buyers. (If you are looking for real estate for your office, these principles do not apply as strongly because owning beats paying rent over the long term.)

WHY REAL ESTATE IS A GOOD INVESTMENT

There are several reasons why real estate has traditionally been an excellent investment, and most of these reasons still apply today. However, there are restrictions you must now consider. To profit today and in the future from real estate, you must be selective about the type and location.

Leveraging

The potential return on your investment can be phenomenal thanks to the wonders of leveraging. Real estate investing is one of the few places where health care professionals should be using leveraging! Leveraging allows you to own a large asset (e.g., a house) with very little of your money and a lot of somebody else's (i.e., the banks). For example, if you put $10,000 down to buy a $100,000 home and the house appreciates 5% per year, then even after just one year the house value is now $105,000 and you have made a 50% return on your initial investment. After five years this translates into over a 250% return!

Leveraging is appealing to those in the top tax bracket because the interest you pay on the borrowed money for investment purposes is deductible. If you borrow money at a rate of 10% and are in the 50% tax bracket, then you reduce the cost of borrowing to only 5%. (However, leveraging lost a lot of its appeal after the 1994 budget with the elimination of the $100,000 lifetime capital gains exemption. Prior to this you could avoid taxes on your investment gains up to $100,000 making leveraging very attractive.)

The trick in making leverage work is to put down as little as possible. Table 7 shows you the different returns on 10% versus 25% down.

Table 7
The Value of Leveraging in Real Estate

Home value with 2% appreciation	% return with 25% down	% return with 10% down
purchase $100,000	-	-
1 year = $102,000	8	20
5 years = $110,000	42	104
10 years = $122,000	88	220

Clearly, the less you put down the more you stand to make (and the less you stand to lose). I have used a rather low annual home appreciation of 2% in this example. If we were to use a 6% return, the difference at five years would be 135% for 25% down versus 338% return for 10% down! The beauty of leveraging is that you actually need very little cash to buy an investment property.

Appreciation

The second most important feature of successful real estate investing which must occur for it to be profitable is appreciation. The gains listed above are just on the capital appreciation of the home. We have not yet considered the fact that during the 5 or 10 years of renting you are paying down the mortgage as well or creating "equity build-up." So when you sell in 10 years, not only is there the capital gains but also the profit from the renters paying down your mortgage.

There are, of course, costs to operating a rental property that must be considered when looking at your return, but as I will show you, these expenses can be kept to a minimum and many are tax deductible. The other neat deal about real estate is that after 10 to 15 years you have beaten inflation because you locked in the price on your home at yesterday's price and are, therefore, paying for your house today with yesterday's non-inflated dollars.

Most profits in real estate have been from capital appreciation, so if you are in an area where you do not expect any appreciation in the near future, you should generally not consider buying a rental property. However, there can be an exception if there is still a demand for rentals in your area. If there is, then you can still make money from rental properties but you will have to be more rigorous in finding the very best deal. Fortunately, in an area where housing prices are low or dropping, you will often be able to get a very good price on a property because of panic selling. Combined with the fact that rents do not usually drop as much as property value, you get to purchase for less but still charge the same rent. What this means is that you will have a surplus of cash each month (rent income will be more than monthly mortgage payment), which you should consider putting on the principal because your personal gain is not going to be capital appreciation but on the equity build up in the home.

But there are the two faults with this strategy. The first is that there will be higher taxation on rental income than capital appreciation so the final return will have to be looked at carefully. The other is that you may end up holding a mortgage that is more than the value of the house if prices continue to drop.

Safety

Safety of your investment is usually higher with real estate than other types of investments because of its physical nature. It is not unheard of for a stock to drop 50%, but it would be very unlikely for housing prices to drop this much in most areas of Canada. When the housing market does drop it affects the upper-priced homes significantly more than the middle-priced homes, and it is the latter in which you should be investing. As well, even when housing prices do drop, rent rates do not drop as much (if at all), so there is some safety cushion built in.

Tax Incentives

Although fewer than in previous years, there still are tax breaks available that make real estate an attractive investment. Under the rules of capital gains, only 75% of gains on real estate are taxed compared to 100% of your investment in a GIC, thus leaving 25% of your gains completely free of taxes. (It is important that you hold the property for five or more years; otherwise the government may view the sale of the property as "flipping" and tax you on 100% of any capital gains.)

The other excellent tax break is in the form of deductions that you are allowed for maintaining the property. The main deductions allowed are interest on the mortgage, any interest on the loan, home insurance, property tax, a lot of accounting and legal fees, general house maintenance and repairs, and part of your auto expenses. There are other deductions available, and I refer the interested reader to a couple of excellent books on real estate investing by Gary Weiss and Douglas Gray that I have referenced in the Appendix.

Another significant allowable deduction is for the home office, if you have one. If you are using part of your principal residence for filing documents on rental properties (bookkeeping); arranging and filing matters related to maintenance of the properties; phoning and interviewing renters and checking their references, etc., then you can claim and deduct a home office expense. This can translate into a lot of tax savings, as much as 15% to 20% of your principal home expenses depending on how big your office is. You can claim a percentage of your principal residence mortgage interest, phone bill, property tax, utility bills, office furniture, filing cabinets, home computer, stamps, stationery, snow clearing, lawn maintenance, etc. The beauty of these deductions is that they may create a loss on the property, which can be put against your salary income.

You may also be able to claim other expenses such as remodeling or home extension if pertinent to the real estate investment management, but this should be reviewed with your accountant. You would probably need two rental properties to safely claim these deductions.

If you live in a province that allows you to incorporate, you should consider doing so if you plan on investing in real estate. The idea is to set up a holding company, in addition to the medical company, through which you would buy the property. This allows you to buy the property with the corporation taxed money (at a 23% tax rate) versus the top marginal rate (50 + %) if you were to buy it personally. If you buy the investment property directly (besides your office/building property) in the corporation, then you stand to lose your status as a "small business corporation" which defeats one of the purposes of incorporating (more on this in chapter 11) and is another reason to consider setting up a holding company.

When to Buy

The best time to buy an investment property is when nobody else is buying or in a "buyer's market." Real estate is cyclical which means the supply and demand goes through cycles of shortages and excesses. Even though the price of the real estate will likely go up over time, your gains will be substantially more if you can buy at a lower price in a buyer's market. This means you have to be patient and wait with your money sitting elsewhere but available (e.g., a money market mutual fund). Unfortunately most of us cannot wait and end up following the frenzy when the economy is booming and buying in the seller's market. This is all right, as long as you get below fair market value for the property.

Several studies have shown that December is the best month to purchase real estate. The most expensive times are between March and June. Use these statistics to your benefit; when you are buying investment properties, unlike the purchase of your principal residence, you have the time to wait and choose.

What to Buy

There are many options in real estate investments, each with their disadvantages and advantages. One good choice for the health care professional is an older home converted into an office plus a rental suite. You can use the office, you get good tax deductions, you have a source of income from the rental suite to offset the mortgage, and you have a watchful eye around the office most of the time (i.e., the tenant).

If you are adventuring outside the converted-home office setup, then I recommend bungalow homes or condos as the choice of real estate investment. The potential gain on the bungalow is better than the condo but the condo requires less maintenance and time (no outside painting, no roof repairs, no furnace maintenance, etc.). Duplexes and triplexes are also good reasonable first-time investments, but depending on the neighbourhood you may attract less than ideal tenants. It has been my experience that you will get the best tenants in a bungalow or condo, saving you many headaches of being a landlord.

The best type of property is without a doubt a bungalow home with a basement suite. The income from both rental floors will frequently cover most of your expenses. However, be careful about local and provincial laws regarding basement suites and renting laws in general. Most basement suites are not registered and are sometimes called "illegal" or "in-law suites." They are illegal because they may not be complying with local bylaws, but in most areas, the local government turns a blind eye to them as long as the tenants aren't disruptive and the neighbours don't complain.

If you are thinking of investing in a condo, be sure you check out the rules that could potentially limit your rental potential. For example, is the condo complex limited to "over-60s"? Are pets allowed? Is it a no smoking complex? Are renters allowed?

The ideal condo is one where the number of rental units in the building is limited to less than 25%. The 75% owner-occupied condos will keep the complex in good shape and will help your eventual resale value. Condos also have monthly fees ("condo fees") and property taxes which are tax deductible and should be worked into your calculations when you are deciding if the deal is feasible (see below). Although the capital appreciation is usually greater for the single-dwelling homes, I think condos will have a great place in the future as the elderly boomers downsize.

Other types of real estate investments that may be worth looking at, but usually only after you have experience with smaller properties, include apartment buildings and commercial buildings. There are both advantages and disadvantages to moving up to these larger types of investments. The disadvantage is the larger down payment, the extra legal and accounting fees, and the likelihood of needing a professional property manager. You will have more local and provincial regulations to abide by and often the complexities and headaches of being involved in a partnership (because of the expense).

On the positive side, there is potential for great gains and potential tax write-offs. The gains come from the fact that there is power (including financial power) in numbers. The more apartment units you have, the cheaper it is to maintain your overhead — whether it is 2 or 40 units they all have the same roof, plumbing system, etc.

An intermediate option is the small commercial building with your office downstairs as well as a few other professionals and upstairs there may be more professionals or even rental suites. This is a little easier to manage and follow than the apartment complex but again often requires a partnership because of the initial setup costs. There are still many more issues to deal with than the simple bungalow and you will need to educate yourself by starting with the recommended reading in the Appendix and seeking the advice of a good realtor, lawyer, and accountant.

Personally, I believe the future of commercial real estate in Canada is bleak. With corporate downsizing, modern telecommunications, and the trend for boomers to move to rural locations, the occupancy rate for commercial real estate is bound to decline.

Should I Use a Property Manager?

You can hire a property manager for dealing with your bungalow or condo rentals, but it will decrease your final return. Property managers usually ask anywhere between 1% and 5% of the monthly rent which adds up over several properties and many years. The fee is negotiable, and it is also tax deductible.

For the smaller forms of rental properties, most health care professionals will be able to handle the property management themselves. If you have larger properties, a property manager is necessary. You will need to find someone you trust who will show the properties, collect the rents, and call on the trades people when problems arise.

Is This the Right Place to Buy?

This is the question that you will be asking yourself over and over just before you consider bidding on a property. Although there is no foolproof way of knowing there are three simple factors to consider that will help guide you to the "right place." These are the location, the home's condition, and the price.

Location is probably the most important factor because you can change the condition of the property but not a bad location. The easiest test to determine good location is to ask yourself whether you could live there yourself. What is the neighbourhood like? What is the access to shopping? Schools? Highways? Keep in mind that you are going to want to sell in 5 to 10 years. Is there any reason why this house would not sell then?

Always try and choose the home that is the average for that neighbourhood or slightly less than average as it will appreciate the most. As well the rent you will get will be no different than the "nicer" more expensive house down the street. I think equally important is the condition of the property; it must be *excellent*. Excellent condition usually attracts excellent tenants which is a big bonus. If the property is not in good shape when you buy, then you will either have to fix it up or pay someone else to do it. The time (sweat equity) and the expense of improving the property are not leveraged like the mortgage, so it comes right out of your pocket. It is tax deductible but the gain is not as great as the fully leveraged ready-to-go home.

Often if I see a good home that has great potential but needs "minor" repairs or painting, I make sure the repair work is included in the contract to purchase, even if this means a higher price, so that the work is done before I buy the house, saving me time and money. If you do the work yourself after you make the purchase, you have the headache of arranging the work and you will lose rental income while working on it. By having it done before you buy, you end up paying less because of the leverage principle.

The same logic applies to including appliances, lawn mower, garden hose, garbage buckets, etc. when purchasing. Negotiate for them to be included in the price otherwise you will pay for them later out of pocket.

Finally, the price you pay is a factor in your decision. Review chapter 3 for advice on how much to pay for property; the discussion there applies equally to investment properties. You can afford to be more selective, however, with the investment property because you aren't buying it for yourself. You can fall in love with a dream home and pay a little extra but you should *never* fall in love with an investment property and let your emotion sway sound financial decision-making.

If you can buy in a buyer's market than you will likely get a better price because the supply is great and the demand is low. Regardless of when you buy you should always aim for below market value. To find out what market value is you will need to look at 10 to 15 other similar homes. By being consistent and vigilant, I have been able to buy all of my properties for 5% to 10% below fair market value. To do this requires time and patience as well as the ability to walk away from a home if the price isn't right.

It can be useful to form a scrap book to follow homes of interest. If you see the right house in the right location and the price is reasonable, then you have to act quickly as there are many others doing exactly the same thing especially in a seller's market (which you should try and avoid).

It is also useful to find out what the city's tax assessment for the property is, but remember these assessments are frequently 5% below fair market value. There are now many real estate companies listed on the Internet including Re/Max and Royal LePage which give quick assessment of homes available in your area and the available statistics on the home.

Once you feel comfortable with the property it is imperative that a home inspector review the house. For the sake of $250, these people can save you a lot of grief. If they think you should get an engineer to look at some settling or an electrician to look at some wiring problems, for example, then do it. Remember that you have to sell this place in 5 to 10 years, and if there is a major foundation flaw you want to know before you buy.

MAKING THE NUMBERS WORK

The numbers have to work to make real estate profitable. Before you approach the lending institutes about a mortgage, you have to first do some number crunching yourself.

First, pick up a mortgage rate table book (available in many supermarkets and in Canadian Tire) that will let you review the different payments per month for different mortgage amounts according to prevailing mortgage rates with different amortization periods. Next, watch the local newspaper's "home and suite rental" section for a few months (even look at a few rental properties as a"potential" renter) to get an idea for what rents are in your area. Be sure to review different types of properties for different locations in the city. An excellent starting point and free source of accurate information is the quarterly report that Royal LePage puts out which gives you the average housing price for your area as well as the yearly appreciation and the average rent charged.

Next you need to start looking at potential properties. When you find one that meets your standards, estimate what the mortgage payment will be per month (based on expected final house price and your down payment). Will the "expected" rent cover the mortgage? You have to be very realistic about your projected rent; I recommend erring on the low side. If the numbers do not add up, then move on.

After going through this process a few times, you will automatically know what amount of rent you will need to cover the mortgage. It is nice if the rent will also cover the property tax that you pay each year as well, but it can still work if it doesn't. (Remember that property tax is tax deductible.) It's also a good idea to ask the lending institution to build the approximate property tax into the monthly mortgage payment so you don't have to scramble each year for the lump sum payment. This can be quite a scramble when you have five or six properties that each have a property tax of $1,000 to $2,000.

Even if the home is in excellent condition and especially, if it is older than 10 years, you should plan on spending 0.5% to 1% of the home's value per year on general maintenance such as furnace upkeep, painting, etc. Expect to pay more for triplexes and fourplexes, and much more again for apartment buildings.

Your best chance for your rental income to cover all of the mortgage costs, property taxes, and the annual maintenance expenses is with a single dwelling with a suite or a well-priced condo. The optimal buy is a three-bedroom bungalow with a one- or two-bedroom suite downstairs with a separate entrance and separate laundry. These are very hard to come by.

Be sure you lower your asking rent if the vacancy rate goes above 5%. Don't lose out on finding renters for the sake of a few dollars a month. The difference between $750 and $725 per month, for example, is nothing compared to missing one or two months' rent.

The final factor to be worked into the numbers is the *rent control* if applicable in your province. Rent control is usually enforced with the larger rental properties but it is something that you should ask the realtor about before buying.

Financing and Mortgaging

The basic information about financing and mortgaging is covered in chapter 3, and you should review that section if you are interested in investing in real estate. However, there are some important differences in your financing strategy when you are dealing with investment rental properties.

One of the major differences, mentioned above, is that you will aim to put down as little as possible in order to maximize the leverage principle. My personal favourite financial lender for investment properties is Royal LePage because they allow 15% down, versus the banks which usually require 25%, and their mortgage options are as good as any of the banks.

If the investment property is going to house your office and you plan to rent part of the building, then you may be wise to put more down, depending on the state of your cash flow and tax situation. In this case, capital cost allowance may be a consideration, and you would be wise to seek the advice of your accountant. If you are in a partnership, then the financing and mortgage arrangement will definitely require the input of a professional.

Most frequently, investors will carry a high-ratio mortgage for an investment property with all the options as discussed in chapter 3. (Do not pay the CMHC fee up front as this will decrease your return when you sell in a few years.) The decisions about the term length, open or closed mortgage and fixed rate or variable very much depends on what the current rates are and when you plan on selling. As you will likely be keeping the property for more than five years, and if the rates remain as good as they currently are, then there is no reason not to lock in for a four- or five-year term with a fixed rate. You will want to make sure the mortgage is assumable so that you can unload it when the time is right without having to pay a penalty or choose a open mortgage around that time or a short closed term.

I have already mentioned the new "rainy day" option being offered by some banks which allows you to miss a month's payment without penalty. This is a vital option for investment property to help your cash flow if you have no renters for one month.

Buydown plans, offered by most institutions, are also very useful because they make the investment property more attractive when it comes time to sell. With a buydown plan, you are allowed to "buy down" your present rate by 1% to 3%. For example, for $1,000, you could change the rate on a $100,000 mortgage from 9% to 7%. Also, don't forget the no-fee early renewal option, which allows you to lock in a low rate of renewal while you are less than 6 to 12 months away from the end of your present term. If you have more than one rental property you should stagger the maturity dates otherwise you could be renewing several properties when the rates are high.

If you are short on cash when you need the down payment, then simply use your line of credit or get a bank loan, but pay it off as quickly as possible. Remember that the interest charged on this is tax deductible. I would not encourage taking out a second mortgage on your principal residence to finance an investment property but you could consider doing this on another investment property that you might already have enough equity built up in it. And don't forget that you will need extra cash ready for all the incidental fees such as legal bills, property transfer tax, etc. (see chapter 3).

The other possible source of funding for your real estate investment is your RRSP. It is possible to borrow funds from a self-directed RRSP. This is a costly affair to arrange and there are strict guidelines to follow, but if the funds are then used for investment purposes (rental properties) then the interest you pay on this loan (back into your RRSP) is tax deductible which is attractive in times of high interest rates and makes for a very cheap investment loan. It is important to weigh the costs of setting this up as well as the lost RRSP gains, and it should be done only under the guidance of your accountant.

When you are dealing in investment properties, you might want to consider using a mortgage broker, especially if you cannot get the support of your local lending institute. Brokers know mortgages well and will usually find you the best deal. They have access to many different sources besides the banks and may be able to find you an institution to back you with a lower down payment. Just be sure to discuss all fees before you hire a broker. In the past, brokers have acquired a bad reputation because of the less-than-scrupulous activities of some. Brokers' fees generally are in the neighbourhood of 1% to 4% of the total amount borrowed. I recommend checking at least two different brokers and comparing the costs before committing to anyone. Remember that their fee is tax deductible.

PREVENTING THOSE REAL ESTATE HEADACHES

There are several potential headaches to real estate investing but most are avoidable. Unavoidable, however, is the time you must put in to find a good property, show properties, collect rent, and maintain the ones you buy.

Looking at several properties is a necessity if you are buying, so you can't save much time there. But once you have tenants in place, there are a few ways to save on the administration and property management chores. First, you can ask for post-dated cheques so you don't have to collect from your renters every month. If your bank doesn't charge for depositing post-dated cheques, you can do that job in one trip as well.

Property maintenance chores can be minimized by providing your renters with the phone numbers of some good trades and maintenance services so that they can make service calls as needed. As long as you have screened the services beforehand, this will save you and your tenants a lot of time. Maintaining such a list all but eliminates the need for a property manager.

Of course, you may choose to relieve yourself of even more responsibility by hiring a professional property manager, but remember that this will cut into your return. I do not recommend using a property manager initially, but you might want to talk to one just to get an idea of what must be done each month. Most real estate offices have a few people who will act as property managers for you or you can look in the Yellow Pages under Property Management. It is very important that you speak to at least three of their clients as references. A property manager's fee is usually 1% to 5% of the gross monthly rent, but this is negotiable.

A common cause of failure in property investing is poor management, which occurs more frequently with apartment buildings or commercial buildings, but is also a factor if you have several smaller rental units. If you do not have the time or personality to handle the job, then get yourself a property manager and draw up a contract with your lawyer's guidance. Remember though, like your other investments, nobody will manage them better than the owner.

Many headaches can also be avoided by getting good tenants in the first place. And you won't get good tenants unless you have good rental properties. Use an "information sheet" asking prospective tenants to list their name and address; next of kin's phone number and address; present and previous employers' names, phone numbers, and addresses; and present and previous landlords' names, phone numbers, and addresses; and finally a couple of references. If after reviewing and checking the references, you have any hesitation or feel like a credit check may be required, then I recommend you move on to someone else. Some experts also recommend asking for credit card numbers, bank account numbers, and social insurance numbers as well, but you may find this important in larger centres only. The most important thing, as in health care, is good screening and prevention by doing your homework first which starts by checking the details on the information sheet. *Always* get the damage deposit on the day that the renters accept otherwise they could renege in a week and you will be left holding the bag with a cancelled ad in the paper. *Always* get the rent in your hand before the tenants enter the house, because once they move in they can be difficult to get out!

Rental agreements or leases vary from province to province, and some provinces have mandatory forms that must be used (e.g., Manitoba and British Columbia). You should familiarize yourself with the basics of tenancy legislation in your province to ensure that all the terms of your rental agreement are enforceable. At a minimum, the agreement should include the maximum number of tenants allowed, the penalty for late payment and bounced cheques, what the tenant's obligations are (e.g., mowing the lawn), when payment is due, whether pets are allowed, and how a termination notice will be served.

One of the biggest headaches in residential properties is the time required in showing the property to prospective tenants. It is wise to look for those who will sign a lease for 6 to 12 months and even consider taking off $25 to $50 per month to entice a longer lease.

SELLING YOUR PROPERTY

Just as buying the right property is important, correct selling practices are equally important to maximize your overall profit. The first concern is timing your sale for when there is a hot market and things are moving quickly (i.e., a seller's market). Try and avoid a winter sale; spring and summer are better.

Generally there are three basic reasons for selling your investment property: you want the money for some other expense, you have decided to invest elsewhere, or you are thinking about turning over the property for a newer model. It is wise to try and reinvest in a younger property after 5 to 10 years because the maintenance bill goes up quite a bit after a home is 20 years old, which will cut into your profit. You may want to keep some properties for income during retirement, but remember that that income will be taxed at 100% compared to the capital gains (taxed at 75%) if you sold the property. The decision to sell should be discussed with your accountant beforehand so it can be tied in with your overall investment plan.

When it is time to sell, you can use a real estate agent or try to sell yourself. In most cases, using an agent will save you a great deal of time and potential headaches. If you sell yourself, you can pocket the commission, which is usually 6% to 7% on the first $100,000 and 2-1/2% to 3-1/2% on anything beyond this.

There are some options that can give you some of the coverage of using a real estate agent without all of the costs. You could opt to pay a flat fee to the local real estate agency to have your home listed on the MLS. This means there is no listing agent and you will still have to pay the buyer's agent the 3% (offer 4% and they will show it even more), but you will save the other 3% on the sale. The difference between 6% and 3% on $200,000 is $3,000, and that adds up to someone who has several investment properties. If you decide to use this method it is wise to rent a lock box from one of the realty agencies so that the agents can show the house at leisure once they have contacted you.

If you are in a really hot market like the one that existed in the Okanagan region of British Columbia from 1990 to 1993, you would probably do well selling without an agent. But as a rule there are many hassles and potential grief trying to sell your own home. I have read one report showing that you will likely get a higher price for your home if there is a realtor involved so your savings may actually be less than doing it solo (but I'm sure there were some biases in the report).

When selecting an agent, don't simply choose the one who convinces you he or she can get a higher price for you. The property has to be priced right to sell, and there is nothing worse than listing your home too high. Often, overpriced homes seem to acquire a "black mark" and they end up selling for less than market value.

The commission for selling an MLS-type listing is and should be negotiated especially if you are selling many homes. Keep in mind, however, that you want to develop a good relationship with an agent, not create resentment, so you must be prudent about this issue and find a mutually satisfactory arrangement. Additionally, remember that if the commission is reduced to 5% then any potential buyer's realtor may also have to take a deduction, which means the house may get fewer showings. One strategy that may appeal to an agent is to negotiate a 2% commission for your agent in exchange for retaining that agent for all your other listings in the future. That way, the buying agent can still be paid the regular 3%. There are many smaller real estate companies that will accept 2% as the selling commission and this is another reasonable option if you are using the MLS type of listing.

House Upgrades

There are many "house upgrades" you can do to accelerate the sale and to maximize the selling price. Some of these are small and inexpensive and others are larger and more expensive. Which ones you opt to employ depends on whether it is the principal residence you are selling or a rental property, what type of market you are selling in, and the urgency of selling. I like to divide these "house upgrades" into no-cost, minor costs, and moderate-to-major costs.

No-cost Upgrades (Sweat Equity)

The initial impression of the exterior of a house is very important, so start there. Make sure the lawn is in good shape and shrubs are trimmed and attractively placed. Replace the front door if needed and fix any squeaks. The house should be clean, uncluttered, and without odor. Put 100-watt light bulbs in all the fixtures (temporarily) and put on all lights and open the curtains when you are showing the house. (Playing classical music in the background also helps.) If there are any odors or pets then have the carpets steam cleaned. If it is a rental property then it may be wise to vacate the home for a few months and show it empty if the present tenants are not tidy.

Minor Costs

Painting the inside and outside of the house is the cheapest and most cost-effective upgrade you can do. Even though it can cost up to $3,000, you will get it back when you sell because the house will sell quicker and without a price reduction. This is especially true for rental properties where the wear and tear has been high. Choose light colours to make small rooms look larger and use neutral tones that will match most tastes and furniture. Consider putting a couple of hundred dollars into some inside and outside shrubs and plants if there are none (you can always take many of them with you afterwards if they are in pots).

Moderate-to-major Costs

The two most important areas are the kitchen and bathrooms. They should be clean, uncluttered, and, if necessary, remodeled. The remodeling can cost you $5,000 and upward but the recovery on these expenses can be 70% to 80% of the original costs. People are turned off very quickly from a home if the kitchen or bathroom is run down.

A recent Royal Bank survey revealed that renovating the kitchen will give you a 73% return upon selling, the bathroom 71%, interior/exterior painting 62%, finishing a family room 56%, and finishing the basement 52%. The real losers as far as getting money back when you sell are adding a pool or hot tub where you will be lucky to get 10% to 20%.

REAL ESTATE INVESTMENT TRUSTS

Real estate investment trusts (REITs) offer another way to invest in real estate without the hassles of being a landlord. A REIT is basically a closed-end mutual fund in that it is a pool of different investors' money focused on real estate. They trade on the TSE similar to stocks and are listed in most newspapers' business sections under "trust units." They may be a good investment for health care professionals in the future because of good returns, quick liquidity, and favourable taxation.

The future of REITS was uncertain up until recently because of the sluggish market, but recent changes has again made some attractive. However, I think there are many other better ways of investing at present for the health care professional and, overall, I do not highly recommend them, unless you see a future in real estate.

Note: REITs should not be confused with real estate limited partnerships where your money is tied up for many years; I recommend staying away from these as well.

10

THE FINANCIAL SPECIALIST

The financial community is well aware of the growing concern that most Canadians have about the economy and their personal financial affairs, and that awareness is reflected in the number of financial companies popping up on every street corner willing to give "the best advice." Financial advising is one of the fastest growing service businesses in North America resulting mainly from the large baby boomer population switching gears from spending to saving and investing. Health care professionals are one of prime targets for these businesses because of our higher-than-average incomes.

As I have said from the outset, you should try as much as possible to educate yourself about financial matters. However, your plan will be enhanced and potentially strengthened by the advice and support of an effective financial adviser. It is very difficult to understand and keep abreast of the yearly budget and tax changes, and most health care professionals have neither the time nor inclination to do so. It is my hope that after you have spent two or three hours with this book, you will understand enough about personal financial planning that you can sit down with the *right* financial adviser and together create an optimal plan.

But where — and when — do you turn to for advice? And how do you choose an adviser and have the confidence that he or she is doing the best for your financial plan? Financial advisers present themselves under many different names and titles, and there is currently very little regulation in the industry, making your choice more difficult. Fortunately, there are guidelines (and questions) available, which are covered here for you to use and to reassure you that your adviser has had the proper training to effectively invest your money.

There are three different types of financial advisers or sources of financial guidance covered in this chapter:

1. *No-cost financial advisers*
2. *Commissioned financial advisers*
3. *Fee-for-service financial advisers*

Some of you will use just one of these types; others may opt for all three at different stages of implementing your investment strategy.

NO-COST FINANCIAL ADVISERS

Banks

Because guaranteed investments such as GICs are so common, the banks themselves will frequently be the initial source of advice for many health care professionals. You should know that as a rule, banks currently rank very poorly in the realm of advisers, but occasionally you will be lucky to meet someone who can actually help you with more then just the bare basics. Generally, the bank "financial adviser" will advise on (and sell you) a variety of their fixed-income, safe but low-yielding investments as well as their own mutual funds which are generally poor performers.

But the banks have finally realized that consumers are demanding better service and are now encouraging their employees to take financial planning courses. More recently, the banks have taken this concept a step further and have developed their own financial course called the Personal Financial Planning/Counseling Program which bestows upon the successful candidate a certificate of Personal Financial Planner. In fact, anybody can enroll in this course; for further information call 1-800-361-7339 (Institute of Canadian Bankers).

Some of the banks offer health care professionals "special" investment management services once your RRSP gets above a certain level (usually around $100,000). This service is generally offered through their trust companies with emphasis on retiring and estate planning. I think you are better staying away from these services and instead hiring one of the other professionals as described below. Use the banks for what they do best — lending money — and not for investment advice.

Professional Investment Groups

Another source of "no-cost" financial advice are professional investment groups (PIGs) representing certain areas of the health care professions. One potential conflict with PIGs is that some of them have their own line of investment products to sell, so they may not always be providing unbiased advice.

The best known PIG is MD Management, which offers an excellent free service to medical doctors. MD Management is a non-profit wholly owned subsidiary of the Canadian Medical Association and has been in operation since 1969. MD Management has financial consultants who are supposed to emphasize planning, not individual products. They all have taken, at a minimum, the Canadian Securities Course and most are working on their Registered Financial Planner (RFP) or Chartered Financial Planner (CFP) courses (see below).

The financial advisers are paid by salary, not by commission, so there is no conflict of interest regarding what type of investment they offer and they are not restricted in where they tell you to invest (e.g., they will advise on mutual funds outside of what is offered by MD Management). Having said this, their group of mutual funds are generally above average performers and some are among the best, such as the international equity MD Growth fund.

MD Management has promised to continue increasing the number of their financial consultants in every province and has recently increased the number of local offices in Canada from 15 to 24 to make themselves more available. They were recently recognized as being one of Canada's 50 best-managed private companies by the *Financial Post.*

I encourage physicians to use the services offered by MD Management. You should arrange a yearly appointment with one of their financial advisers, preferably one with either the CFP or RFP designation, and ask that a written investment plan be written for you. I have been told that they give the same excellent advice to family members of doctors (who are also allowed to invest with them). For younger health care professionals especially, as well as those with less than $100,000 in their RRSP, I strongly recommend using mainly these services. Once your portfolio is larger, I think the commission-driven financial advisers may perform better for you, simply because there is more incentive. You should also consider continually meeting with the M.D. Management (MDM) financial consultant yearly to get a second opinion on your plan.

There are one or two chartered accountants working with MD Management in most provinces who are also financial consultants; they are the ones you should seek out once your portfolio gets above $100,000.

Medical doctors have available to them a monthly publication called *Strategy,* which is published by the Canadian Medical Association and MD Management. This free newsletter contains excellent information on many aspects of personal financial planning specifically related to doctors and other health care professionals. It is also available to any other health care professionals for $60 per year (or simply ask one of your doctor friends for a copy). For more information, call 1-800-267-9703, and remember the cost is tax deductible.

Dentists have access to the Canadian Dental Service Plan Inc. which administers the retirement savings plan as well as different types of insurance. It also has regular newsletters worth reading.

Some of the other health care professionals have formed alliances with specific financial advisory companies and they in turn may offer better services (and prices).

COMMISSIONED FINANCIAL ADVISERS

There are many different types of commission-driven financial advisers willing to give you advice. Because of poor provincial regulations, almost anybody can call himself/herself a "financial adviser." The list of different titles being used by these advisers is endless, but with the help of this chapter you should be able to weed through the maze quickly and zone in on the real professional investment advisers.

The more common titles that you will come across include "broker," "stockbroker," "discount stockbroker," "mutual fund dealer," "financial planner," "investment dealer," and simply "investment professional." Some only advise where to park the funds, others just park the funds (discount stockbrokers), and most do a bit of both. Your choice depends on the size of your portfolio, your age, and your purpose for investing.

If you are using a financial adviser with a title different from what is described below, you should ask him or her why they do not have these particular qualifications. The exception might be some of the titles used in the insurance business, but I have listed the important designations for that industry in chapter 5.

Mutual Fund Dealer

The designation of mutual fund dealer describes a person with a very narrow selection of investment vehicles. Those who work at the trust companies, insurance companies, and banks sell a limited number of mutual funds; others offer you a whole array of different funds depending on where they work.

These dealers can give you advice on mutual funds, but often not on any other aspects of personal financial planning such as stocks, bonds, estate planning, insurance, etc. Keep in mind that it is very hard for someone to recommend an investment product without knowing how it fits in with the remainder of your investment plan. Some fund dealers also offer other types of investments, but they may still fall short of being full service (i.e., offering all investment products that your portfolio may call for).

Stockbroker

A stockbroker, sometimes called a full-service broker or, simply, a broker, is a person who can trade securities on the stock exchange. Although traditionally linked to stocks, most brokers will now sell you any type of financial product.

A certified broker will have completed the Canadian Securities Course, offered by the Canadian Securities Institute, and the Conduct and Practices Handbook for Securities Industry Professionals course. If you want to make sure you are dealing with a legitimate broker, ask if he or she is a member of the Investment Dealers Association of Canada (IDA) which regulates all licensed brokers. Alternatively, phone 416-364-9130 and ask yourself.

I strongly recommend choosing a broker with one of the large investment firms such as RBC Dominion Securities, Midland Walwyn, Nesbitt Burns, etc. These large firms attract good, honest brokers and their individual dealings are monitored regularly within the company. These larger firms also have the deep pockets to do good research and can offer a whole array of financial vehicles from blue chip stocks to mutual funds to strip bonds.

You should meet with several brokers at different firms before making a final decision. The ideal broker is one who has already been through a significant bear market which, at the time of writing, means at least eight years' experience. Always discuss up front what the commission is on each type of investment transaction and remember that in many cases this is negotiable. Generally, a full-service broker charges 1% to 2% on stock trades and 2% to 5% on mutual fund transactions. Most health care professionals are "afraid" to negotiate and that is why the brokers love us. Just remember when you negotiate that you want a fair price, but you don't want to alienate the broker, and you often get what you pay for.

A good example of potential abuse is the commission range that has been charged on strip bonds. It can vary from 2% to 8% depending on market conditions, and if this is not discussed up front, your return could be substantially lower then it should be.

Brokers now realize that many clients want advice on all aspects of personal financial planning and are now referring to themselves as investment advisers to try and attract more business in this very competitive field. To legitimately wear this hat, however, they should have completed (or at least enrolled in) the Certified Management Investment course. (see below)

Discount brokers are certified stockbrokers, but the commission you pay is generally less (although now, many full-service brokers will match the discount price for certain types of investments). Depending on what you are buying, the commission can be as much as 80% cheaper than the full-service broker. Discount brokers moved into Canada in the mid-eighties and their share of the market has been growing steadily. Estimates are that they are already doing up to 25% of all Canadian stock trades and this will likely increase because of the knowledgeable baby boomers who are becoming thrifty investors. Generally, most health care professionals should stick to the full-service broker, although if you are willing to do some reading and you plan to follow the buy and hold strategy of investing, then there is nothing wrong with using a discount broker.

All of the major banks offer these subsidiary services including the recent newcomer associated with Canada Trust. The TD-Green Line is the largest claiming between 60% to 70% of all the discount business (since the buy out of Marathon Brokerage Discount Services). It has just recently acquired the fourth-largest American brokerage firm (Waterhouse Investor Services Inc.) making it one of the biggest in North America. TD is also the only major bank that has not established a full service brokerage house.

The cheapest discount brokerage firms are those offered through the Bank of Montreal (Investor Line) and the Scotia Discount Brokerage. It is even cheaper if you do your ordering by an automated system or the new on-line service offered by the Green Line (MicroMax).

One step "above" the regular broker status offered by the Canadian

Securities Institute is the designation of Certified Financial Planner (CFP). The designation is earned by taking the Canadian Investment Management course (CIM), which will soon change its name to Professional Financial Planning course. Then there is a further course that brokers can take which leads to the top distinction, the Fellow of the Canadian Securities Institute (FCSI).

Traditionally, the brokers who had taken these extra courses dealt with accounts larger than $200,000 and usually charged a flat rate based on a certain percentage of your portfolio value (1/2% to 2% depending on the size). But more brokers are pursuing this certification simply to allow them to be better personal financial planners and investors. The recent federal budget dealt a serious blow for advisers who were charging a percentage rather than straight commission because the charge for their RRSP services are no longer tax deductible. But because of a backlash from the financial industry, Revenue Canada is considering modifying these rules further? Because of this confusion, it is best to get the most recent details from your accountant or call Revenue Canada at 613-957-8953. This is all the more reason for the health care professionals to learn about personal financial planning themselves.

Another type of broker arrangement being offered by most brokerage houses is the *wrap account.* In this arrangement, you are charged a pre-set percentage of your portfolio value, usually 1% to 2%, for advice and implementation. This puts the client on a level playing field with the broker because the more growth the client achieves, the greater the reward for the broker. The idea is now there is no incentive to churn (excessive trading), just to perform.

The two largest Canadian wrap accounts are offered by Nesbitt Burns (NB Freedom Plan) and Richardson Greenshields (Sovereign Investment Program). The advice and investment plan is tailored specifically to meet your demands and is discretionary. There are many different versions of the wrap account with some being set up so the broker has full control of buying and selling and others where you must be first contacted to discuss the deal. A problem with some of these accounts has been double billing, where you end up paying a fee on certain mutual funds or stock in addition to the wrap account fee. This "double fee" needs to be discussed up front if this type of arrangement interests you.

Wrap accounts are usually for those with over $200,000 in their portfolio and where the investment slant is more on stocks then mutual funds or bonds. Many wrap account financial advisers also provide guidance in other areas of personal financial planning such as estate planning and insurance. Many of the mutual fund companies now also offer wrap accounts, but their choices of investments are often limited. There has been many recent changes made by the federal government regarding the fees for RRSP/RRIF WRAP accounts. At the time of writing (Aug '96), it appears best to pay the WRAP account fee with funds from within the plan and not outside. Because of the government ambivalence on RRSP/RRIF fees it is best to speak to your accountant about this.

Professional Money Managers

Professional money managers are companies that manage very large sums of money such as group pension plans. Some may look at private accounts with assets over $200,000 and will charge you a percentage similar to the wrap accounts.

Financial Planners

There are two reasonably good financial planning organizations that offer training for *overall* financial planning which is exactly what the busy health care professional needs. The Canadian Association of Financial Planners bestows the designation of Registered Financial Planner (RFP), and the Canadian Institute of Financial Planning grants the Chartered Financial Planner (CFP) designation after completion of six different courses over approximately two years covering all areas of financial planning.

The only problem with using a CFP/RFP is that you may still have to use your broker (or discount broker) as many cannot sell stocks (directly) but they can usually deal with mutual funds. But as many brokers are now taking these courses, you may be lucky enough to find a stockbroker with a CFP designation. The commission they charge is variable from a straight fee for advice about your RRSP, life insurance, or retirement, but more commonly the commission is based upon what you buy through them.

Because of the lack of regulation and the many confusing titles financial advisers use, a new financial regulatory body, the Financial Planners Standard Council of Canada (FPSCC), was recently formed in Canada. This body hopes to bring some uniformity to the "fractured" financial planning industry and will bestow the designation of Certified Financial Planner (CFP) to successful candidates who meet their requirements and pass their exam. Those financial advisers who already hold the designations of chartered financial planner or registered financial planner and graduates from the insurance industry who have their chartered financial consultant designation will be grandfathered into the new organization. You may recall that the Canadian Securities Institute already offers its members a certified financial planner designation, which will also be recognized by the FPSCC.

In my opinion, the perfect financial adviser would be somebody with a certified financial planner designation (CFP) who also has a university degree in economics, commerce, or accounting, has at least eight years' experience in investing, and has completed the Canadian Securities Course. The medical doctors will be happy to know that MD Management has many financial consultants working with them who already meet these criteria.

FEE-FOR-SERVICE FINANCIAL ADVISERS

Fee-for-service financial advisers should have the above-mentioned qualifications as a minimum because with the present poor regulations you could end up paying for nothing. The charge is usually on an hourly basis and you can expect to pay between $100 and $200 per hour.

This type of adviser can be very useful for the health care professional who feels comfortable investing with a discount broker complemented with fee-for-service advice. But remember that the guidance will only be as good as the qualifications. If you are buying stocks, you want to make sure that the adviser is also a broker.

Some health care professionals with large portfolios may want to use these financial advisers for a second opinion from time to time. As a general rule, though, fee-for-service financial advisers are not regular "stock pickers" and if they are working as independents they do not have the deep pockets for stock research that some of the commissioned brokers have.

SO WHICH FINANCIAL ADVISER DO I USE?

For medical doctors, the answer is easy. Use the financial consultant with MD Management. Try and get one with the CFP designation. Even better is one of the accountants working with the local office who also has the CFP designation.

After your portfolio grows above $100,000, you may want to bring in the commission-driven spirit, preferably a broker with the CFP designation or at least one who has enrolled in the course. You will have to do some shopping, but start with referrals from your friends. Bring along the list of questions at the end of this section.

MDM is planning on setting up its own self-directed RRSP branch in the near future, which will be very attractive to medical doctors. Again, however, the commission-driven spirit may be lacking.

For other health care professionals, choose a financial adviser who is a CFP right from the start. If you opt for no-load mutual funds early in your portfolio, then you will likely have to pay for the services of the CFP but not if you use load mutual funds or a combination. Most CFPs can sell you mutual funds, so they will get their fee from the commission and trailer fee. It certainly would be a wise decision for MDM to consider offering its services to other health care professionals besides doctors. Hopefully, this will happen in the future.

Once you get to the stage of considering a self-directed RRSP, it would be helpful if the adviser is also a broker so that when it comes time to venture into stocks you do not have to change financial adviser.

Once your portfolio is more than $75,000 to $100,000 you should become more selective. Because I recommend individual stock investing above this level, I would look for a CFP who is also a registered broker. At this point you will have a self-directed RRSP and maybe some assets outside the RRSP. Whether you opt for the commission, wrap account, or fee-for-service type of remuneration is up to you. I think the commission-driven broker is the best choice initially.

You may also consider using the "combination approach" mentioned earlier, which maximizes your returns using a combination of broker/CFP for your RRSP investments and a discount broker for your non-RRSP investments. But this arrangement is suitable *only* if you have an interest in investing and you are willing to follow the investments regularly.

As a guide to help you choose the best financial adviser for you, I suggest using this checklist of questions as a starting point for each potential candidate. Arrange to meet at least two to three different financial advisers. Your choices will often be recommendations from friends.

CHOOSING THE CORRECT FINANCIAL ADVISER

1. *Is the first meeting free?*
2. *What designation or accreditation does he or she have? Specify that you want someone with the CFP (or RFP) designation and at least eight years' experience in financial markets. Bonuses are a broker's licence, CIM certification, background in accounting, economics, or a business degree.*
3. *If you are looking at commission-orientated services, are the fees negotiable? Ask what he or she cannot sell you directly.*
4. *If you are investing in mutual funds, is there any bias based on the trailer fees or other perks that the mutual fund companies offer? (Of course, the answer will be no, but by asking you are making that person aware that you know about these conflicts of interest.)*
5. *Can you have an example of a written financial plan that has been prepared for others? Will the same service be provided to you? Review the plan to see if it covers most of the topics covered in this book.*
6. *Will he or she provide the names and numbers of three clients for references, two of whom are not health care professionals?*
7. *Can you meet once per year (or more frequently) in your office to go over last year's results and a future plan? At this meeting you should ask if your asset mix allocation is appropriate and what new financial trends are emerging that you should be aware of. This type of discussion will help keep the financial adviser interested and alert to your portfolio.*
8. *What are the adviser's personal investment ideas? Are they similar to yours?*
9. *Does the financial adviser carry liability insurance?*

10. *How can you measure your performance each year? For example, your mutual funds' performance should be above average and your stock return average should be above the TSE-300.*

CHOOSING AN ACCOUNTANT

Choosing the right accountant is one of the most important decisions the health care professional must make. This is especially true if you are incorporated. All accountants will tell you how much you owe, but the good accountant will tell you how much he or she has saved you. If your accountant is not saving you money then look for another.

If you are meeting with your accountant just a couple of times a year in the month before taxes, you are not likely saving any money. The more frequently you meet with your accountant, the more expensive the bill is, but it is usually worth it. Proper tax planning is an essential part of personal financial planning for health care professionals and a good accountant can save you thousands of dollars over the years. While you are already aware of some of the tax-planning strategies, such as RRSPs, and spousal RRSPs, there are many other important issues your accountant can help with, such as income splitting, incorporating, and estate planning (see chapter 11).

Before approaching the local corner "tax specialists" or "accounting services", check out their qualifications. The Yellow Pages list many outfits that are willing to do your yearly tax return and provide accounting services, but not all are suitable for health care professionals, especially the self-employed ones.

You should be looking for an accountant who has been trained and has earned one of the professional designations of CGA (Certified General Accountant), CMA (Certified Management Accountant), or CA (Chartered Accountant). CMAs and CGAs charge less than CAs, and in most cases will be suitable for health care professionals for at least the first few years. CGAs and CMAs have taken specialized courses, usually at the college level, and are generally quite knowledgeable about personal taxes.

If you have an annual income over $100,000 or a large, complicated portfolio, you should seek the services of a CA. And all health care professionals should consider using a CA if they are incorporated, if they are at the stage of buying their own office, or if they have excess money after the extra mortgage payments and maximum RRSP contributions. All

CAs have a university degree and have completed further specialized courses after that. The price you will pay is usually based on an hourly rate ranging from $100 to $150 per hour.

My personal experience with the CAs is that they are only as good as you push them to be. You have to repeatedly ask if you are optimizing income-splitting abilities and if there are any other reasonable ways to reduce your tax bill. I call my accountant frequently so I know where I stand from a tax perspective now and in the future. I think it is wise to send your questions to your accountant by note or fax before a meeting so he or she can prepare ahead of time.

If your portfolio is very large and complex (i.e., it holds trusts, real estate property, an incorporated business, and a holding company) you might find it worthwhile to hire a tax lawyer. As they charge between $200 to $400 per hour, I recommend you hire one every couple of years; don't rely on a tax lawyer to take care of your routine accounting needs.

There are many ways to find an accountant but the best is from recommendations by your colleagues. After you have two or three names, set up interviews with each and then make a decision. Tell each what your financial plan is to give him or her a sense of your direction. You should also ask up front what the charge will be and whether the accountant will be doing most of the work or if he or she will assign it to an associate (often a junior).

NOTICE:

11

WHAT YOU NEED TO KNOW ABOUT TAXES

Canada has one of the most complex tax systems in the world and Canadians pay one of the highest level of taxes in the world! As you would expect from such a complex topic, very few actually understand the tax system. Although many accountants claim to understand it all, they certainly have a hard time explaining it to others. How many times have you dozed off (with your eyes open or course!) as your accountant tried to explain some fine point of tax law to you?

Even so, I still think it is important for health care professionals to have a basic comprehension of Canadian taxes, especially those who are self-employed. Figures show that from 1961 to 1991 the average Canadian family's home expenditure on taxes of all kinds went from 33% to 45% of total gross income. With these trends sure to continue, most health care professionals want to know more about the legal ways to minimize and reduce taxes.

The Income Tax Act is over 1,500 pages long, so what follows is a *very* condensed and simplified version on what you must know. The rest we will leave up to the tax specialists.

PERSONAL INCOME TAXES

The tax reform in 1988 created three personal tax brackets: 27%, 40%, and 50% (give or take a little for individual provincial differences). These rates reflect a combination of federal tax levels, which are fixed at 17%, 26%, and 29%, plus provincial tax rates which vary. Also, there are many different provincial surtaxes included in the above figures which are now "permanent temporary" taxes. As an approximation, those earning less than $30,000 pay 27% on their taxable income.

Individuals earning more than $30,000 and up to $60,000 pay 40%, and the unfortunate people who earn above $60,000 pay more than 50% back to the government on every dollar earned over $60,000. Along the way there are many incremental increases that differ from province to province which create a "progressive" tax system. For example, in British Columbia, the marginal tax rate is set at 54% which kicks in at $78,000, compared to New Brunswick where it is 51% which kicks in at $91,800. To keep things simpler, I use the above-mentioned averages throughout this chapter.

The highest tax rate that you pay is referred to as your *marginal tax rate*. For most health care professionals, this means giving back over 50% of every dollar earned above $60,000. Your *effective tax rate* is the overall average of the various tax brackets which gives you a net tax rate on your total earned income. Your effective tax rate is the actual percentage of your income that you pay in taxes. The more you earn, the closer the marginal rate is to the effective rate. For example, if you have an income of $500,000, approximately $440,000 of it is taxed at 50% or above!

Let's look at an example to put these numbers into perspective. When an individual in the highest marginal tax bracket invests outside the RRSP and achieves a reasonable return of 10% with a GIC, the tax department will take 50%, reducing the return to 5%. If we then factor in inflation at 3% to 4%, the *real return* is reduced to 1% to 2%. This shows why it is critical to have a basic understanding of taxes and how they can affect your investment return because, as you will see later, not all forms of income are taxed the same.

OTHER FORMS OF INCOME AND TAXES

There are numerous sources of income and each has different tax implications. The most common sources of income outside of your employment income are interest income, Canadian dividend income, and capital gains income.

Interest income comes from many sources, such as bonds, GICs, savings accounts, term deposits, and T-bills. This type of income is taxed at your highest marginal rate just like your personal income (i.e., 50% to 54% for most health care professionals depending on the province). Interest income is said to be the safest form of income but also has the highest tax rate. If these types of investments are held in an RRSP, taxes are deferred until they are withdrawn.

Dividend income, earned through ownership of stock in Canadian companies, is taxed in a more favourable but complex manner because of the dividend tax credit. This tax credit is next to impossible for the average person to calculate, but we can make a few comparisons to give you an idea of how it works. At a marginal tax rate of 53%, the return on $1,000 of dividend income would be $700, but only $530 from interest income after tax. For health care professionals in the top tax bracket, a good estimate is that the tax rate on dividend income is 36% (differing from province to province by 1% to 2%) which shines when compared to interest income. (Note that if the dividend is earned from shares of a company which is non-Canadian, this tax credit does not apply and any dividends will be taxed as interest income, but you will still get the capital gains tax benefit if applicable — see below.)

Capital gain refers to the gain or appreciation that has occurred between the time you buy and sell capital property. This includes, among other things, stocks, mutual funds, real estate, and precious metals. (Capital gains realized on the sale of your principal residence are exempt from taxation.)

Only 75% of capital gains are subject to tax, so if you have a capital gain of $1,000 then the you pay taxes on $750. Assuming a top marginal tax bracket, that translates into approximately $620 in your pocket. This compares to interest income where at the top marginal tax rate of 53% you would take home only $530! For those in the highest tax bracket, the effective tax rate on capital gains is about 40% (subject to some provincial differences).

You can see why you ought to seriously consider capital gain investments over interest income investments. Remember that not only do you come out ahead in taxes, but the historical performance of capital investments has been superior to interest investments. The other excellent feature of capital gains is that it is second only to the RRSP as a means of deferring taxes. You do not have to pay taxes on the gains until you realize them. And the capital gains tax benefit applies to both Canadian and non-Canadian companies, so investments in global mutual funds benefit.

Keep in mind that these rules apply for investments made outside the RRSP because inside the RRSP there are no taxes. It is, therefore, routinely advised that your portfolio be set up so the tax favoured investments are outside the RRSP (i.e., capital gains and Canadian dividends) and the less-favoured tax investments go in the RRSP (i.e., GICs, bonds, and interest-earning investments).

Always remember to consider the after-tax return when comparing the different types of non-RRSP investments. As a rough guide, keep the figures 52%, 36%, and 40% in your head as the top taxation level for interest income, Canadian dividend, and capital gains respectfully. Another rough rule you can use to compare *pre-taxed* returns on these three different types of investments is that 10% interest income equates to about 7.75% dividend income, and 7.69% capital gain income (assuming a top marginal tax rate). As you can see the most favourable tax investment is the dividend, but the best performer when net return is considered is the capital gain simply because it has historically given the highest return overall.

The *lifetime capital gains exemption* which once existed is of little relevance now. The government once allowed a lifetime tax exemption of $500,000 on capital gains, which was then reduced to $100,000, and then was subsequently eliminated completely in February 1994. There are still some exceptions such as certain private corporations and farms, but even these are currently being reviewed and may also be eliminated.

If you were holding capital gain investments such as growth mutual funds outside the RRSP prior to February 1994, you may still be able to take advantage of the lifetime capital gains exemption, but if you have left it this long you will have to be content with a penalty for late claims. Ask your accountant about the "transition rules" if they apply to your portfolio.

HOW TO REDUCE YOUR TAXES

There are many ways that health care professionals can and should legally minimize their tax bill. I cover the more common and easy-to-understand methods below and also touch on some of the creative "tax shelters" that some health care professionals fall prey to. If you want more detailed information, refer to the reference books listed in the Appendix.

Tax Credits and Deductions

The first way to minimize your tax bill is to make sure you are taking advantage of all tax credits and deductions available. A tax deduction is something that you get to subtract from your income *before* calculating your taxes; that is, it is deducted from your gross income and the savings is directly tied to your marginal tax rate. For those in the 50% tax bracket, this means a 50 cent savings on every dollar, whereas those in the 25% tax bracket save only 25 cents.

Tax credits are deducted *after* your tax calculation and, therefore, come directly off the taxes owed. Both deductions and credits are valuable, but tax credits are fairer to the person with a low income because they aren't influenced by your marginal tax rate. This is why your accountant should be putting tax deductions in the hands of the higher income earner and most tax credits in the hands of the lower income earner.

The three main credits that you should be familiar with are charitable donations, donations to federal and provincial political parties, and medical expenses.

Charitable donations receive a federal tax credit of 17% for the first $200, which for the high-income health care professional equates to about a 29% overall tax savings once the provincial tax break is included. For donations above $200, you get a 29% federal tax credit, which equates to about a 50% tax savings for the health care professional once the provincial tax savings are included. The combined tax savings on a donation of $1,000 would be about $430.

You should make sure that you combine all family charitable donations so that the amount is always over $200 to get your best tax break even if this means skipping a few years and using carry forward rules. The maximum contribution has recently been increased from 20% to 50% of your net income.

Donations to federal and provincial political parties are treated extremely well with a credit of 75% on the first $100, 50% on the next $450, and 33% on the next $600 (with some provincial differences). No credit is given for political contributions above $1,150.

The credit for *medical expenses* is based on your income and equals 17% of your medical expenses that *exceed* 3% of your net income. In other words, you can claim this credit only if your medical expenses are more than 3% of your net income. The maximum annual credit offset, however, is only $1,614. Generally, the income level of the health care professional is too high to claim this, but if you have a low income earning spouse, you may be able to take advantage of him or her taking the credit. You can pick any 12-month period to maximize the amount. You can include prescriptions, eyeglasses, additional health insurance, and travel insurance.

There are many tax deductions available for health care professionals, especially those who are self-employed, are they should be claimed each year. A good accountant will help identify these; an overly busy or lazy one will not. The deductions for those few health care professionals who are incorporated are more complex and are discussed later in this chapter.

The best available deduction for both the self-employed and employed health care professional is, of course, the RRSP. For the health care professional making over $80,000, the $13,500 allowable maximum yearly contribution means a savings or "refund" in taxes of approximately $6,700!

Deductions on the office include office rent, interest on any business loans, interest on office mortgage (a great reason to buy your own office), salaries, phone and fax bills, utilities, insurance, supplies, stationery, cleaning, and office furniture and equipment. Office furniture and equipment is deducted over several years as they depreciate. (Depreciation for tax purposes is referred to as *capital cost allowance.*)

Client and staff entertainment costs are 50% deductible. The cost must be incurred for the purpose of "earning income from business," which is open to broad interpretation, and you should consult your accountant if your are unsure of what expenses apply.

If you are self-employed, your *automobile expenses* can be deducted. The deduction applies to trips from the office to the hospital or to home visits, but not for driving from your home to the office. The deductible expenses includes insurance, operating costs, maintenance, and depreciation. This depreciation calculation is complex and encompasses the capital cost allowance equation.

There are limits on how much can be written off as far as the cost of the car. For owned vehicles, the limit is $24,000 before GST and PST. For leased vehicles it is $650 per month. If financing is involved there is a limit of $300 per month on the deductibility of interest. Finally, you have to keep a mileage log to back up your claim; otherwise you have to be prepared to lose the deduction if you are ever audited.

Moving expenses are deductible if you move for work or university training. If you have to sell your house to move, the real estate commission can be included in the total costs when calculating this deduction.

Child care expenses (including some summer camp programs) and babysitting costs can be claimed against the income of the spouse with the lower income if these costs are incurred for the purpose of enabling that spouse to work.

Professional dues and the *fees for medical conferences and education seminars* are deductible.

There is a long list of other deductions such as the cost of this book or any other book or periodical that helps you run your business. Your accountant should be claiming all of these each year. I have listed a couple of good references in the Appendix for those who would like to know more about deductible business-related expenses.

The deduction for a home office should be investigated by every health care professional, even though the restrictions on it can make it difficult to claim. The restrictions state that your home must be your principal place of business or used to see patients or clients regularly. If you do research work at home, you may be able to take the deductions. If you have two or more rental properties, your need for a home office is more legitimate because you need an office from which to do your bookkeeping, phone tenants, and arrange mortgages and insurance plans.

Finally it is worth noting that although money borrowed to top up your RRSP is not deductible, any interest on money borrowed to invest outside the RRSP is deductible. The general wisdom is that if you have any money invested outside the RRSP, you should cash it and apply it toward any personal debt (e.g., mortgage) or to top up your RRSP. You can then borrow the same amount and invest it again, but now the interest is deductible.

The Family and Income Splitting

The basic principle of income splitting is that two people pay less taxes then one on the same amount of income because of our incremental progressive tax system. These measures assume that you are married (or have children) and that one spouse is a high income earner (usually the health care professional) and the other is a low income earner or homemaker who will become an employee of yours. Income splitting allows you to divert taxable income into the hands of a family member who is in a lower tax bracket than you. If you can take a $60,000 single income and convert it into two $30,000 incomes, it will reduce your tax bill by 30%.

There are several methods of income splitting. The basic one for the self-employed health care professional is to pay the other spouse (or family member) a reasonable salary for services such as bookkeeping, secretarial support, accounting, filing, office cleaning, etc. — anything that helps your health care practice. This in effect puts some of the gross family income into a lower tax bracket with the effect being less taxes. The other benefit to income splitting is that by paying your spouse (or child) an income, he or she can set up an RRSP, which provides another potential savings for the family.

Another option is for the spouse to set up a business (consulting, cleaning, etc.) for which you pay for his or her services. In this case, your spouse should also be able to make deductions for a home office, providing another tax savings. In this case, it is important that to be legitimate, the services your spouse provides must be available to other businesses and professionals, not just to you and your practice.

The other "mandatory form" of income splitting is investing in a spousal RRSP, which was covered in detail in chapter 4. This does not so much decrease your annual tax bill but can reduce your retirement income tax bill up to 15%.

Beyond these income-splitting techniques, Revenue Canada's *attribution rules* may apply. These rules basically state that you may get taxed on property or assets transferred or given to another family member if the purpose was to reduce your tax bill. There are three considerations when it comes to income splitting and the attribution rules.

First, if you give money or property to your spouse for the purposes of investing, any capital gains, dividend income, or interest earned on this money or property will be taxed in your hands.

Second, if you give money or property to a minor (under the age of 18), the same rules apply *except* that any capital gains are taxed in the minor's hands. This plan can be used to your advantage by investing in an equity mutual fund that emphasizes capital growth. It is an excellent means of building up an education fund for the minor and a means of decreasing the family tax bill. This is a great way to income split, especially if you have 2 - 4 children.

Third, the attribution rules do not apply to an adult child who is 18 years or older. If you give (not loan) the adult child money or property to invest, any income or gain will be taxed in his or her hands. But remember, once given it is no longer yours (otherwise attribution kicks in). Many parents are nervous about giving money or investments to their children in case they misuse it and in these cases a trust (see below) may be a helpful alternative.

There are many other creative ways to use the family to decrease your tax load. For example, if you give $10,000 to your spouse and he or she invests it at a return of 10%, you will have to pay taxes on the $1,000 return but *not* on any money earned on the $1,000 if it is reinvested. This "interest on interest" (or second generation income) is something to consider if your spouse is in a lower tax bracket because the tax bite on the reinvested income will be lower.

You can also "loan" money to your spouse at the current prescribed government rate which can then be invested, and any income earned on it will be taxed in his or her hands. Your spouse then makes regular interest payments to you. To save on taxes, your spouse must be in a lower tax bracket and the earned income should be as a dividend or capital gains in order to optimize the tax benefit. Although you have to pay taxes on the interest that your spouse pays to you, he or she gets to deduct this interest because it was borrowed to invest.

You can also loan your spouse money to start up an unincorporated business (e.g., bookkeeper, researcher) and any income earned from that business will be taxed in his or her hands.

Other methods of income splitting are available but are often considered "aggressive" and require the input of your accountant. As a general rule, the more aggressive the strategy the higher the accounting bill and the more likely there will be an audit, and for most audits you end up incurring additional accounting fees and paying some additional taxes. Keep in mind, too, that the rules are constantly changing and not in your favour. Aggressive tax strategies could leave you with a big accounting and tax bill and nothing else to show.

KISS PRINCIPLE — Income Splitting

1. *A spousal RRSP is an essential investment for most health care professionals.*
2. *Paying your spouse and child a reasonable salary is a must for most health care professionals who are self-employed.*
3. *A growth equity mutual fund is an excellent means of income splitting and an even better way to put aside money for a child's education.*
4. *As a general rule, put most non-RRSP investments in the name of the lower income spouse from the start (including the house).*
5. *Consider giving assets to your children before you die to avoid heavier taxes and probate fees on disposition of your estate (see chapter 14).*

Making Use of Trusts

For health care professionals, the main uses of trusts are to provide a means of income splitting (including aiding in children's education) and to reduce taxes and probate fees upon your death. Most health care professionals will want to consider a *domestic trust,* which is also referred to as a personal, private, or family trust. There are other forms of trusts that are not dealt with here (e.g., offshore trusts).

A trust is set up when a *trustee* (usually you) holds property for the benefit of the *beneficiary* (usually a family member) of that trust. The person transferring the property into the trust is called the *settlor.* Property can be real estate, stocks, mutual funds, bonds, partnership interests, etc. In simple language, a trust is a means of your transferring assets to another family member and continuing to have some control over those assets or income that is generated. Any income earned is then taxed in the hands of the lower income earning family member.

The major disadvantage to a trust is the cost associated with setting it up and maintaining it. The set-up fee ranges from $2,000 to $4,000, and then you will be charged an annual management fee and an accountant's fee for preparing the yearly income tax for the trust. You will have to sit down with your accountant before setting up a trust to determine if it is financially worthwhile. A general rule is that trusts with assets under $100,000 are probably not cost effective, especially those held outside of a corporation. (Corporate trusts are covered later.)

One of the major advantages of trusts prior to 1996 was the ability to keep earned income within the family trust free of taxes because you could "pretend" that income had been paid out to the beneficiaries. This rule was called the preferred beneficiary election, but it has been eliminated. Now family trusts must distribute any interest income or dividend income earned in the trust to the beneficiaries; otherwise income accumulating in the trust will be taxed at your top marginal rate. However, distribution of income to the beneficiaries is still usually beneficial because of their low or non-existent tax rate. Most people with trusts are now simply rolling over the earned income into a equity mutual fund to save for children's education or living expenses.

Capital gain income in the trust does *not* have to be distributed unrealized, so many will now focus future trust investments in growth type investments. An excellent investment for the trust for physicians has been the MD Growth mutual fund which has had minimal interest or dividend income and above average capital gains.

Another recent change to trusts is that as of 1999 any trust in existence for 21 years will be deemed to have disposed of all assets at fair market value and taxes will then have to be paid on any earned income. Prior to this you could extend the trust beyond this period. (More is said about trusts in chapter 14.)

TAX SHELTERS

Many health care professionals have had bad experiences with so-called tax shelters and have realized that these adventures are not good investments. Even with the tax breaks available, it is possible to end up losing money. A simple rule for health care professionals to follow is that a tax shelter should be considered only if there is a good chance of profit *after* the tax benefit is accounted for. And you will find that very few tax shelters, if any, fit this bill.

Tax shelters and *limited partnerships* have been synonymous for health care professionals for many years. Limited partnerships often invest in things such as real estate, Canadian movie productions, mining and oil interests, and gas exploration. These were reasonable investments in the 1970s and 1980s, but because of changes to the tax system they are no longer. Over 90% of these limited partnerships have been money-losing ventures over the last 10 years; so *stay away* from them. If your broker or financial adviser offers you one, get another opinion to ensure someone is looking out for your best interests.

You may hear about the mutual fund limited partnerships which cost less to take part in and have had some good returns since their introduction in 1987. Even so, I do not recommend them and would choose other safer and more reliable investments.

Another tax-sheltered investment that health care professionals have been plagued by are the *labour-sponsored venture capital corporations* (see chapter 8 on mutual funds). As a general rule, stay clear of these. Some health care professionals may be disappointed by this advice because one of these funds (Canadian Medical Discoveries Fund) has been very helpful in financially assisting medical research in Canada. But since the 1996 budget changes, these funds have lost just about all attractions for health care professionals.

Probably one of the best tax shelters remaining is in the form of *tax-exempt life insurance* (discussed in chapter 5 where the emphasis was on life insurance). If you have your mortgage paid off and you have maximized your RRSP, then these policies can be good tax shelters. The problem is that many health care professionals are buying these policies too early in their careers. It is a much better investment to put the extra money on your mortgage before looking into one of these plans. But once the mortgage and RRSP are taken care of, these tax-exempt policies have their merit, especially if estate planning is important. You can take money out during the retirement years or you can borrow against the equity built up in the plan. If the main purpose is tax sheltering, then opt for a low face value and the "last-to-die" option, which will lower the premium and maximize the tax shelter.

As mentioned earlier, there are many different options available with these plans and the most important is the guarantee on the future administrative costs and the insurance rates. Also find out what is not guaranteed or what is variable when comparing plans. But I must reiterate: never lose sight of why you are buying this type of insurance.

Finally, the newest hot tax shelters are the Royalty Trusts which have favorable taxation treatment, but again, there is no guarantee on the return. These are attractive investments however in times of low interest rates.

If you do invest in some of these other "aggressive" tax shelters, you should do some reading on the alternative minimum tax that applies to them, which basically prevents you from paying too low a tax bill. (See the list of books for further reading in the Appendix.)

INCORPORATION

The option to incorporate a health care practice is available in some provinces only. At the time of writing, only Alberta, British Columbia, New Brunswick, Prince Edward Island and Yukon have allowed (some) health care professionals to incorporate. The benefits of incorporating also differ from one province to another, with British Columbia and New Brunswick currently have the most attractive features. The health care professionals that most frequently seek to be incorporated are medical doctors, dentists, chiropractors, and veterinarians. Other health care professionals reading this book may be able to incorporate, but you should check with your provincial association or accountant first.

There are two main reasons to consider incorporating: for the potential tax savings through tax deferral and income splitting and to limit legal liability. For health care professionals, the main reason is the potential tax savings as we all carry liability insurance and our governing bodies do not allow us to avoid liability by hiding behind the corporate umbrella.

Structure

By forming a corporation, you create a legal entity distinct from you. You will own the shares of the company and the company in return becomes the legal owner of your health care practice. All in one step you become the director, company officer, shareholder, and employee. By leaving money in the corporation, you can benefit from the more favourable tax rates (see below). If you cannot leave money in the corporation, because of personal debt for example, then, as a general rute you should not be incorporating at this time.

The tax benefit occurs because the tax rate within the corporation is substantially less then your personal tax rate, so by leaving the money in the corporation you are essentially deferring taxes until you draw the cash out. Ideally, this will happen after retirement when you are in a lower tax bracket.

There are different means of distributing the corporation money out to you, including through salary, capital dividend, dividend, or loan. If you distribute money as a salary, it is paid directly from the corporation and you are taxed on it as any employee in the normal fashion. If the corporation distributes its profits through a dividend, a preferential tax level is applied. For individuals in the top tax rate, the benefit will only be about 3% by the time all taxes are paid and this benefit may not cover the cost of setting up the corporation. If, however, you can pay this dividend to another shareholder, such as your spouse, who is in a lower tax bracket, then the savings start to show.

The company can also pay out money in the form of a capital dividend; 25% of the company's capital gains can be paid out tax free to the shareholder. The other option to distribute money is through a loan to you or another shareholder; this scheme can be complicated, but beneficial if done properly.

There are other more complicated methods of taking money out of the company which should be discussed with your accountant.

Advantages to Incorporating

The potential advantages of incorporating are many. The main one is the tax savings, thanks to rules that apply to Canadian-controlled private corporations such as health care practices. The combined federal and provincial tax rate on Canadian corporations is approximately 23% on the first $200,000 of taxable income (different provincial rates range from 18% to 23%). Anything earned above $200,000 is taxed at approximately 46% in the corporation. (In case you are wondering, you cannot have more than one corporation in order to benefit from the $200,000 limit.) This tax rate is far better then the marginal tax rate of 50%-plus!

For example, if your practice is unincorporated and you have $10,000 in pre-tax dollars, you will pay about $5,200 in taxes with the top marginal tax rate leaving you with $4,800. But if you were incorporated, you would only pay about $1,800 in taxes leaving $8,200 for re-investment. At some point you will draw this money from the company and, therefore, much of the "tax savings" is actually in the form of tax deferral. But there are favourable ways to get money out and to unwind the corporation.

Incorporating may also allow further income splitting. Unfortunately, income splitting through payment of dividends to shareholders is only possible in British Columbia and New Brunswick as these jurisdictions allow family members (non-health care professionals) to be shareholders. If the family member receives no other form of income, he or she could receive up to approximately $24,000 per year of dividends without attracting personal income tax in British Columbia (except for the company's 23% tax rate). But because of the recent federal court's decision on the "Newman Case" it is prudent to make sure that the family member is "contributing" to the corporation.

Health care professionals in these two jurisdictions may also benefit from the use of family trusts. The family trust can own shares of the corporation, enabling further income splitting through payment of dividends, and you still have control of the funds in the trust by being the trustee. Less funds are needed in the incorporated trust to make it feasible ($25,000) because of the lower taxation and ongoing fees. The more children you have (and hence trusts), the more beneficial this can be. There is a great amount of flexibility with what can be done with trusts that own shares of a corporation and your lawyer and accountant should be able to assist you in this area.

Corporations can pay family members a reasonable salary for services rendered (e.g., office management or filing) and the money can then be invested for things such as future education. Since this salary will be earned income, it will enable the family member to set up an RRSP, which could also be used for education costs later on.

Incorporating allows for better budgeting because salaries and taxes are paid monthly. There is also a means of providing a retirement allowance and a tax-free death benefit through the corporation.

With the recent change in rules requiring self-employed health care professionals to pay taxes based on the calendar year, eliminating the opportunity to defer taxes by establishing a favourable fiscal year, incorporation offers another small advantage. As of 1995, unincorporated businesses must start reporting deferred income and start paying taxes on it. The more you have deferred the harder this will be to do. The deferred amount must now be recognized over the next 10 years at a rate of 5% in 1995, 10% through to 2003, and 15% in 2004. The amount recognized each year is added to income and taxed at the prevailing marginal tax rate.

If you are incorporated then this calendar year does not apply unless if you are a member of a partnership. In an incorporated business, you can still defer taxes, although before you incorporate you would have to pay any outstanding taxes which could be large if you have already been deferring income.

The possible benefits of using a universal life insurance policy within the corporation was mentioned in chapter 5. Within the corporation this would cost you less up front as the company uses 23% tax dollars to pay the premium, whereas most non-incorporated health care professionals would be paying with 54% after-tax dollars. The end beneficial payout would be the same. Under current tax law, at the time of death, the face value of the life insurance policy and gains within the policy are paid out to the corporation free of income taxes. Money can then be paid tax free to the family using capital dividends.

Disadvantages to Incorporating

There are disadvantages to incorporating as well. The main one occurs only if you incorporate before you pay off your mortgage and all personal debts. If you do, you may be tempted to take money out of the company to pay down your mortgage leaving nothing in the corporation to avail of the tax benefits. You would then be out of pocket because of the extra accounting and legal fees.

As a rule, *do not* incorporate until you have the house nearly paid off (or all personal debt) and can expect to leave at least $25,000 to $50,000 per year in the corporation. The annual tax saved on the $25,000 to $50,000 should offset the expenses of incorporating and the annual filing fees incurred by the company. If you have two or more children and an income over $250,000, then the issue of family trusts must be factored into this equation.

There is also a cost to incorporating. The ranges on the cost are great and you should get an estimate before hand. The combined legal and accounting fees for starting the corporation can be anywhere from $2,500 to $7,500. There is also the application fee to the professional licensing body ($500 to $1,000) and the ongoing yearly fees for the accountant ($1,000 to $2,500) and lawyer ($100 to $400). Further, if you are going to put one or more members on a salary, you must now pay workers' compensation and the extra accountant's fee for setting everything up.

Once you decide to incorporate you should shop around for different opinions on who can provide you with good service, and *always* get an estimate in advance on the price to incorporate and the recurring annual fees. You have to make sure you get an accountant that you feel very comfortable with as you will have to totally trust his or her opinion on the tax matters and planning that will take place.

Financial Planning Options Within the Incorporated Business

You have several options concerning reinvesting the money left in the corporation. The corporation can hold stocks, mutual funds, real estate, etc. The investment vehicles you choose will be based on when you anticipate winding down the corporation and whether you will be requiring the funds in the near future or if you can leave them in for many years.

As of 1995, many of the advantages of holding investments through the corporation were eliminated. You still get the preferred taxation on the $200,000 but now taxes on the resulting income earned ("investment income") in the corporation has been changed, and you should discuss the tax implications of these changes with your accountant and financial adviser. Basically, interest income and dividend income earned within the corporation are taxed the same as if these investments were held personally. The only difference is that the corporation will be entitled to a refund on a portion of the taxes when dividends are paid out to the shareholders. The capital gain investments are, therefore, the best type of investment (if held long term) because you will not be paying tax on the gain until you realize it, ideally in your retirement when your personal tax rate will be substantially lower. There is also the capital dividend which would allow 25% of the corporation's capital gains to be paid out tax free to the shareholders making this more attractive.

The attribution rules for health care professionals who have incorporated are different then what was discussed earlier. This is where your accountant or tax lawyer will be of great assistance.

The plan for winding down the corporation should be put in place well in advance. You do not have to wind down the corporation just because you have retired. In fact, it is at this time when you are in a lower tax bracket that the corporation can pay you a salary and/or dividends resulting in less tax. Ideally, you will be winding down the corporation when you are in a substantially lower tax bracket which will create definite tax savings.

You will have to decide whether it is possible to sell the business assets or to sell the shares of the business or just simply wind down the business (because of no buyers). The best option is to sell shares because of the tax preference allowed with the capital gain on these shares through the $500,000 capital gain exemption that still exists for small businesses (and farms). The excess funds that have built up in the corporation must then be dealt with. These funds may be used for income between retirement age and the age at which the RRSP must be unwound (69). If the company terminates your job, then there is an allowable "severance pay" that can be rolled over into your RRSP. As you can see, there are many options that need to be discussed with your accountant.

Holding Companies

A holding company is another company created mainly to allow assets to be funneled into it from the medical company. In other businesses, this is done to secure assets from creditors but there are other reasons as well. Because the rules related to retaining the identity of the Canadian-controlled private corporation (for purposes of the tax break on the $200,000) are very strict, a holding company can help the health care professional. If you end up with too much non-business related assets (e.g., real estate, stocks) in your medical corporation, you may risk losing the $200,000 tax break. Setting up a holding company can reduce this risk. The idea is that dividends can be paid from the medical company to the holding company without any tax effect, which is very useful if you are considering, for example, investing in real estate which can be purchased with corporate taxed money (23%) rather then personal taxed money (54%). The 1995 federal budget, however eliminated many of the advantages of investment income earned within the company. This and the other benefits, such as estate planning, of setting up a holding company should be discussed with your tax adviser.

In those provinces where health care professionals are not allowed to incorporate, you may want to look into a *professional management company*. This company is set up in the name of a family member and provides services such as bookkeeping, administrative work, and research to the health care professional. The idea is to try and have this company incorporated in order to avoid the attribution rules mentioned earlier.

There are other creative ways for health care professionals to incorporate in those provinces that have restrictions. For example, you might be able to incorporate the laboratory aspect of the practice. Or if you are a dentist, you may try to incorporate the x-ray or hygienist aspect. This option is definitely something that must be discussed at length with your accountant or tax lawyer to see if it makes sound financial sense for your situation.

KISS PRINCIPLE — Incorporation

1. *As a rule do not incorporate if you have not paid off your mortgage or any other large personal debt.*
2. *Try and leave as much money as possible in the corporation and invest in growth vehicles over interest or dividend-earning vehicles.*
3. *Go through the advantages and disadvantages with your accountant to make sure you will come out ahead.*

THE SNOWBIRD AND TAXES

If you have taken up the "snowbird" lifestyle, that is, fleeing from the long Canadian winters for a few months of the year, you should seek some professional tax advice. Both the Canadian and U.S. governments have been cracking down on snowbirds who have been avoiding taxes but continue to use their countries' services regularly. If you are spending more than 183 days per year in the United States, you will be considered an American taxpayer. This calculation is based on the average stay over three years. Even if the average is 121 days you have to file with the IRS. An excellent source of information on this topic is *The Canadian Snowbird Guide*, by Douglas Gray.

AUDITS

The government has up to three years after the date of assessing your tax return to perform an audit. Many health care professionals are audited, so be sure to keep all records and receipts well organized.

You must keep all records for a period of six years. Furthermore, you must know why you claimed any deductions in the return you submitted.

There are certain "types" that tend to attract audits:

1. *Self-employed people, especially those who are incorporated.*
2. *Those who earn six-figure incomes.*
3. *Anyone whose deductions are higher then average. Deductions should stay below 40% of your gross income.*
4. *Health care professionals claiming home office deductions.*
5. *Anyone with low tax payments for whatever reason.*
6. *Limited partnerships and other fancy "tax shelters" and real estate investments.*

Most audits conclude with your paying additional taxes. If you are audited, it is important to remain cooperative and polite. Better yet, let your accountant deal with the auditors on your behalf.

NOTES:

12

DEVELOPING THE RIGHT PORTFOLIO FOR YOU

Your investment portfolio will be influenced by considering three main issues:

1. *Your investment objectives*
2. *Your risk tolerance*
3. *Your age*

This chapter provides very general guidelines for balancing these three issues and developing your personalized portfolio. Keep in mind that these guidelines will vary substantially depending on your personal circumstances; you will still have to sit down with your financial adviser to create your own individual investment portfolio that suits your specific needs. The married neurologist who "graduates" at the age of 35, $50,000 in debt, after doing a two-year sub speciality in stroke in addition to an internal medicine degree will want a different investment portfolio than the 35-year-old single dentist who has been practising for 10 years. The neurologist will have the $50,000 university debt and a new mortgage compared to the dentist who has no mortgage and a very large RRSP and non-RRSP portfolio. Even though their ages and occupations are similar, their investment objectives and tolerance levels will likely be very different.

YOUR INVESTMENT OBJECTIVES

You cannot create an investment portfolio without first having an idea of your immediate, short-, and long-term investment objectives. In chapter 1, I painted a bleak picture for the average Canadian who is presently carrying high personal debt and who has only put aside 5% to 10% of what will be needed to retire in 20 years. Lack of an investment plan is probably the number one complaint most financial advisers have about health care professionals. Because health care professionals generally make good salaries, they are never in need while they work. The problem is that some day they will want to retire and there will no longer be the steady cash cow. This comes as a shock to many near retiring health care professionals. The end result is usually postponing retirement.

A recent survey of medical doctors, *1995 Physician Resource Questionnaire,* brings home the financial malaise that exists, I am sure this is also a good reflection of other health care professionals. This survey indicated that only 20% of doctors felt that they had any real skill with managing their investment portfolio, but only 50% were obtaining assistance from financial advisers. In doctors under the age of 35, where implementation of a investment plan is so vital, 91% felt that their financial knowledge and training was poor. Women were the most neglectful subgroup, which is unfortunate as they comprise such a large percentage of health care professionals.

The earlier you sit down with a financial adviser and develop your plan, the more likely it will materialize. If you leave the investment plan until your late forties or fifties, you may be in for some unpleasant surprises, the most common being that your dream of retiring early is shattered.

When there is a lack of funds or your nest egg is less than optimal, your options are limited. You can earn more per year, which is hard and stressful; spend less, which is possible but difficult; save more, which is possible especially past age 40 but difficult; pay less taxes, which has its limits; get higher returns on your investments, which is what this book is about; or postpone your retirement, which is the most frequently chosen option by default.

Your investment objectives will dictate what type of investments are required in your investment portfolio. The investment plan will usually have short- and long-term objectives. If you are under 40, your short-term plan could be for making extra payments on the mortgage and maximizing the RRSP. Paying off the mortgage should come before any non-RRSP savings/investment program. As well, you would want to include in the plan the need to put cash aside for proper disability and life insurance. If you are over 40 your short-term plan may be to save a down payment for a ski chalet or a cottage or to take that exotic extended vacation or simply to remodel your home.

The long-term plan for those under 40 might be to retire early and have a cottage on the lake paid for which you plan to retire in. Children's education may be part of your long-term plan. The long-term plan for those over 40 might be building on the present retirement nest egg or estate planning for your children and grandchildren with universal life insurance.

As a rule, short-term plans deal with funds that will be needed in less than five years. Anything longer is considered long-term investing. The length of time that you will be investing (or requiring) the cash will dictate the type of investment vehicle. The shorter the term the less risks you can take and, therefore, the less return you will get. If you are investing long term you can afford to make riskier investments that can result in higher returns. Some people are not comfortable with this risk, even with time on their side, and will only want to invest in safe, low-yielding vehicles. Others will want a mixture.

Short-term investments need a safety feature to give you the peace of mind that the cash will definitely be there when it is needed. Most short-term investing would be outside the RRSP (unless you are nearing retirement which is covered in the next chapter). The type of investment can be any of those covered in chapter 6, such as the GIC or term deposit, especially if you are very unsure of the future markets and if present rates are high.

If you will require the funds in less than one year, then money market mutual funds are another virtually risk-free way to go. If you are looking at two to five years and want a higher return, then mortgage mutual funds (or potentially bond mutual funds if rates are high or dropping) can be a good option, but consider switching over to a safer investment in the last one to two years. But remember that both mortgage and bond mutual funds can have poor years so if you are not willing to take this risk then the more conventional, relatively risk-free investments are a better choice.

If the funds are outside an RRSP, then you could consider the preferred dividend mutual funds which have stable returns, good safety for the principal, and lower tax implications. Another option for short-term investing is mortgage-backed securities and preferred stock from blue chip companies. All of these investments are discussed in chapters 6 and 8.

If your investment objectives are longer than five years, then you can afford more risk with your choices including equity mutual funds, balanced mutual funds, or individual stocks. If the period is greater than 10 years, I would choose a larger percentage in equity mutual funds, and if you are planning for in between 5 to 10 years, I recommend a mix of these according to your asset mix allocation (see below). This is not to say that you cannot use these vehicles for shorter term needs, but then you risk having to sell when the market is down when your return could be low or negative.

The other important aspect to creating an investment plan in accordance with your objectives is to reassess it every year. Your objectives may change with changing personal circumstances such as the arrival of children, receiving an inheritance, the need to remodel the house, or a change in the market conditions. I have preached the buy and hold strategy throughout this book, and it remains the golden rule, but there should be some portfolio adjustments made each year if need be. Asset mix allocation calls for a specific mixture of stocks (or mutual funds), bonds, and cash at any one time, but the mix can be altered slightly now and then to take advantage of current market conditions.

YOUR RISK TOLERANCE

Your tolerance for risk is very personal and only you can assess it. Your personal investment risk level may vary from time to time and will be influenced by many factors including current interest rates, level of inflation, expected age of retirement, and number of years of retirement. Some people will have no choice but to take on a higher risk level than they feel comfortable with because their nest egg is much too small for their investment plan. These are usually the health care professionals who procrastinate on their financial plan only to find out in their fifties that things are not going well.

Personally, I have a high risk tolerance when it comes to investing. This is likely a reflection of my "nature," my present financial situation, my financial knowledge, and my young age. My present portfolio is about 95% growth investments even though the "experts" say that I should be in the 70% to 80% range. But because I have a very ambitious investment plan to retire before age 50, I have decided "to go for it"! But I am doing this within reason. By this I mean that 1993 to 1996 have been very good years for growth investments, so I adjusted my asset mix allocation to increase my holdings in those types of investment vehicles during this period. In late 1996 and early 1997, I will likely reduce this exposure if the markets take a down turn. I will still take advantage of dollar-cost averaging during this period, but I will increase my cash-equivalent (and perhaps bond) holdings slightly.

You should have an asset mix allocation appropriate for your age and investment plan, which should be arranged under the guidance of a financial adviser. If you are not on track with your investment plan, then one of your options is to accept more risk and invest in vehicles that should give you higher returns. If you cannot take this step because it is simply not in your nature, then you will have to incorporate one of the other listed options including postponing your retirement. If you opt to accept a higher risk investment portfolio, it should be done under the guidance of a financial adviser and the increased risk should be "reasonable" and prudently managed.

Your risk level should decrease with age, but at times when the we have an extended bull market, you may want to increase your risk exposure slightly to capitalize on some of the movement. The key is to manage the risk effectively.

YOUR AGE

Your age is probably the single biggest determinant of which investments you choose for your portfolio, but there is still great variability depending on your investment plan and risk level. A standard rule is that the percentage of growth investments in your investment portfolio should equal 100 minus your age; conversely, the percentage of guaranteed investments should match your age. But these percentages can vary by 20% to 30% depending on your particular circumstances. In the example above comparing the 35-year-old neurologist and the dentist, the neurologist would probably have more growth investment exposure because he has more catching up to do. But he may decide to retire later and keep a lower growth investment exposure if his risk tolerance is low. As a general rule, the more money you have banked toward your required nest egg, the less risk you need to take. Unfortunately human greed frequently alters this rule.

Age 20 to 30

Time is on your side, and 80% to 90% of your investment portfolio can be in growth investments to gain maximum returns. The other 10% to 20% can be split between bonds and cash (i.e., GICs, term deposits, T-bills, Canada Savings Bonds, and money market mutual funds).

At this age I would use mainly money market mutual funds as your source of cash. Cash is important to take advantage of buying opportunities. Bonds are important for times of interest rate declines and when rates are high and stable. These three types of investment vehicles form the basis of asset mix allocation, which is discussed below.

If the market is about to turn down, then you may want to consider slightly increasing your cash holdings, allowing you to later buy cheap stocks or mutual funds. If you are using a pre-authorized contribution plan, you may want to redirect this monthly buy into a money market mutual fund for a few months and then buy the cheaply priced growth mutual funds that have dropped in price. But this should only be attempted by those knowledgeable enough and comfortable with this minor form of "market timing." A preferable option is to simply leave the PAC in place allowing you to buy mutual funds or stock cheaply as the price drops (i.e., dollar-cost averaging), and then use the cash already in your portfolio to buy more.

You will not likely have any money outside your RRSP at this point and if you do it is probably slated for the new home down payment. I would focus RRSP investments mainly in mutual funds at this stage. A good no-load mutual fund is optimal, but you may want to mix this with either a rear-end mutual fund or front-end mutual fund to take advantage of the services of a financial adviser whose commission will be provided by the load fund.

Age 31 to 40

Your RRSP value is now in the $30,000 to $75,000 range and you probably have little if any money outside your RRSP because you have just bought a home. Now is the time to be reviewing your investment plan. You probably have some idea of when you would like to retire and you know what your present debt is. Having some rough figures about how much you will need when you retire (see next chapter) will assist you in choosing the correct vehicles for your investment portfolio. If your present path will leave you short, then one of your options is to keep your percentage exposure to growth investments high.

The recommended percentage exposure to growth investments at this age is 60% to 70%, but this can vary by 10% to 20% depending on your circumstances. I recommend still focusing mainly on mutual funds. As mentioned in the chapter on mutual funds, you will want to be dealing with two to three different mutual fund companies and holding six to nine different mutual funds to allow for diversification of both funds and fund managers' investment strategies and to minimize administrative costs.

A self-directed RRSP is not yet required if you are just holding mutual funds (although some would disagree) but it is something that you can consider once your RRSP gets above $50,000 if you are going to be buying blue chip stocks. Any extra money should be going on your mortgage and maximizing your RRSP. If you are fortunate enough to still have extra cash, then the best option is a global mutual fund which provides income mostly in the form of capital gains. This will likely give you the highest return (over five or more years) and you will get to defer taxes until you realize the gains.

Age 41 to 50

Your RRSP portfolio is probably now in the $75,000 to $150,000 range and you are starting to build up a non-RRSP investment portfolio as well. By now you are very content because you can see the light at the end of the tunnel or, you are very anxious because you just don't know where all the money is going. If the latter, remember that it is never too late. You just have to be more proactive and start making things happen or push the retirement back a few years.

You *must* have a financial adviser at this point to help with the large nest egg and to make sure you are on track with your investment plan. Most recommend that if you are on schedule then you should shift your portfolio so that 50% to 60% is now in growth investments and the remaining 40% to 50% is in the safe guaranteed investment vehicles. Some recommend lower exposure growth investments for this age group, which I think is wrong. Remember at this age you will likely have at least 30 to 40 years ahead of you! This means that inflation is still going to eat away at your nest egg and if you go on the defence too early, you could come out short at the age of 70.

Your RRSP is still mostly invested in mutual funds but now is the time to give serious consideration to blue chip stocks. The global mutual funds are still the best choice for a large percentage of your non-RRSP assets, but you want to keep a proper asset mix allocation there as well and start including some blue chip stocks. Some experts recommend keeping your RRSP and non-RRSP investment portfolio similar, but I don't think this makes sense. First, you should avail of the global markets as much as possible and there are no limits outside the RRSP. Second, we know that the rule is to keep interest-bearing investments within the RRSP and dividend and capital gains income producing investments outside in order to optimize taxes. Both of these factors mean that the types of assets held in your RRSP and non-RRSP will be different.

Do not forget that the combination of using a broker (for RRSP) and discount broker (for non-RRSP) may be the optimal way to invest at this point *if* you are willing to put in the time to follow your investments. This is especially true if you are using the buy and hold strategy. Otherwise, let your financial adviser take care of the whole portfolio.

Age 51 to 60

Most of us are now only 5 to 10 years away from retirement, so preservation of capital is becoming the main aim. The size of your RRSP investment portfolio will likely be $150,000-plus, and many health care professionals will have investment portfolios significantly larger than that. Your non-RRSP investment portfolio is also growing quite nicely.

This is a time when too many health care professionals go on the defensive with their investment portfolio. Protection is important, but there are varying degrees of defence. To slip into total hibernation with staggered GICs could be dangerous. At this age, I think you should still have 40% to 50% exposure to the different growth investments. The first $100,000 might be in the mutual funds and anything above in individual stocks. The type of stocks (i.e., growth or income) will be tailored to your investment plan as well as present market conditions.

Because your exposure to guaranteed investments is 50% to 60%, you will now be looking at more bonds and cash equivalent investments. A great option for within your RRSP are the strip bonds that were covered in chapter 6 because of their excellent returns and safety. Mortgage-backed securities are another good safe form of investment providing above-average return.

The non-RRSP portfolio will still be the inflation fighter with 50% to 60% growth investments, but the type of mutual funds and stocks you now choose will be more defensive. You will be aiming at utilities, banks, gas, and pipeline common stocks as well as preferred stocks because of preferential tax treatment.

For health care professionals who have built up equity in their home, you may want to consider selling, realizing the tax-free capital gain, and adding the amount to your retirement fund. But many health care professionals do not want to sell or downsize, which is all right if the nest egg is otherwise healthy. There could be trouble, however, if the equity in the house is a major part of your retirement plan for which you hope to collect on down the road. Remember that top-end housing prices could very well take a dive around your retirement years leaving you empty handed. Most financial experts agree that the days of great appreciation for large homes in urban cities are over, and future prices will decline. Further, you can be sure that local councils and provincial governments are going to continue with sharp rises in property taxes on these larger homes. For these reasons, if you are or will be house rich and cash poor at this age, you should consider downsizing and investing the difference sooner rather then later. (There are other options such as the reverse mortgage and home equity loan, which are covered in the next chapter.)

Age 61 and up

Many health care professionals will be retired or semiretired at this point and will be depending on the income being produced by their nest egg. It is wise to use your non-RRSP investment income initially and use your RRSP only when you have to. This allows continued tax deferral and tax-free growth within your RRSP up to age 69. Your decision about how to unwind your RRSP should be foremost in your mind now especially if interest rates are high, allowing you to lock in some good rates.

Input from a financial adviser is a must at this stage to help monitor your overall portfolio and to consider the issues of selling your house, arranging the investment portfolio to provide regular income when needed, estate planning, and looking at the options for unwinding the RRSP. (Financial options for retirement are covered in chapter 13.)

Asset Mix Allocation

Asset mix allocation refers to the ratio or percentage of the two major investment sectors that you should have in your investment portfolio at any one time. These two areas are, of course, the guaranteed investments (bonds & cash) and growth investments. Repeated research has shown that it is not the individual type of mutual fund, stock, fund manager, or market timing that makes you wealthy, but the mix of different types of investments.

It has been shown that 80% to 90% of your return is determined by having the right asset mix allocation, which of course evolves with time. This logic will be meaningful to you only if you correctly assume that nobody can time the market all the time. If you could, then you would consistently pick stocks such as Diamond Fields (Voisey Bay) and Bre-X. But as we all know, this is not the case. So the best alternative is to have a proper asset mix allocation which is basically a mixture of stocks, mutual funds, bonds, and cash at all times. The percentage of each to be held at any one time is influenced by several of the factors discussed already. Table 8 shows you why asset mix allocation is important.

Table 8
Canadian Capital Market Total Rates of Return (%)

Year	Stocks	Bonds	T-bills
1983	**35.5**	11.5	9.6
1984	-2.4	**14.7**	11.6
1985	**25.1**	21.2	9.9
1986	9.0	**14.7**	9.3
1987	5.9	4.0	**8.5**
1988	**11.1**	9.8	9.4
1989	**21.4**	12.8	12.4
1990	-14.8	7.6	**13.5**
1991	12.0	**22.1**	9.8
1992	-1.4	**9.8**	7.1

As you can see in Table 8, the top performing type of investment differs from year to year. If you are a "market timer," you would try to predict what is hot each year but as you know, few (if any) can do this. In fact, studies have shown that market timing, specific investment vehicle choices, and specific stock picking choices account for only 10% to 15% of your total return on average. That is why the "buy and hold" strategy is recommended. But more important, you can see that if you had a mixture of these different types of investments for each year, then you would be holding some of your portfolio in the winner's circle (and therefore less in the loser's circle) at all times. This is the basic logic of asset mix allocation and it is the most effective and prudent strategy for managing risk.

The second thing you need to know about asset mix allocation is that the heavier the balance is weighted in growth investments, the better you will do if your investment plan is longer than five years. However, you still need an asset mix of other investments even if only 10% to 20% of your portfolio.

The basic asset mix allocation recommended by most professional money managers is 45/45/10 for equities/bonds/cash equivalents, but these percentages will vary by 10% to 35% depending on the current market environment and the issues discussed in this chapter. As well, even though two different investors may opt for this 45/45/10 investment portfolio, the aggressiveness of each can be very different depending on the specific types of investments held within each class. For example, stock from the Bank of Montreal and a junior oil company would differ enormously as would bonds from each company.

The asset mix allocation can be, but does not have to be, readjusted by 10% to 20% each year to take advantage of the different market cycles. This strategy has been referred to as passive asset mix allocation, which is different then the dynamic asset mix allocation, which calls for regular portfolio readjusting. I do not recommend the dynamic form as it is similar to the market timing strategy which even the experts have trouble with.

A passive type of asset mix allocation example would be if you and your financial adviser believe that 1997 is going to be another great year for stocks, then you may want to increase your asset mix of growth investments from 60% to 70%. The remaining 30% should still be in guaranteed investments just in case you are wrong. Another example would be if you expected declining interest rates you may want to increase your bond/bond mutual fund exposure. On the other hand, if rates were increasing you may want to consider decreasing your bond exposure and increasing your cash exposure (money market mutual funds).

The younger you are the more flexibility you have with this readjusting. Let me stress that we are still sticking with the buy and hold strategy; readjusting should be looked at as fine tuning and again done with the guidance of a financial adviser.

Remember that much of the gain in the market occurs within a very small number of stock trading days (less than 1%) so the buy and hold is the best guarantee that you will be in the market during these few crucial days. You will continue to benefit from dollar-cost averaging if you are using a PAC program, and your fine tuning will just enhance your strategy. If you are using a PAC program, an easy way to readjust the asset mix allocation is simply to change where the PAC goes for a few months in order to increase or decrease the assets.

Finally, your asset mix allocation will have to be altered every couple of years as your age and personal circumstances change. Remember, though, that as a general rule you should hold stocks and mutual funds for at least two years before unloading them and only then if the company has changed or your investment plan has. Trading or switching more frequently puts the odds in favour of you losing.

DIVERSIFICATION

Diversification is another aspect of your portfolio that you must pay attention to if your investments are to thrive. Diversification is somewhat similar to asset mix allocation but it takes the issue closer to the root of the actual selection of individual investments. Diversification should be considered at three different levels:

1. *Diversification by asset class (i.e., cash, stocks, and bonds)*
2. *Diversification within each asset mix (i.e., different types of stocks and bonds)*
3. *Diversification by country*

You could also include diversification by investment strategy (e.g., top down or bottom up), but the best method is the buy and hold strategy. But once your portfolio is over $100,000 you could ask your financial adviser to also diversify your investments by investment strategies as well.

Diversification of stocks refers to different types of stocks that perform differently depending on market conditions. Review chapter 7 for more information. Bonds were covered in chapter 8; remember the basic rule of buying using the "ladder approach."

Diversification by country both within the RRSP and outside is also vital to optimize your return. Canada represents only 2% to 3% of the world's stock market capitalization and the average Canadian market return has been below the world's average market return.

The best way to achieve diversification by country is through mutual funds. In fact, a combination of mutual funds allows the health care professional to have instant diversification on all three of these levels. A typical portfolio might contain a balanced mutual fund (containing equities, bonds, and cash), a money market mutual fund (T-bills and cash), and a global mutual fund (foreign content).

When considering the diversification of your portfolio, remember you have to consider your entire portfolio: that is, your principal residence (often your biggest investment), your RRSP, and your non-RRSP investments. If you own a $1.5 million house, you may consider it a great asset, but it isn't so great if your total portfolio is valued at $2 million because you are over exposed in real estate.

WHAT TO DO WHEN YOUR PORTFOLIO IS OVER $100,000

I think the overall best investment vehicle for the average busy health care professional is mutual funds. Once your portfolio (mostly RRSP) reaches the range of $75,000 to $100,000, you might want to consider looking at adding blue chip stocks to your portfolio. Some health care professionals with high risk tolerance and/or an aggressive investment attitude may want to look at stocks before they have $75,000 in the RRSP. But keep in mind that to achieve adequate diversification in individual stocks you will need at least $50,000. If you decide to move into individual stocks, then I recommend keeping your existing mutual funds intact, especially if they are performing well, and simply adding your stock selection to them. Remember that with mutual funds, you pay 1% to 3% in commission per year, versus the one-time initial 1% to 2% commission charged on blue chip stocks. You could, therefore, be ahead 1% to 3% *every* year if you hold blue chip stocks. The future contributions (maybe with the PAC program) should be used to develop a good diverse selection of stocks across the five sectors as discussed in chapter 7.

Whatever you do when your portfolio reaches this level, the most important piece of advice I can give the average health care professional is to get professional assistance and guidance. Studies have shown that investors who use a professional financial adviser do better in the long run then those who do not. Just make sure you choose the correct financial advisers.

WHAT ABOUT YOUR NON-RRSP INVESTMENTS?

As a rule, you should not have any money invested outside your RRSP if you are not maximizing your extra mortgage payments (preferably paid off) or if you have not maximized your RRSP. Most health care professionals will not be making any non-RRSP investments until they are in their forties. Many financial advisers recommend keeping a similar asset mix for both your RRSP and non-RRSP. But you may recall that I have already stated that you should try and keep your interest-bearing investments within your RRSP and growth outside because of the favourable taxation. And remember that you have the opportunity to hold more than 20% foreign content outside your RRSP which should be taken advantage of.

As a result of these two opportunities, your non-RRSP will have more growth investments than your RRSP. For those under 45, this non-RRSP investment portfolio may be in mainly growth investments. Once you are over 45, how much of the non-RRSP you keep in growth investments will depend on your need for the money invested. It is general wisdom that in the early retirement years you use the non-RRSP funds to allow optimal tax deferral in the RRSP. If you will require the non-RRSP money in these early retirement years, then this will dictate the types of investments. This is where the use of preferred shares (or even relatively safe regular dividend-paying common shares), for example, would be a good choice in terms of return, safety, and favourable tax treatment. You will still require some money in the safer guaranteed investments, however, such as the GIC and term deposits because of the "absolute" guaranteed steady income.

Mutual funds are a great place to invest your non-RRSP money (see chapter 8). You should optimize your foreign content by investing in global mutual funds which can represent up to 50% to 60% of your non-RRSP portfolio depending on your age. Many mutual fund companies offer the systematic withdrawal plan (SWP) to attract investors who will be using this money as a means of income in retirement. You can set up a SWP at any time, but most wait until retirement before using the SWP for income to bridge the time between early retirement and age 69 when they must unwind the RRSP.

With a SWP you can withdraw up to 10% of the original investment every year without incurring any commission fees. This plan can be set up so that you will get a monthly paycheque, and the taxation is at about

38% rather then 52% because it is in the form of realized gains (assuming your SWP is set up with an equity mutual fund). Additionally, if funds are withdrawn soon after setting up the plan, the taxes are even lower because part of the income is from the original principal invested. An example from some of the better funds such as MD Growth reveal that if you had put $100,000 in this SWP mutual fund in 1984 (from the sale of your house, for example) and withdrew $10,000 every year from 1985 up to 1995, then you would still have about $207,000 in the account in 1995!

Don't forget that the "spousal contribution" also applies to non-RRSP money if the other spouse is in a lower income bracket or will be later in life. You may want to put a major share of your non-RRSP investments in your spouse's name so that any income will be taxed at a lower rate. Remember that the idea is to split the wealth so that the tax bite later will be in two names rather than one, which will likely mean lower taxes overall.

WHAT TO DO WITH ANY INHERITED MONEY

Currently, there are no inheritance taxes, but many feel that this will change because of the billions of dollars that are expected to be passed on over the next decade of which the government would like a piece. The question for many will be what to do with this lump sum of money?

As a starting investment, the best place is a money market mutual fund or a short-term cashable GIC. This will give you safety and some return while you review your whole financial portfolio in light of receiving this sudden lump sum.

Next you should pay off any personal debt starting with credit cards, car loans, line of credit, etc. Next comes the mortgage either with extra monthly payments plus the annual 10% or, if feasible, one lump sum payment plus the penalty cost. Remember that these types of debt are very expensive because you are paying for them with after-tax dollars, so it is next to impossible to get a better investment return then simply paying them off.

The next thing to do is to maximize any unused RRSP contributions. You may have purposefully skipped a couple of years in anticipation of the inheritance which can be wise. Then only problem with this strategy is that nobody knows how long the RRSP carry forward rules are going to last.

If there is money left over after accomplishing all these feats, then consult with your financial adviser. One consideration for any "extra" inheritance money is to set up a spousal trust assuming that your spouse is in a lower income bracket. This is another form of income splitting that will minimize your future tax bill.

INVESTMENT CHOICES WHEN YOUR PORTFOLIO IS LESS THAN IT SHOULD BE

If you are in this predicament, your options are, unfortunately, limited. The solution will depend on what age you realized that your investment portfolio was off track. The later in life this happens, the more likely the answer will be postponing your retirement. Very few of us can work any harder, in fact most health care professionals should be working less.

The next most viable option is to save more, which means spending less. You may also optimize your returns by investing in other vehicles that you are reasonably comfortable with and will provide higher returns. Higher returns, however, means tolerating higher risk and will require the input of a financial adviser who understands your situation and is able to manage your investment portfolio.

The following are other considerations that you and your financial adviser may want to consider.

1. *Increase your exposure to equity investments such as mutual funds (especially global mutual funds) or stocks. Many health care professionals have too much exposure to the fixed-income investments.*
2. *If you are house rich and cash poor, consider selling and downsizing (or renting) and investing the difference.*
3. *If you do not want to leave your house and are mortgage free, consider borrowing against the equity in the house (i.e., a reverse mortgage) and invest this money (global mutual fund) outside the RRSP. The interest on the money borrowed (about 8%) will be tax deductible, giving you a very cheap loan (about 4%). If this is invested in a good global mutual fund, you can probably expect 13% to 16% annual return over the next decade. This strategy is optimal when interest rates are low.*

4. *If you need a forced savings plan, then take out a $20,000 to $30,000 loan from your line of credit each year, and invest it (global mutual fund) outside the RRSP every year. The interest rate on the line of credit is usually low (8% at present) and is tax deductible, giving you an even cheaper loan. The key to this strategy is to pay off the line of credit every year which is your forced savings plan.*
5. *If you have more than five years, you may want to consider increasing your exposure to some of the more aggressive and volatile mutual funds such as the emerging market mutual funds or resource mutual funds. These can give excellent returns, but are very high risk and should be done under the guidance of a financial adviser.*

There are many other alternatives such as leveraging, but these are very, very risky and I would recommend them only if you and the financial adviser are well versed in the possible downside.

Putting It All Together

There are many factors that need to be considered when looking at your overall financial portfolio. Besides everything that has been discussed in this chapter, you will want to take a holistic approach which includes considering all aspects of your financial well being, and not just your investment portfolio.

There are six different and equally important pillars that must be looked at when considering your overall financial portfolio: your investment portfolio (discussed here), your personal debt (including your mortgage), your insurance plans, your will and estate planning, your financial adviser, and, if applicable, funding for the children's education. Personal financial planning is most effective when all the pillars are considered together. Each affects the others and if one is not balanced then it can throw the whole portfolio off.

KISS PRINCIPLE — Investment Portfolio

1. *Find a reliable financial adviser.*
2. *Develop an investment plan early in your career.*
3. *Don't overexpose yourself to guaranteed investments, especially past the age of 50. Remember, most people cannot afford not to take some risk.*
4. *Stick to your asset mix allocation and diversify those investments.*
5. *Stick to the buy and hold strategy. Equity mutual funds and stocks require at least two years and preferably five.*
6. *Cash is good in the investment portfolio to avail of buying opportunities.*
7. *Mutual funds are excellent choices for every health care professional. They can be the only type of investment in your nest egg up to $100,000. After this you should consider blue chip stocks.*
8. *Global equity mutual funds are excellent choices for every health care professional.*
9. *Consider regular dividend paying blue chip stocks once your portfolio gets above $75,000 to $100,000.*
10. *Aim for 6 to 10 stocks diversified across the different economic sectors.*
11. *Dollar-cost averaging and the preauthorized chequing/contribution (PAC) plan is a great way to invest both inside and outside the RRSP.*
12. *Reassess your investment portfolio and the asset mix allocation yearly.*
13. *Make sure that your mortgage, RRSP, insurance, and will are taken care of.*

13

PLANNING FOR RETIREMENT

This chapter is of more immediate importance to those in the 45- to 65-year range, but I strongly encourage all health care professionals to take the time to review it. (Note that this chapter does not consider corporate pension plans as most of readers will be self-employed. I strongly encourage those who have a pension plan in place to learn more about it as soon as possible to understand what role it plays in your investment plan.)

Thinking about retirement often becomes a priority for the busy health care professional after 5 to 10 years in a practice. Retirement can mean different things for different people. Some will semi-retire; some will retire from one job only to move on to another; others will start travelling; and others will be content to fish at the cottage (if there are any fish left). Regardless of your choice, it will require an investment plan that will reflect the time frame and the means of achieving healthy wealth.

It cannot be overstated that you must start early with your retirement plan. The earlier you give consideration to your retirement plan, the more likely it will be successful. If you are currently in your thirties or forties, you can probably plan on 30 to 40 years of retirement. Without government help, this is going to require a large nest egg. An early investment plan is the only way to achieve it unless you are fortunate enough to inherit a large sum of money.

Before looking at how much you will need to retire, let's first review the "dream plan" that hopefully no health care professional under the age of 50 is counting on.

The Dream Plan: "The Government May Help"

If you are 10 or more years away from retirement, you should not be relying on any future government help for your retirement. The government is broke because of outrageous and inappropriate spending by previous governments. The government retirement resources that are currently in place will likely rapidly erode over the next 5 to 10 years and will be available only to those in the very low income brackets. The above-average income earners, such as health care professionals, will have to pay more into these plans, despite likely not benefiting from them. Fortunately, the government recognizes these future shortcomings and has allowed generous RRSP contributions, but even this is now being tampered with. In the future we are going to have significantly fewer working people and more retiring people, so that by the year 2030, Canada will have one of the oldest populations on the earth. How is the succeeding younger population going to feel about paying higher and higher taxes for government retirement plans when they know that they will most likely not benefit from them?

There are basically two government systems in place now: the Old Age Security (OAS) and the Canada Pension Plan (CPP). In Quebec, there is also the Quebec Pension Plan (QPP), which is not discussed here, but the numbers are similar to the CPP.

Old Age Security (OAS)

Old Age Security (OAS) is an indexed pension that most Canadians start receiving at the age of 65 (not before) even if they continue working past this age. It is taxed like all good things in Canada. Eligibility is based on the number of years you have lived in Canada and not whether you have worked. To collect you must have been a resident for at least 10 adult years.

You should apply for the OAS 6 to 12 months before turning 65. The maximum payment was about $390 per month as of 1995; to achieve this level requires at least 40 years of residency in Canada.

There are a number of federal (and some provincial) supplements available in addition to the basic OAS if your income is low enough. The best known is the Guaranteed Income Supplement (GIS) and the Spousal Allowance with its many variations. It is very unlikely that any health care professional would be eligible for either of these.

Nobody knows the future of the OAS. Since its inception in 1952 it has had a downward trend. The OAS took its first hit during the Mulroney era with the introduction of the "clawback." For those retirees receiving more than $53,000 per year (or as a couple over $78,000 per year) there is a 100% clawback and below these amounts there is a declining sliding scale down to about $45,000. The federal budget in 1996 proposed more changes to the OAS beginning in 2001 when it will be replaced with a "senior's benefit." Other future changes are inevitable, but for the health care professional, the bottom line is that there will be less — perhaps no — government retirement support in the future.

Canada Pension Plan (CPP)

The Canada Pension Plan (CPP) differs from the OAS in that those who benefit do so because of mandatory contributions that are made by employees and employers. What you get in retirement is proportionate to what you have put in up to a predetermined maximum. If you are employed, you and your employer contribute equally to CPP. If you are self-employed, you pay a portion and so does your company.

The original idea of CPP was to provide regular income in retirement, but this is now in jeopardy. You can also receive CPP benefits if you have been severely disabled, and your family can also collect a certain amount in the event of your death.

The CPP is indexed to inflation so the amount you (or your employer) pay into the plan has steadily increased — as have the benefits. As of 1996, the amount you paid as a self-employed health care professional was about 5.6% for yourself and 2.8% for each of your employees. This percentage is applied toward the salary up to a maximum of about $35,000. The real numbers are $1,786 for you and up to $893 for each employee.

The CPP maximum benefit at the age of 65 was $714 per month for 1995. You can collect CPP as early as age 60 or as late as age 70; if you take it earlier the payments are less (up to 30%) and more if you take it later. The decision for when to collect should be based partly on your tax bill because you have to pay taxes on the CPP payment.

The combined maximum government retirement benefit in 1995 for OAS/CPP was about $1,100 per month. The maximum CPP disability pension was $839 per month in 1994 for those whose disability was severe and prolonged preventing any future gainful employment. Additionally any child of a disability claimant gets $160 per month up to the age of 18 or 25 if attending post-secondary school. These figures should make health care professionals sit up and take notice the next time any patient seeks your signature for disability CPP at the age of 35 with three young children.

There is also an estate payout and spousal benefit if the contributor dies. The lump sum death benefit paid to the estate is about $3,500. The surviving spouse gets a percentage of your CPP benefit based on age and number of dependants. This amount will likely be decreased for the high income health care professionals over the next few years.

The future of the CPP is unknown. Realizing the financial hole that the CPP was in, the federal government has been increasing the percentage of CCP contributions that you must pay each year by about 0.25% since 1992. It is estimated that by the year 2016, the CPP payment will have to be at least 10% of whatever the indexed maximum CPP benefit will be then (another reason to retire early I would say).

As the population ages, there is going to be incredible pressure on the pension plan fund. When the CPP was created in mid-sixties, the ratio of workers to retirees was 7:1. It is now 5:1 and in the near future it will be 3:1 thanks to our excellent medical services and decreasing birth rates. In fact the CPP has been drawing on its principal since 1994 because the government is now paying out more than it is taking in. Most experts believe that if there are not radical changes brought in place soon, by the year 2015 the $40 billion government nest egg will be empty.

What we know for sure is that health care professionals as a whole, especially the self-employed, will pay more into this plan for themselves as well as their employees and almost definitely receive less (if anything) in return! Another reason to start taking personal financial planning seriously I would think.

HOW MUCH WILL I NEED?

The tables in this section will give you a reasonable approximation of the size of the nest egg you will require to retire at your chosen age. These are approximations only because there are many variables that could change between now and then (e.g., change in inflation rate, variable return rate, number of years of retirement). It is a good idea to do three calculations: the most likely and hopeful scenario, the best scenario, and the worst scenario.

Step 1: Determining Your Annual Retirement Requirements

Determining your annual requirements is best approached by thinking of what you would need in today's dollars if you were to retire tomorrow morning. This should be somewhere between 60% to 80% of your present salary excluding your overhead. For example, if your salary is $100,000 per year and after overhead (and before taxes) your salary is $70,000, then a reasonable retirement income might be $50,000.

The amount you choose depends on the type of lifestyle you desire in retirement. If you plan to do a lot of travelling to exotic places, then you may require more than 80% of your present net income. If you plan to spend most of your time at home or at the cottage, then 60% may suffice.

Now you need to calculate what this amount will equate to after inflation is considered if the time to retirement is more than 5 to 10 years. Remember that inflation reduces the value of your money according to the "rule of 72 in reverse." With 4% inflation every 18 years your nest egg value decreases by 50%.

From Table 9, select your expected required income from the first column and match it with the years until retirement to find what you will require in yearly income in "tomorrow's" dollars assuming a 4% inflation rate. For example, I expect to require $60,000 per year when I retire in 15 years, which translates into a future yearly income of $108,000 after taking inflation into consideration. The number you calculate is your "number 1."

I strongly recommend not including any OAS/CPP payments in your calculation for any health care professional retiring after the year 2006. If you may receive another pension from work, then it should fit into the calculation.

TABLE 9
Future Annual Income Required (Number 1)

Income Required	Years Until Retirement 10	15	20	25	30
$40,000	59,000	72,000	88,000	107,000	130,000
$50,000	74,000	90,000	110,000	134,000	162,000
$60,000	89,000	**108,000**	131,000	160,000	194,000
$70,000	104,000	126,000	153,000	187,000	227,000
$80,000	118,000	144,000	175,000	214,000	260,000
$90,000	133,000	162,000	197,000	240,000	292,000
$100,000	148,000	180,000	219,000	267,000	324,000

Step 2: The size of the nest egg required

Now that you know how much annual income you expect in retirement, you must next calculate the size of the nest egg required to generate this yearly income. This requires an estimate of the number of years until retirement as well as the investment return you expect to obtain on your investments during your savings years. From Table 10, find your "number 2" and multiply it by "number 1" to get the size of the nest egg required to make your investment plan a reality. Because I would like to retire close to 50, then I will require at least 30 years of retirement funding so my "number 2" is 15.1. To calculate my nest egg size, I multiply $108,000 (number 1) X 15.1 (number 2) = $1,630,800.

TABLE 10
Nest Egg Size (Number 2)

Expected % Return	Number of Years of Retirement 16	18	20	22	24	26	28	30
8%	12.8	13.8	14.8	15.7	16.5	17.3	18.0	18.6
10%	11.3	12.0	12.7	13.3	13.8	14.3	14.7	**15.1**
12%	10.0	10.6	11.1	11.5	11.8	12.1	12.4	12.6

Step 3: Size of present nest egg

This step will allow you to see what the shortfall is between your present nest egg size and the one that you will require in retirement. You again have to estimate what you hope to achieve on future investment returns and the number of years until retirement.

By using Table 11, you will find a "number 3" which, when multiplied by your present RRSP nest egg, will tell you the future value of your present nest egg. As an example, I hope to retire in 15 years and I hope to achieve an annual investment return of 10% so my "number 3" value is 4.2. I then multiply this 4.2 (number 3) X $130,000 (present RRSP value) = $546,000. This means that by just using my RRSP I will require $1,630,800 (step 2) - $546,000 (step 3) = $1,084,800 more in my nest egg at the time of retirement if my investment plan is going to work. This is very possible if I continue to maximize my yearly RRSP contribution plus my non-RRSP nest egg. If I manage to achieve 12% or more on my investment returns (which I should be able to) then I will easily reach my goal by age 50.

You need to do the same calculation for any non-RRSP investments that you have but decrease your expected return by 2% to 4% when using these tables. This is because even though your gross return is 10%, your after taxes return is only 6% to 8% depending on the type of investment. Add this amount to your RRSP figure which will give you your present overall shortfall.

TABLE 11
Current Nest Egg Value At Retirement (Number 3)

Expected Return	Number of Years Until Retirement 10	15	20	25	30
6%	1.8	2.4	3.2	4.3	5.7
7%	2.0	2.8	3.9	5.4	7.6
8%	2.2	3.2	4.7	6.8	10.1
10%	2.6	**4.2**	6.7	10.8	17.4
12%	3.1	5.5	9.6	17.0	30.0

A good financial adviser will have access to computer programs that will give this information instantly if you prefer. This can be done with any inflation rate and return rate that you choose.

The final step is to figure out how much you will have to contribute to your nest egg on an annual basis between now and retirement to meet your investment plan objectives. From previous chapters, you know that the earlier you start building the nest egg the easier it is. There are calculations that can be done showing you exactly what you should save per year to allow retirement at "age X" based on what your present nest egg value is. Medical doctors can take advantage of the new software offered by MD Management, *Personal Retirement Projector,* which will give you these figures.

The annual savings range "should be" from 10% to 15% of your net income if you start at age of 25 compared to 18% to 20% if you commence saving at age of 35. This is a lot of money for those paying university debt, mortgages, etc., but if you consider your mortgage as an investment plus your monthly RRSP, then you may find that you are already putting away 5% to 10% each month. As a general rule, most health care professionals should aim for 5% to 10% of their income after expenses have been paid. Then in the later years when the house is paid for, you can increase the savings percentage to the 15% to 20% range.

WINDING DOWN YOUR NEST EGG

When it comes time to consider winding down and thinking about specific retirement plans, you should consider the help of a financial adviser as mandatory. However, understanding the basics will allow you to knowledgeably examine the pros and cons of each and choose among the different options. This section provides a good overview, but the exact numbers you will need will require more reading and consulting on your part. A good reference book on this topic is *Retire Right,* by Kirk Polson and George Brett.

Time to Cash Your RRSP?

As mentioned in earlier chapters, you should try to postpone unwinding your RRSP until age 69 to take full advantage of the tax-free compound growth. Instead you should use your non-RRSP investments in the early retirement years. Remember that you can continue contributing to your spouse's RRSP up until he or she turns 69 regardless of your age. And if you are employed and there is a "lump sum" retirement payment, it should be rolled over into the RRSP to defer taxation.

You can unwind your RRSP at any age but it *must* be done by December 31 in the year you turn 69. It is wise to start checking out the different options at least one to two years before then. There are basically three options for unwinding your RRSP:

1. *Cash the RRSP and pay the taxes*
2. *Purchase an annuity*
3. *Transfer the funds into a Registered Retirement Income Fund (RRIF)*

Any combination of these three options is possible; the most common is a combination of annuity and RRIF.

If you are an "employed" health care professional and contribute to a pension plan (locked-in), then you have the option of purchasing a life annuity or transferring the pension funds into a life income fund (LIF) or locked-in retirement income fund (LRIF). These options should be discussed with your financial adviser or an insurance broker; they are not covered here.

The first option, cashing in the RRSP, is one very few take because the tax bite is the highest. However, if you do opt to take all or some cash out of your RRSP, there are ways to do it to help ease that bite. The best method is to take out a maximum of $5,000 at a time, which will result in the institution where your funds are holding back only 10% for taxes. If you withdraw higher amounts they hold back more (e.g., on $15,000 it is 30%). It would be better to take out three separate $5,000 withdrawals then $15,000 at once.

The Annuity

An annuity is a contract with a financial institution where you exchange your nest egg for a guaranteed series of payments. The institution will pay you a monthly (or quarterly or semiannually) income for life or a specific period of time. The two main types are term-certain annuities, which pay for a specific number of years, and life annuities, which pay for life. Only life insurance companies sell life annuities; banks, trust companies, credit unions, mutual fund companies, and even some stockbrokers sell term-certain annuities. Because each institution is limited in the type of annuity it sells, you have to check with at least two different institutions before you buy.

The term-certain annuity (also called fixed-term or fixed annuity) is a popular plan where the payments are usually guaranteed until age 90 or any term less then this. After 90 you are on your own. One benefit of this plan is that if you die before 90 then your spouse will continue to receive the payments until you would have turned 90, and if you both die before 90 than the estate will receive any remaining payments. It is best to take this type of annuity out in the name of the younger spouse in order to provide coverage for both until age 90. Remember though that if you live past age 90 (and one in five persons who are now age 65 will do so), you will have to find income from another source.

The life annuity (also called straight life) provides benefits for life regardless of how long that is. You can opt for single-life annuity or joint-life annuity which covers both spouses and is advisable if you are married. (Joint-live annuities are also referred to as joint and last survivor.) You should consider a guaranteed payment period (10 to 15 years) so that if you both die prematurely the payments will not stop to the family or estate, resulting in a loss. Such a guarantee lowers the monthly benefit slightly, but is well worth it if estate planning is important to you.

If you take a life annuity with a guarantee to age 90, the only difference from a term-certain annuity (other than lower income) is that if you live beyond 90 you still get benefits. The single-life plan pays more than the joint because the payment period will likely be less.

If you already have adequate life insurance in place or your children are already financially secure, then a life annuity without a guarantee is appropriate. A universal life insurance plan is probably the best option if estate planning is important, but by choosing a life annuity (or term-certain annuity) with a long guarantee, you can further complement the estate plan. The universal life insurance has more attractive tax benefits both from the tax-free growth of the investment and the tax exemption on the payout. There is now, however, an "insured annuity" available that provides both life annuity and term insurance which is passed on tax free to the estate. Compared head to head, I think the universal life insurance is the better choice as far as estate planning goes.

Some Options and Scenarios to Think About

1. *There are many, many options available for annuities. The more you get, the less monthly benefit you receive. As a rough rule, a single life annuity pays the most followed by the joint life annuity, followed by those with guarantees. Term-certain annuities frequently have the lowest benefit because of the estate payout. But the exact amount is variable depending on your age and present health.*
2. *If you are single, a widow, or widower and there is no need for an estate plan, look at single life annuity.*
3. *If you are married and there is no need for an estate plan, consider joint life annuity.*
4. *Most other circumstances require the guarantee option with the life annuity to make sure you or the estate gets out what you put in. Choose a guarantee of 10 or more years.*
5. *The indexing option on an annuity is very important if you are a young retiree.*
6. *Consider buying your annuities over several years (ladder approach) to avoid locking in at low rates. If interest rates are quite high a few years prior to your retirement, consider a "deferred annuity," which allows*

you to purchase an annuity (before you actually need the cash) when interest rates are high and the payout benefits are deferred. You may, for example, consider this at age 65 even though you do not need the cash until age 69, simply because the rates are so good.

7. *Most important: shop around as the premiums vary by 2% to 4% at different institutions. Similarly, small fluctuations in interest rates can make big differences. A 1% difference in the interest rates can mean a 5% to 6% difference in your monthly premium. Once you have bought a plan you are stuck, so shop very carefully.*

Registered Retirement Income Fund (RRIF)

A Registered Retirement Income Fund (RRIF) is an RRSP in reverse; that is, you reverse the plan from savings to spending. There are no contributions allowed; instead you must make regular withdrawals. You can set up a RRIF at any age although it is wise to delay until 69 if you can. The investment vehicles allowed are virtually identical to those used in the RRSP, making the transition easy. You are only taxed on funds removed and what remains inside can continue to grow tax-free. New rules introduced in 1986 and 1993 allow more flexibility with the RRIF making it very attractive for health care professionals. In 1987 only 10% of retiring Canadians were using a RRIF compared to 60% in 1995.

You can withdraw as much as you wish but there are minimum withdrawals that must occur. (The requirement to collapse it completely by age 90 has been removed; you can now structure your RRIF to allow income for life.) The minimum withdrawal amount past age 69 is based on age, which is then reflected as a percentage of the RRIF's value that must be paid out that year. Each year the percentage increases, which is why it is wise to set the RRIF up in the name of the younger spouse. Table 12 shows you some of the minimum withdrawal percentages for different ages.

If you decide to use the RRIF prior to the age of 69, then the calculation for minimum payout is based on the total assets in the RRIF divided by the difference between 90 and your (or your spouse's) age. If you have taken out a RRIF prior to 1993, then the "old rules" apply up to age 77, which means lower early minimum payments. After 77 the new rules take effect.

TABLE 12
Minimum RRIF Payments

AGE	RRIF after 1992 (% of total RRIF)	RRIF before 1992 (% of total RRIF)
65	4.00	4.00
71	7.38	5.26
75	7.85	6.67
80	8.75	8.75
85	10.33	10.33
90	13.62	13.62
95	20.00	20.00

You can tailor different payment schedules to suit your needs with either monthly, quarterly, or semiannual payout benefits. The more frequent the payment schedule the lower the return, so if you are not in need of the monthly cheque, choose semiannual or annual payments.

Most people withdraw more than the mandatory minimum benefits because they need the income, but you do not have to if you have another source of income. This strategy is preferred because than the minimum withdrawal plan can allow your RRIF to continue growing for many years (assuming the return on the investment is greater then the minimum payout) as well as deferring taxes. You can get a computer printout estimating your future return, but it is very important that your estimate be on the conservative side when doing these calculations.

The advantage of the RRIF is the control and flexibility that you have to change investments. Once you own an annuity, you are locked in regardless of what happens to interest rates and inflation. You can have more than one RRIF (e.g., one based on bonds and another on treasury bills), and you can always transfer funds from an RRIF into an annuity which is especially nice if interest rates go up. If the interest rates are low, do not lock into your RRIF for longer than one year if you are using fixed-income investments. If the interest rates are high a few years before your actual retirement age, then consider buying a "deferred RRIF" similar to the deferred annuity.

Like RRSPs, RRIF plans are offered by banks, trust companies, credit unions, mutual fund dealers, and insurance companies. You will have to decide if you want a managed RRIF, which banks and insurance companies offer, or a self-directed RRIF, which many institutions offer. The managed RRIF is similar to the annuity with the exception that you are not locked into the plan (although some annuities now allow you out for a penalty). The self-directed RRIF can be a good choice if you enjoy dealing with financial matters, but at this stage all health care professionals should have a financial adviser to assist with all decisions.

Make sure you name your spouse as the beneficiary to your RRIF so it can be rolled tax-free into a RRIF for him or her (or annuity or an RRSP if he or she is under 69). The other option is to name your spouse as the successor annuitant so that he or she continues to receive the RRIF payout. If you are the last surviving parent, you may want to name the children as beneficiaries. Make sure you ask and compare what rules, fees, and limitations there are for naming children as beneficiaries at each institution as there are significant differences.

Remember that institutions may push the sale of a certain product, not because it is necessarily better for you but because it is all they sell. Be sure to visit more than one bank or insurance company before you buy. You should check into the charges that can be incurred if you want to change the RRIF within the same company or even to another company. Compare the fees for taking out extra cash (small and large lump withdrawals), canceling, moving to an annuity, and switching investment vehicles.

Investments for the RRIF

The type of investment in your RRIF will depend on whether you choose the managed RRIF where the investment vehicles are chosen for you or the self-directed RRIF where you (and your financial adviser) will have to make the decision. A proper asset mix allocation is the key to a successful RRIF, just like it is with the RRSP, to provide optimal security and a hedge against inflation. The exact investments you chose will be determined by many factors such as your age, expected number of years of retirement, and the amount you have managed to accumulate.

As a rule, you should try to leave your RRSP untouched until age 69. If you are retiring in the 55- to 60-year age range, then most likely you will have both an RRSP and non-RRSP portfolio built up. You will need to consider the effects of inflation and likely have to be more aggressive with your pre-retirement investment plan then someone who is retiring at 65.

As you get older, your asset mix allocation will put greater emphasis on the guaranteed vehicles such as GICs, bonds, and T-bills. But to help cover inflation, the average 65-year-old retiree should still have 30% to 40% of his or her portfolio in growth vehicles and the remainder in safe income producing vehicles. Remember that even at the age of 65 you will likely have 20-plus years of retirement, which is more then enough time to ride out most stock market/equity mutual fund fluctuation. These percentages can vary by 10% to 20% depending on the size of your nest egg and your risk level. As a rule, the larger the nest egg is in pre-retirement, the less emphasis you need to put on growth investments.

The GIC is the most common choice for a major chunk of the RRIF because of the insurance coverage, safety, and flexibility. Remember that CDIC will cover up to $60,000 of assets for both the RRSP/RRIF and non-RRSP as long as the maturity date is five years or less. Insurance companies insure investments with maturity terms up to 20 years. Do not forget the ladder approach to purchasing GICs. If the rates are low at the time of maturity then you should put that portion in a T-bill or money market mutual fund until they improve.

Many people are tempted to initially buy long-term GICs with 10- to 20-year maturities because they offer higher returns, but if you need the cash sooner, you will have to pay a stiff penalty. Consider the "redeemable" GIC for a portion of your investment if there is a chance that you may require the funds before the maturity date.

Other good safe investments for the RRIF are bonds, especially strip bonds. Remember that strip bonds are mostly from government bonds and are, therefore, extremely safe, and there is no limit on this "safety coverage" unlike the $60,000 limited insurance on the GICs. As well the strip bonds do not lock you in, allowing you to sell them at any time if need be. Remember that if you are using conventional bonds as a means of income, you will probably require six different bonds as most only give income semiannually. Canada Savings Bonds are also good at this time because of their flexibility.

Mortgage-backed securities are a bother in an RRSP because of the constant issue of having to reinvest the monthly interest, but this is a benefit in the RRIF because of the usual need of steady income. The "closed" form provides slightly less income then the "open" type and is probably preferred in the RRIF for convenience and dependability. Like the strip bond, mortgage-backed securities are also virtually 100% guaranteed and unlike the GIC there is no upper limit. You require a self-directed RRIF for strip bonds and mortgage-backed securities. (All of these safer types of investments are covered in chapter 6.)

Mutual funds are a major type of growth investment for the RRIF, and there are some that are quite safe. Money market and mortgage mutual funds are the most conservative, but bond and balanced funds are also excellent choices. The balanced mutual funds are particularly good for the younger retiree who has to be aware of the effect of inflation over 20 or more years.

The insurance companies' segregated funds are also worth considering because of the insurance guarantee they offer. A portion of your RRIF can also be in an equity mutual fund depending on your age, risk level, and financial needs.

The last type of RRIF investment is the Canadian blue chip company with a good record of regular dividends. You would keep any preferred stocks in your non-RRSP portfolio to avail of the tax benefits. If you stick to the safer sectors such as utilities, pipelines, and financial institutions, you will receive good returns, regular dividends (if needed), and capital appreciation. But choosing stock for your nest egg at this age definitely requires the input of a financial adviser and stock broker.

Do I Choose the Annuity Or the RRIF?

There is no simple answer to this question. There are many variables in each person's situation, so here I simply provide general comments about the pros and cons of the two different programs. Because this decision is such a serious one, I advise seeking the help of a financial adviser with experience in this aspect of personal financial planning.

The RRIF is probably the better choice if you also have a non-RRSP nest egg. The non-RRSP portfolio can provide "backup" in case the potentially higher-risk RRIF does not perform. The RRIF allows more flexibility and choice and you can always move into an annuity later (when rates are high) or jointly. The RRIF flexibility allows for better estate planning than the annuity as well as better tax planning.

The disadvantage of the RRIF is that there are no guarantees on the return unless you stick with long-term guaranteed investments. There is also the hassle of constantly monitoring the investments even with the assistance of a financial adviser.

The advantages of the annuity is that once purchased there is no further hassle. You just sit back and collect your guaranteed income.

This is a good choice for the health care professional who does not have the concern of estate planning. An annuity is also the best option for those who do not have a non-RRSP portfolio and those who have long life expectancy.

The disadvantage is that an annuity is a poor hedge against inflation, although there are now some plans that address this with an indexing option. The recent declining sales of annuities has forced some companies to allow the option of cashing in an annuity and getting a cash settlement rather than being locked in for life.

Many people elect to have both types of plans. This can be done by dividing your RRSP equally and putting 50% in both plans or any variation that suits your needs. Others use the RRIF early in retirement to hedge against inflation, and then when high interest rates roll around, convert some of the RRIF into an annuity. Others use the RRIF in early to mid-retirement and then switch to the annuity for the later years because their income needs are much lower and predictable.

The Annuity/RRIF Broker

It is probably best to find an independent broker rather than one attached to a insurance company or bank because of the potential conflict of interest. The independent broker can shop around for you and provide you with a computer-generated comparison of different companies. Your financial adviser may be able to help you or recommend someone in his or her office with expertise in this area. You should make sure that they have at least five years' experience in the annuity/RRIF field.

The other option is to look in the Yellow Pages under Retirement Planning or Annuities, which will provide more than an adequate selection. The banks or their affiliated trust companies can offer good plans, but the advice given is generally poor (although improving). It's better to get an independent broker to look at the bank's plan.

The RRIF/annuity broker gets handsomely reimbursed on a percentage basis of how much money you "spend," and this is paid by the institution from where the annuity/RRIF is being bought. For example, if you are buying a $75,000 annuity, the salesperson/broker gets on average a 2.75% commission. There is no other fee or charge with the annuity. The RRIF, on the other hand, can have extra charges attached to it besides the commission fee.

Approach two or three brokers and get quotes from each. Just remember that the highest return may not be the best plan and you need to check the fine print especially regarding flexibility of RRIFs. The broker you choose will likely result in a long-term association, so it is worthwhile choosing properly from the start. If you are not happy, then switch your RRIF to another broker!

And now some final points...

1. *Once you turn 65, you get an annual $1,000 tax credit for any payment from the annuity or RRIF. This is a reason to set up a spousal plan so you both can take advantage of the credit. It may also be a reason to unwind a small portion of your RRSP at this age.*
2. *Remember that you and your spouse can each have an annuity and/or RRIF.*
3. *Do not forget that if you make a spousal contribution in the three years prior to converting the spousal RRSP into a RRIF (or annuity) the payout could result in extra taxes.*
4. *Different institutions offer different vehicles: Only insurance companies offer life annuities and banks can only offer term-certain annuities. Banks and trusts offer mostly RRIFs. Get three to four different opinions before you jump.*
5. *Check on the safety of your deposit. As a rule there is insurance coverage for most annuities, but RRIFs depend on the investment vehicle within them.*
6. *You cannot make a decision about which plan you want until you take the time to sit down and do a present and expected budget.*
7. *Regardless of whether you chose an RRIF or annuity, you should shop around as 1% over 20 years makes a difference.*

NON-RRSP INVESTMENTS AND RETIREMENT

You want to make sure that your whole investment portfolio is arranged to give you the lowest tax break, meaning that your investments outside your RRSP/RRIF contain the capital gain and Canadian dividend income vehicles and within the RRSP/RRIF are the interest-income investments. However, you will obviously have to have some income-producing investments outside the RRSP/RRIF if you will be relying on them for early retirement income.

As has already been discussed, your investment vehicle options include GICs, bonds, mortgage-backed securities, mutual funds, and stocks. Strip bonds would not be used outside the RRSP/RRIF (although they can be okay if interest rates are dropping) but preferred Canadian stocks are an excellent choice because of the steady income and preferred tax treatment. Mortgage-backed securities generally produce higher yields then GICs, and bonds higher than mortgage-backed securities, but this generality depends on the variables discussed earlier.

Balanced, bond, and money market mutual funds are also excellent types of investments. The systematic withdrawal plan mentioned earlier is an excellent way to receive steady income, growth, and a hedge against inflation. Make sure you set up the withdrawal plan to suit your needs (e.g., monthly, quarterly, etc.).

Blue chip stocks should be considered as well for non-RRSP/RRIF investments in retirement. Common stocks that provide a 3% to 5% dividend yield translates into 5% to 7% after tax if they are Canadian, and there is the capital appreciation on top of this which can give you close to a 10% annual return. Some investors worry about the stock price fluctuation but this is not an immediate concern for you as you are only interested in the dividend income at this point.

The other option to consider is an annuity. By buying a "prescribed annuity," you can defer some taxes in the early years when your income might be higher. Annuities may provide higher returns then GICs or term deposits in the early years because of more favourable taxation. They also carry deposit insurance if bought through an insurance company (life annuities) but not through other financial institutions (term annuities). Again if estate planning is important, make sure you get a guarantee payout period.

YOUR HOME AND RETIREMENT

Deciding what to do with your principal residence when you retire can be difficult. Some health care professionals may want to stay in their home regardless of the size simply because they enjoy it so much. For others, remaining in the old house will be for sentimental reasons and to be able to accommodate visiting children and grandchildren. Most health care professionals will not be house-rich and cash-poor and will not be forced into any decision, but unfortunately some will not have this freedom. If you are still paying off your mortgage when you are in your late fifties, it may make sense to sell the house (maybe very soon) to capture the capital appreciation and put it toward your retirement nest egg. Make sure the home is in both spouses' names so you both can invest this money, allowing for income spitting.

The *reverse mortgage* was mentioned briefly in earlier chapters as a means of staying in your house and recouping some of the equity built up. The income from the reverse mortgage is tax free. There are many different versions offered by many different institutions. The banks offer something similar called the home equity loan, whereas the insurance companies offer the reverse annuity mortgage. The reverse mortgage option is really for those who love their home and do not want to leave it but require some cash.

Basically, a reverse mortgage works this way: An institution (usually an insurance company) allows you to take a mortgage (say $100,000) out on your paid home (valued at $350,000). You can just take the cash or, more commonly, buy an annuity from the institution which gives you income for life (or a predetermined time period). During this period you do not make any payments and the annuity payments are tax-free. The catch is that when you die the house is sold and the proceeds are used to pay off the mortgage that you took out. And when you die in 10 years, the house value may have gone up to $400,000 which you or the estate captures minus the mortgage payment. The older you are, the more income you will receive because the payback period is closer and more predictable.

If you decide to go this route, make sure you get a guarantee on the annuity (10 or more years) so that your spouse or estate will benefit in case you die prematurely. Also make sure that you will never owe more then the home is worth in case of a real estate crash. Additionally, the family should have the option to keep the house when you die if they take over the mortgage that exists on it.

If you do not want an annuity, the other option is to simply approach the bank and take out a mortgage on equity built up in the house. You could then invest this money outside the RRSP making the mortgage interest charged tax deductible. The present five-year rate of 8% would be reduced to 4% to 5% on your mortgage after the tax deduction, which is not a bad loan rate. If you, for example, took out $100,000 and put it in a good systematic withdrawal plan, you could add an extra $10,000 to your annual income before taxes and still have the same roof over your head.

KISS PRINCIPLE — Calculating Your Retirement Needs

1. *An investment plan is mandatory and the calculations in this section are a good place to start. A plan should be started in your thirties.*
2. *Spending requirements will likely go down substantially after age 75 which can be factored into the calculation.*
3. *Life expectancy is going up so plan on an income until at least age 90. Plan on at least 30 years of retirement if you are nearing retirement at the age of 60. If you are younger, your life expectancy will likely be even higher by the time you reach 60.*
4. *If you are an employed health care professional then you may be eligible for a pension which should be discussed with your financial adviser.*
5. *If you are now more then 10 years away from retirement do not count on OAS/CPP in your calculations.*
6. *If you are 1 to 10 years from retirement, factor in the present "clawback" and likely future increases in clawbacks in the OAS/CPP.*
7. *Pick conservative numbers for your investment return when using the above tables.*
8. *As a very rough rule most 30- to 40-year-olds will require a $1.5 to $2 million nest egg; most 40- to 50-year-olds will require about $1.2 million; and 50- to 60-year-olds will require about a $1 million nest egg.*

NOTES:

14

ESTATE PLANNING (OR PROTECTING YOUR FAMILY'S INHERITANCE)

Estate planning is the process by which you plan in advance how and when your assets are to be passed on when you die. If you do not have a proper plan, then needless amounts of your hard-earned money may end up in the wrong hands (i.e., the government) or there may be a lengthy delay in distributing the assets. Having a plan in place for your inevitable death is an important and final step in personal financial planning. There are three major reasons for estate planning: to leave the assets you want to the people you want, to pay for the cost of your death, and to lessen the tax burden.

It is a very individual decision whether you leave an inheritance to your family, spend it all before you die, or leave it to a charity. In this chapter, I cover the more common means of leaving an inheritance; if you wish to leave a large amount to a charity, you should review your plan with your accountant.

Finally, it is important to appreciate that as your family and estate assets evolve, so may your estate plan, and so you should conduct a regular review of your plan every couple of years.

LEAVING WHAT YOU WANT TO WHOM YOU WANT

The most important aspect of estate planning is to make sure that you have an adequate will. Your will covers vital matters such as how your assets are to be divided among family members, who the beneficiaries are for the RRSP/RRIF and life insurance, and who will act as executor of your estate. Your will also plays a role in covering the costs of your death as well as minimizing the tax burden (see below).

Other issues that should be covered in your will include burial instructions, contingent beneficiaries in case you and your spouse die at the same time, and a contingent executor. Remember that if you do not have a will dictating your wishes, then the settling of your estate may be very prolonged and complicated. See chapter 5 for more on preparing your will.

THE COST OF DYING

Most people have no idea about what it costs to die. First, there are the obvious costs: funeral or memorial service costs and legal fees for executing your will regardless of what you decide to do with your assets. But there are other less well-known costs as well.

First, the *deemed disposition rule* means that the government deems that you have disposed of all capital assets (mutual funds, stocks, real estate, etc.) at fair market value at the time of your death. Accordingly, taxes have to be paid on these "realized" gains by you or your estate. For example, if you bought a cottage for $50,000 in 1975 that is now worth $250,000, your estate will owe taxes on the capital gains of $200,000. The more unfortunate situation is where the estate is asset rich and cash poor, which often results in the forced sale of the cottage to pay the taxes on the estate. This can be a real hit to the estate if the real estate market is flat at the time of the sale.

There are different ways to provide for these death costs. The simplest is to leave enough money in the estate to cover all the costs. Alternatively, you could arrange for life insurance to be paid to your heirs tax free. These strategies are reviewed in chapters 5 and 11 and, as mentioned there, they are very complex and must be carefully selected.

Some annuity plans can provide money for the estate, but only if the guarantee is long enough. The other option is to get an "insured annuity" where you buy the life annuity plan with a built-in insurance plan that provides tax-free dollars to the beneficiary upon your death.

Another way to provide estate funds is with the RRIF Maximizer. This is an RRIF with slightly lower benefits which allows for the additional purchase of life insurance (called joint second-death) which, upon death, is passed on tax-free to the estate.

All of these options should be discussed with the family in advance to see what the wishes of the potential heirs are. If using life insurance as a means of funding a large estate, then it may be appropriate to ask the heirs to pay for the insurance.

LESSEN THE TAX BURDEN

Probate fees

Probate fees are fees paid to the government to verify that the will is legal and the estate is distributed properly. All the provinces except Quebec charge probate fees. Probate fees are paid with assets from the estate and are based on a percentage of its total value. Prudent estate planning can reduce probate fees and the other legal fees that accompany them.

The easiest way to reduce probate fees is to reduce the amount of assets going through the estate. If you do not name a beneficiary (and contingent beneficiary) in your will for your life insurance policy, RRSP, and RRIF, then your estate will owe more in probate fees because these will go through the estate before your family receives them. Similarly, if property is solely in your name, it becomes part of the estate and must be probated. However, if you plan ahead and put all your property/assets into joint ownership, it automatically passes to the joint owner without probate.

Gifting

Gifting (or transferring) refers to passing assets on to the family before you die. Gifting decreases the amount of assets going through the estate, which means lower probate fees. You should review the discussion of attribution rules in chapter 11 before embarking on transferring or gifting assets as there are different tax implications depending on whom you gift to. You will have to pay tax on any gains realized up to the point of gifting, but after that gains will be taxed in the hands of the receiver as dictated by the attribution rules.

A popular plan has been to transfer property (such as a cottage) to a child or grandchild and then any future capital gains will be taxed in his or her hands. Even better, the child or grandchild might claim the property as a principal residence and avoid any capital gains tax. The downside for you is that for tax purposes, the cottage has been deemed sold at the time of transfer and you would have to pay tax on any capital gains appreciated up to that point. And, of course, you lose legal rights to the property. If you wish to continue having input on the ownership of the cottage, you could gift it to the family through a living trust which still results in the lower probate fees and tax deferral. Gifting is an excellent way to decrease the families overall taxes.

Trusts

Trusts were covered in chapter 11 as a means of income splitting. They are also very useful for estate planning. The living trust avoids probate fees because you essentially transfer assets before you die. There are numerous "creative slants" on the use of trusts in estate planning (e.g., "estate freezing") that should be discussed with your accountant and financial adviser if you have a large estate and want to optimize your tax plan.

Do not forget that the estate can make one final contribution to the RRSP of the deceased in the year of death (if the deceased is under 69) which then can be passed on to the spousal beneficiary, which decreases the probate bite.

Some health care professionals with very large estates may want to consider setting up a holding company in another province that has lower probate fees because there are significant differences. You will incur legal and accounting fees, but if the estate value is greater than $1 million, this strategy may be financially beneficial.

The rules for estate planning for corporations are complex and require the input of an accountant experienced in this matter.

15

CHILDREN AND FINANCIAL PLANNING

The older baby boomers have been very fortunate as far as saving for children's education is concerned. Up until 1992, the federal government provided a family allowance to every Canadian family, which was frequently rolled into a savings plan for education. But like everything else in that era that was good, it is now gone. It is now the responsibility of the parent to put aside funds for children's education.

You can be certain that with reduced federal transfer payments added to provincial financial restraint, educational grants will soon be a thing of the past and tuition fees will continue to skyrocket over the next decade. It currently costs about $6,500 to $8,000 per year for university education (including room, board, and tuition) in Canada which totals to $26,000 to $32,000 per child over four years. What's more, universities have been given the go-ahead to increase tuition fees by 20% over the next couple of years. If your children's education savings plan is for 15 to 18 years down the road, then with inflation and government cutbacks, conservative estimates put the cost in the $15,000 to $20,000 range per year or $60,000 to $80,000 for just a four-year program!

We as professionals know the value of education and, therefore, most will want our children to pursue post-secondary education. The statistics certainly indicate the importance of a university education: the average income for a university-educated family is $80,000 versus $52,000 for the high-school educated family. Further, the unemployment rate is substantially lower (approximately 7%) for those with a university education. The bottom line is that you need to start an education savings program today and you need to choose the best one.

FUNDING CHILDREN'S EDUCATION

There are several ways to save for your children's education, and I review the pros and cons of several here.

Registered Education Savings Plans

There are two basic Registered Education Savings Plans (RESPs) that most people have heard about: the "pooled" scholarship trusts and the self-directed RESP. The premise behind these plans is that contributions are not tax deductible but any earnings can accumulate tax-free until withdrawn. All money in the RESP can grow untaxed until withdrawn and then it is taxed in the hands of the student (who will likely pay little, if any, taxes).

There are many different "pooled" scholarship RESPs, but two in particular are quite popular. These are the University Scholarship of Canada and the Canadian Scholarship Trust Foundation. These are mandatory savings plans where funds are pooled together and require regular monthly contributions up to age 18. If the funds are not used for education, then you forfeit the income earned but you still get back the principal contribution. Your money is pooled with other parents' funds and invested (mostly) in fixed-income type investments.

There are many options in these pooled RESPs that you must compare before signing on the dotted line. You should ask about enrolment fees, whether the student can defer his or her education for a few years, if the student can take time away from his or her studies, if there is a transfer option to another beneficiary, and what the maximum number of payments to the beneficiary is. Generally, I think RESPs are poor education savings plans because of the low returns they will generate in the future (because of low interest rates) and because if your child does not go to university you lose all earned income.

The self-directed RESPs are offered by banks, trust companies, and a growing number of mutual fund companies and brokerage houses. The contributions are not tax deductible, but the savings plan grows tax free until withdrawal. Money that is later withdrawn is taxed (not the principal) in the hands of the child which is minimal or nill. Contribution maximums have recently been increased to $2,000 a year and the maximum contribution time is 21 years allowing for a maximum contribution of $42,000 (similar to the pooled). The final size of the fund depends on the investment return you achieve. There is no carry-forward for missed years.

If the designated child does not attend a post-secondary institution, then most firms allow you to switch beneficiaries, which is an important option. If the savings are not used for post-secondary education, then you will lose everything but the principal you put in. (Be sure to check on the plan's definition of post-secondary education.)

This RESP is a better choice then the scholarship trust, but I would still not recommend it because of the potential financial loss if your child does not attend a post-secondary institution (which is currently a 30% chance). There are many limitations, restrictions, and extra fees that you must inquire about if you are going to use this type of RESP.

Developing Your Own Plan

The options covered in this section require that you have an understanding of the attribution rules (see chapter 11). Generally, your investment vehicle should be mainly slanted toward capital gains income because this is taxed in the hands of the child when realized. If your education savings plan earns interest or dividend income, it will be attributed back to you resulting in a top marginal tax assault.

Probably the best way to set up an "education fund" is to use a good growth or equity *mutual fund* which emphasizes capital appreciation. It is best to use one of the global equity mutual funds recommended in chapter 8. The physicians have to look no further then the excellent MD Growth mutual fund. Additionally, if there is any interest income earned you can keep track of the "interest earned on the interest" which will be taxed in your child's hands.

Remember to switch the fund (or part of it) over to an income mutual fund or other safe type of investment in the two to four years before it is required in order to guarantee the safety of the assets. You should regularly crystallize the capital gains along the way while the child has no or low income rather than realizing the whole amount when he or she begins university, which could result in a large tax bill. Because each child has an annual basic personal tax exemption, it is possible for each to earn close to $8,500 per year in capital gains tax-free.

The advantages of this type of education savings plan are the flexibility, historically great returns, low taxation, and no loss if the child does not go on to a post-secondary institution. You should register the funds in the child's name, but add the words "in trust" on the application form. (Some companies will not allow this and instead require that you set up an official trust with a lawyer.) Because there are no limits on this type of "education fund", it is a great way to income split, especially if there are several children.

Another option is to invest directly in individual *stocks* through a discount or full-service broker. Some discount brokerages are offering special rates for education funds such as the TD Green Line. Probably the best way to invest in individual stocks for your children's education is through a dividend reinvestment plan or DRIP program which was covered in chapter 7. You will pay tax on the initial dividend income but any reinvested dividends as well as any capital appreciation will be taxed in the child's hands.

The DRIP should be registered in the child's name. To do this you first must apply for a social insurance number for the child. It is best to set up the initial stock buy "in trust" then write to the company to register with the DRIP. Emphasis should be on common stock for the favourably taxed capital gains as well as Canadian companies to avail of the dividend tax credit, although the child will be paying little if any tax when he or she realizes the gain for university. It is important to have a couple of different stocks to allow diversification, and within three or four years of requiring the cash be sure to switch the stocks over to safer ones if need be.

Some companies also offer *deferred preferred* shares for the children's education savings plan. With deferred preferred shares, the dividend payments are deferred and allowed to accumulate tax-free until you cash them. When you decide to sell the stocks, the dividends are taxed in the hands of the child. The beauty of these shares (like the equity mutual fund) is that you can cash them at any time without a penalty if you need emergency cash.

Insurance Company Plans

The insurance companies also offer a variety of education savings plans. There are many similarities to RESPs, such as tax-free compounding and lower taxation rates if the child collects the savings for education purposes. But there are also some "advantages" over RESPs.

The Savings Endowment for Education and Development (SEED) program, for example, guarantees awarding of the investment even if the child does not attend university, has no limitation of contributions, and guarantees a minimum return. The present guaranteed return, however, is only 3% of the total. Additionally, not many parents can afford to put away more than the present RESP maximum contribution of $2,000 per year so that eliminates those "advantages."

Another life insurance education plan utilizes universal life insurance and is called the "self-completing" education plan. It allows you to put aside savings that will grow tax-free and provide money for the child's education as well as providing life insurance. The funds withdrawn for the child's education are taxed in his or her hands. A good feature about this plan is that if the child does not go to university, you can just leave the plan as is or withdraw it for other purposes (but then it is taxed in your hands).

I do not recommend buying this type of life insurance solely for education savings, but if you are purchasing universal insurance, then this can be an added bonus. Universal life insurance plans held within the corporation can also provide a means of funding a child's education if set up properly.

As a general rule, I would not use any of the life insurance policies for your children's education simply because they are not as good as the equity mutual funds or the DRIP program already discussed. As well there are many possible variables, restrictions, and extra fees that make them a complicated way to save.

Trust Fund

You could also set up a children's trust for educational savings. You should factor in the cost of setting up the trust ($2,500 to $5,000) and the annual accounting fees, as well as what this money would have grown to in an equity mutual fund at 10%-plus return over 10 to 15 years. These types of trusts are useful for those health care professionals fortunate enough to be able to incorporate, but as discussed earlier, some recent changes (and potential future changes) have made this less attractive. In general, you need about $25,000 in an incorporated trust or $100,000 in an unincorporated trust to make it worthwhile, which is a lot of cash up front, especially if you have two or three children. Discuss this option with your tax specialist as everyone's case is different.

OTHER DECISIONS ABOUT YOUR CHILDREN'S EDUCATION

The question always arises: should you pay down the mortgage before saving for your children's education? If you are in the early stages of paying your mortage (i.e., years 1 to 7 on a 25-year term) and cannot afford both the extra mortgage payments and a contribution to the education fund, then you are better off putting it on the mortgage because this is when the interest percentage on the mortgage is at its highest.

After this amortization period, the decision will depend on your mortgage rate and the investment return you hope to get on your chosen education fund. Most experts would say that to be worthwhile contributing to the education fund, you would want to be earning double your mortgage rate. Because this is very hard to accomplish (i.e., you currently need a 15% return), you should pay most of the mortgage before starting an education fund. Fortunately, many health care professionals' salaries are high enough that they can make extra payments on the mortgage as well as contributing to an education fund.

The second question is whether you should maximize your RRSP or contribute to the education fund. Because nobody knows what will happen to the RRSP contribution limits, it is best to maximize those contributions and worry about the education fund later. This is certainly true in the early years of your RRSP. Do not be tricked into believing that the enormously generous RRSP carry-forward rules will still be available a few years from now; many think they will not be.

TEACHING YOUR CHILDREN ABOUT PERSONAL FINANCIAL PLANNING

Child rearing is a very expensive proposition. It is estimated that it currently costs about $6,000 to $8,000 per year to raise a child up to the post-secondary education level. Over 18 years, this will cost you at least $108,000! Then the post-secondary education costs begin!

I think it is safe to say that the average health care professional does not have the time (or the know-how, up until now) to even consider properly educating their children about financial matters. If your parents did not educate you at an early age, then you will likely pass on this debt of ignorance to your children, which is a big mistake. I would be willing to bet that if more parents took the time to educate their children about basic financial matters they and the children would greatly benefit over the long run. Speaking from personal experience, a better comprehension of financial matters would have been very useful in my earlier years of my medical training and especially in those first couple of young "rich" years after graduating.

This financial education should be started at a very young age. It could start with an explanation of what an allowance is for, rather than just handing over a weekly amount. Suggest allocating a portion of the child's allowance to savings and the rest to spending. Routine chores should be distinguished from "work" chores. Setting up an account at the bank and explaining earned interest is very useful.

Many of the banks have special accounts available for children with no charge chequing, no service fees, and they provide a special bank book and card. Introducing them to the different household bills and showing them the banking transactions that pay for these bills is informative.

There are now a couple of books on the market as well as software for kids that help them understand personal finances. I recommend a book by Gail Vaz-Oxlade called *The Money Tree Myth* which provides many useful suggestions for parents on how to educate their children. The bottom line is that an introduction to finances will do absolutely no harm and likely benefit you in the short term and them in the long run (maybe they will even turn off the lights or shorten the time in the shower a bit!).

NOTES:

16

YOUR OPTIONS FOR BUYING A NEW VEHICLE

THE FOUR OPTIONS

There are basically four options available when it comes to acquiring a "new" vehicle. The most economical option is to buy a pre-owned vehicle that is two to three years old. It is very useful if the vehicle has an extended warranty included, but you should never buy this yourself. This pre-owned option will likely only be pursued by those health care professionals under age 30, which is unfortunate because the savings are enormous when compared to the other vehicle-buying options discussed below.

The next option is to pay the full amount in cash up front, which is difficult for most because of the large cash layout, but it is the next best option after buying a pre-owned vehicle. Even if you cannot pay the full amount, it is wise to put down as much as possible and the rest on your line of credit because it is substantially cheaper then the next two options.

The third option is to arrange financing through your own bank or through the dealership. This type of financing is similar to home financing in that you take out a "mortgage" on the vehicle. This means that the shorter the amortization period the less interest you will pay. You should check the deal offered by the bank before checking with the car dealership.

The final option is leasing. Leasing is now big business which is why the banks want in on this action. The value of new car leasing grew from $5.1 billion in 1989 to $9 billion in 1994. In 1994 there were 245,000 new vehicles leased in Canada which represented 50% of all new cars sold. Vehicle leasing has become very competitive and complex. Because of the poor legislation, consumers have to shop around to know what they are looking for.

LEASE OR BUY?

To help you decide between leasing or buying a vehicle, there are now several companies that will sell you software that help with the analysis. Rob Lo Presti of OrangeSoft has developed a one-page checklist for $5 and computer programs for $45. They will also give you a similar computer analysis of almost any office furniture equipment.
Phone 1-800-647-8693 for more information.

As a rule, leasing costs you less per month then buying and there is little or no up front cash required. But you will most likely pay more over the long run with leasing over any form of buying. Whether you opt for the "open-end" (possible buy back) or "closed-end" (no buy back), you will likely pay more for the leased car compared to both buying the car outright with cash or financing the buy. In a recent comparison by Rob Lo Presti published in the *Globe and Mail* of leasing a new car every three years starting with a 1995 Honda Accord EX to buying a new car every five years using normal financing, the difference at the end of 15 years was dramatic. The car buyer comes out ahead by almost $35,000. When the tax implications of the self-employed health care professional are taken into consideration, the difference is not as marked but still favours buying.

Prior to 1991, leasing was very attractive to the self-employed health care professional, but many of these advantages are no longer present. In fact leasing now loses on almost all head-to-head long-term comparisons (over 10 years) with buying a vehicle. As it currently stands, the self-employed health care professional can deduct up to $650 (plus taxes) a month for leasing charges versus $300 per month for interest deductions on a loan. There is also the yearly depreciation allowance if you buy the vehicle, up to a maximum of $24,000 plus taxes.

If you buy through the corporation, then the entire amount of the lease can be written off. Most after-tax calculations for the self-employed person shows that in the short run (less than three years) leasing means less cash but after this buying the vehicle by almost any means is the winner.

The main "advantage" of leasing is the lower monthly payments which "allows more cash flow." But if your cash flow is this tight, then you are probably spending too much. However, if lease payments fit your present financial picture, then it may be the better choice for you, at least in the short term.

Leasing is also a reasonable consideration for those who want to drive an expensive car or want to have a new car every two to three years. If you want to eventually own your own vehicle, choose the "open-end" lease and keep the car for a few years, which will save you money in the long run. But if you do not mind keeping a vehicle five or more years, then buying is the cheaper method.

Take the following list of questions with you when you go lease shopping as a starting point. The final decision should be based on the final cost and your cash flow needs.

Leasing Checklist

1. *What is the penalty for early cancellation of the lease?*
2. *What is the penalty for going over the "kilometre allowance" with the closed-end lease?*
3. *What is the suggested list price of the car? (This will allow you to compare financing versus leasing and you can obtain this information for a small fee from the Automobile Protection Association: 1-416-964-6774.)*
4. *Are there any "excessive wear and tear" charges or specific insurance requirements?*
5. *What are the additional administrative costs?*
6. *What is the residual value?*
7. *Is there coverage for vandalism and theft or is this extra?*
8. *Can anyone else drive the car? Are there any limitations on where you can go?*
9. *Are there any other fees, restrictions, or obligations that I do not know about?*

NOTES:

AFTERWORD

THE IMPORTANCE OF FRUGALITY

Have you ever wondered why so many health care professionals complain about their lack of cash flow or overall poor financial situation despite salaries that push them into the top 5% to 10% of all Canadian income earners! Many literally fear salary freezes or clawbacks because they are on such a fine financial edge. How do the other 90% to 95% of Canadians get by?

There is definite truth to the adage "the more you make the more you spend." The easiest way for the health care professionals to save money is to spend less — that is, exercise some frugality. This section does not apply to all health care professionals, and others may find it too repulsive to read. But having been brought up in a frugal family, town, and province, I have an inherent knack for living with prudent frugality and I would like to share with you some of what I have learned.

The four biggest expenses for the average health care professionals are housing, transportation, food, and overhead. For some health care professionals, vacation, and entertainment expense would also have to be added to the list. This is where the biggest savings can be made if you are frugal. Of course, the biggest Canadian family expense (especially for health care professionals) are taxes, which we have limited ability to curtail. But one of the easiest ways to reduce the amount of taxes you pay is to simply spend less and save more. This way you avoid many, many taxes (e.g., GST, PST).

Canadians are now only managing to save 6% to 7% of their disposable income as compared to 18% in 1982. It is interesting to look at the biggest difference in spending habits between the average-income Canadian family and the high-income family. On home purchases we spend 100% more; on food 20% more; on transportation 100% more; on clothing 100% more; and on recreation 150% more. You can see that most of the extra bucks go into nonessentials. Any health care professional can save thousands of dollars per year by reducing their expenses in such areas as housing, transportation (vehicle and its costs), and recreation.

The House

You should seriously consider the cost of any new home and subsequent mortgage payments. We are now definitely spending more on homes in the 1990s than we did in the 1980s. In the mid-eighties, the average percentage of mortgage debt to total personal debt was 36%; in 1995 it was 65%. Why are we spending so much more on homes yet our family size is decreasing? The choice of your home is very personal, but it is important that you buy within your means, keeping in mind that future income will probably drop and other expenses (property taxes, children's education) will increase.

In the early to mid-eighties, buying a larger-than-needed house was a "good investment" because housing prices were rising so much. This logic is now probably faulty as future home prices (especially so-called monster homes) will remain level or even drop. If you need more room, the best option is to renovate and build up. It is likely that the days of consumption will slowly turn into "deconsumption" and keeping up with the Joneses will no longer be in vogue.

The Automobile

For the new graduating student (even the seasoned health care professional), it is absurd to buy a new vehicle for $20,000 to $30,000. With today's competitive automobile market, vehicles are easily lasting 10 years (150,000 to 200,000 km) especially if you change the oil and filter every 5,000 to 10,000 km. The average annual expense for owning and operating a midsize new 1996 car is $8,000 to $9,000. This covers financing, depreciation, insurance, taxes, maintenance, gasoline, and licencing fees. This amount is higher for the larger top end vehicles and double that amount if you have two vehicles. You can substantially lower this cost by choosing a pre-owned vehicle or at least considering a pre-owned vehicle for one of the two (or three) family cars.

The best bang for your buck is to buy a pre-owned vehicle that is two to three years old which you can often get for 50% off the original price tag. New vehicles automatically drop 25% in value the minute they leave the dealership's parking lot. By buying a pre-owned vehicle, you can save $10,000 to $15,000, which can be put toward one of your other expenses or the RRSP. This is especially important to those younger health care professionals. The $10,000 saved and invested at the age of 25 with a 12% return would allow for an extra $300,000 in the nest egg by age 55!

The best place to find a pre-owned vehicle is through the local newspaper. The secondhand car dealerships are usually over priced by 15% to 20%. The best deals can be found at the end of summer or during the winter. By looking in the winter you also get firsthand experience of how the automobile operates during cold months. You then must get the local dealership mechanic to examine the vehicle (for $50 to $100). They will be able to tell you what is still covered under the regular and extended warranty as well as any foreseeable problems with the vehicle. You do not have to reveal this information to the owner but rather use the report to barter a lower price. Make sure you check to see if there are any liens against the car before the final transaction.

I recommend using the *Lemon-Aid Used Car Guide* by Phil Edmonston, which is an annual publication showing the pros and cons of each vehicle and what to look for when buying a pre-owned vehicle. You should mention some of the common problems that are listed about the vehicle in this book to the mechanic who is going to examine the vehicle for you.

For those of you who *must* have a new car, I recommend giving either Auto Hotline in Mississauga or Automobile Protection Association in Toronto a call (416-964-6774); for $25 you can find out the wholesale cost for most vehicles sold in Canada. With this information, you can approach the dealer starting with this price rather then the over-inflated sticker price and avoid needless amounts of haggling.

Recreation

This is a difficult area to generalize on but health care professionals do spend plenty on all types of recreation. From the ski chalet to the expensive restaurant dinners, many health care professionals spend 150% more then the average Canadian family. These recreational activities are big stress releaser for many health care professionals. I leave it up to the individual to review your financial plan; if it is off track, this may be the place to curtail your spending and increase your savings. Just remember that all these expenses are paid with after-tax dollars, so the $100 meal requires your earning $200.

NOTES:

APPENDIX

Where To Get More Information

BOOKS AND NEWSLETTERS

Here I have listed recommended books and newsletters according to the chapter topics, although some of the books recommended for specific areas of reading also contain other useful information.

Chapter 1

Books:

Beck, Nuala. *Shifting Gears.* Harper Collins Publisher Ltd.

Chapter 2

Books:

Dominguez, Joe and Vicki Robin. *Your Money or Your Life.* Penguin Books.

Chapter 3

Books:

Baker, Murray. The Debt-Free Graduate. Harper Collins Publisher Ltd.

Foot, David with Daniel Stoffman. Boom, Bust and Echo. MacFarlane, Walter & Ross.

Turner, Garth. 2015 — After the Boom. Key Porter Books.

Silverstein, Alan. Home Buying Strategies for Resale Homes. Stoddart Publishing.

Chapter 4

Books:

Kelman, Stephen. *RRSPs 1996.* Penguin Books.

Pape, Gordon. *Buyer's Guide to RRSPs.* Prentice Hall, Inc.

Vaz-Oxlade, Gail. *The RRSP Answer Book.* Stoddart Publishing.

Chapter 5

Books:

Bullock, James and George Brett. *Insure Sensibly.* Penguin Books.

Gray, Douglas. *The Canadian Snowbird.* McGraw-Hill Ryerson Ltd.

Paterson, Dr. J. *Russian Roulette: Gambling with Disability.* (Self-published. Tel: (403) 237-5772.)

Chapter 7

Books:

Beck, Nuala. *Shifting Gears.* Harper Collins Publisher Ltd.

Carter, Ted. *Successful Stock Market Speculation* Mistaya Publishing Ltd.

Cook, David and Susan Highstone. *The Pig and the Python.* General Publishing

Dent, Jr., Harry. *The Great Boom Ahead.* Hyperion.

Fox, Douglas. *Exploring Options.* Penguin

Graham, Benjamin. *The Intelligent Investor.* Harper & Row.

Hagstrom, Robert. *The Warren Buffet Way.* John Wiley & Sons.

Hall, John. *Options, Futures and Other Derivative Securities.* Prentice Hall.

Lanyi, Andrew. *Confessions of a Stockbroker.* Prentice Hall.

McKeough, Patrick. *Riding The Bull.* Key Porter Books.

Newsletters:

Canadian Shareowners Association newsletter at (519) 252-1555 or 1-800-265-9543

The Investment Reporter. MPL Communications Inc. & Marpep Publishing Ltd. (416) 869-1177

Investor's Digest. MPL Communications Inc. (416) 869-1177

The Money Letter. Hume Publishing. 1-800-733-4863

Chapter 8

Books:

Pape, Gordon. *Buyer's Guide to Mutual Funds.* Prentice Hall, Inc.

Newsletters:

The Canadian Mutual Fund Adviser. MPL Communications Inc. & Marpep Publishing Ltd. (416) 869-1177

Chapter 9

Books:

Foot, David with Daniel Stoffman. *Boom, Bust and Echo.* MacFarlane, Walter & Ross.

Gray, Douglas. *Making Money in Real Estate.* McGraw-Hill Ryerson Ltd.

Turner, Garth. *2015 — After the Boom.* Key Porter Books.

Weiss, Gary. *The Small Investor's Guide To Making Money In Canadian Real Estate.* Stoddart Publishing.

Chapter 10

Books:

Rogers, Kelly. *The Insider's Guide to Picking the Best Money Managers.* by Kelly Rogers.

Courses:

The Canadian Institute of Financial Planning @ (416) 865-1237

The Canadian Securities Course @ (416) 364-9130 for information.

Chapter 11

Books:

Deloitte and Touche. *How to Reduce the Tax You Pay.* Key Porter Books.

KPMG. *Personal Tax Planning Guide.* Carswell Thomson Professional Publishing.

Newsletters:

The TaxLetter. Hume Publishing. 1-800-733-4863

Chapter 13

Books:

Gray, Douglas. *The Canadian Snowbird Guide.* McGraw-Hill Ryerson.

Kerr, Robert. *The Only Retirement Guide You'll Ever Need* Penguin Books.

Longhurst, Patrick and Rose Marie Earle. *Your Pension: The Complete Guide to Pension Planning in Canada.* Doubleday Canada Ltd.

Polson, Kirk and George Brett.*Retire Right: The Practical Guide to RRIFs, Annuities and Pensions.* Penguin Books.

Chapter 14

Books:

Doulis, Alex. *Take Your Money and Run.* Uphill Publishing Ltd.

Lumsden, Jack with Sue Lumsden. *Sudden Wealth.* Uphill Publishing Ltd.

Also see chapter 11 references

Chapter 15

Books:

Vaz-Oxlade, Gail. *The Money Tree Myth.* Stoddart Publishing.

by Gail Vaz-Oxlade

Chapter 16

Books:

Edmonston, Phil. *Lemon-Aid Used Car Guide.* Stoddart Publishing.

SOFTWARE

There are many software programs now available that cover most aspects of personal financial planning. Some are specific to certain investment such as stocks and mutual funds (e.g., InvestorBase and Portfolio Tracker) and others give more generalized advice on all aspects of personal financial planning.

A couple that are highly recommended are *The Wealth Creator* and *Asset Architect.*

THE INTERNET

There are many places on the Internet where you can get information on every aspect of personal financial planning. Many sites such as the banks and mutual fund companies will offer you free service; others will charge you a monthly or per-use fee. The growth rate of these Internet financial services is tremendous, but because there is little regulation there are many pitfalls.

There are a couple of new books that will help guide health care professionals through investing and getting personal financial advice on the Net. *The Worth Guide to Electronic Investing* by Jim Jubak provides an excellent guide to "cyberinvesting." This book takes you through all the steps of electronic investing as well as providing a review of over 100 other electronic investment programs both on line and on disc. I highly recommend this book for any health care professional interested in computer-assisted personal financial planning. Another book is the *Investor's Guide to the Net* by Paul Farrell.

There are far too many sites for me to go into any detail here, but I can make a few suggestions. An initial freebie to start with is the Canadian Corporate NewsNet (CCN NewsNet) which focuses mostly on news releases by different companies and associations. CCN also allows you to navigate through the wide array of investor's resources that are now being offered by providing direct links with most of these. CCN NewsNets address is *http://www.cdn-news.com.* Another is The PAWWS Financial Network site: *http://pawws.secapl.com* offering free stock quotes and Canada StockWatch (*http://www.canada-stockwatch.com*). Thomson Financial Services at *http://www.marketedge.com.* provides a variety of services dealing with stocks and mutual funds. The Fund Library at *http://www.fundlib.com* deals specifically with mutual funds.

A few services that deal with personal financial planning that are worth checking out are Financial Services Network, The Treasury Management Page, and The Global Network Navigator Personal Finance Page.

The future of placing direct stock and mutual fund orders through the Net via online brokers seems to be promising with the TD's Green Line discount brokerage leading the way. It is quite likely that we will see a an actual on-line stock exchange quite similar to Nasdaq in the near future. This will allow trading without the services of a broker but again there are many, many pitfalls for the inexperienced investor.

Index

PRESCRIPTION FOR WEALTH — ORDER FORM

Discover how easy personal financial planning can be for any health care professional.

A great gift idea for any health care professional student or friend.

- Yes, I would like to order_______copy(ies) of *Prescription for Health* at $23.95 each. = $ ___________
- Add $4 for shipping and handling for first copy and $2 for each additional copy. = $ ___________
- Add 7% GST for each copy ($1.96 each) = $ ___________

Total payment to Crowne Rock Publishing = $ ___________

Payment options

☐ Cheque/money order enclosed (payable to Crowne Rock Publishing)

☐ Bill my credit card (Visa only)

Card number:

Name on card: ______________________________Exp. date: __________

Signature of cardholder: ____

Address:____________________________City ________________________

Prov._______________________________Postal Code __________________

Phone: (   ) ____________________Fax: (   ) ________________

Mail to Crowne Rock Publishing
R.R. #6, Site 11A, C18
Vernon, BC V1T 6Y5

OR

Phone:(250) 545-1137 Fax:(250) 558-6137
Toll free (orders only) 1-800-567-7955

(Have your Visa number ready)

Discounts available for students (25%) & for orders of 5 or more books.
Comments welcome
EMail : tcurran@nohr.org

G.S.T. # 899560353

PRESCRIPTION FOR WEALTH — ORDER FORM

Discover how easy personal financial planning can be for any health care professional.

A great gift idea for any health care professional student or friend.

- Yes, I would like to order_______copy(ies) of *Prescription for Health* at $23.95 each. = $ ___________
- Add $4 for shipping and handling for first copy and $2 for each additional copy. = $ ___________
- Add 7% GST for each copy ($1.96 each) = $ ___________

Total payment to Crowne Rock Publishing = $ ___________

Payment options

☐ Cheque/money order enclosed (payable to Crowne Rock Publishing)

☐ Bill my credit card (Visa only)

Card number:

Name on card: ______________________________Exp. date: __________

Signature of cardholder: ____

Address:___________________________City ________________________

Prov.______________________________Postal Code _________________

Phone: (   ) ______________________Fax: (   ) ________________

Mail to Crowne Rock Publishing
R.R. #6, Site 11A, C18
Vernon, BC V1T 6Y5

OR

Phone:(250) 545-1137 Fax:(250) 558-6137
Toll free (orders only) 1-800-567-7955

(Have your Visa number ready)

Discounts available for students (25%) & for orders of 5 or more books.
Comments welcome
EMail : tcurran@nohr.org

G.S.T. # 899560353